PELICAN BOOKS
British Society Since 1945

Arthur Marwick is Dean of Arts and Professor of History at the
Open University. Born in Edinburgh, he has for many years
lived in Hampstead. He studied at Edinburgh University and
Balliol College, Oxford, and has taught at Aberdeen,
Edinburgh, and the State University of New York at Buffalo.
He has written widely on recent social history particularly with
reference to war and social change, class, and film. His books
include *The Deluge: British Society and the First World War*,
Women at War 1914–18, *Class: Image and Reality in Britain*,
France and America Since 1930 and *The Nature of History*.

THE PELICAN SOCIAL HISTORY OF BRITAIN
General Editor: J. H. Plumb

Already published:

Roy Porter: *English Society in the Eighteenth Century*
John Stevenson: *British Society 1914–45*
Joyce Youings: *Sixteenth-Century England*

Titles in preparation:

José Harris: *Britain 1870–1914*
Margaret Spufford: *English Society in the Seventeenth Century*

Arthur Marwick

British Society Since 1945

Penguin Books

PENGUIN BOOKS

Published by the Penguin Group
27 Wrights Lane, London w8 5TZ, England
Viking Penguin Inc., 40 West 23rd Street, New York, New York 10010, USA
Penguin Books Australia Ltd, Ringwood, Victoria, Australia
Penguin Books Canada Ltd, 2801 John Street, Markham, Ontario, Canada L3R 1B4
Penguin Books (NZ) Ltd, 182–190 Wairau Road, Auckland 10, New Zealand

Penguin Books Ltd, Registered Offices: Harmondsworth, Middlesex, England

First published 1982
Reprinted 1982, 1984, 1985, 1987, 1988

Printed and bound in Great Britain by
Cox & Wyman Ltd, Reading
Filmset in Monophoto Bembo by Northumberland Press Ltd,
Gateshead, Tyne and Wear

Contents

Editorial Foreword

Historians respond to the problems of their time almost without being conscious of the process, and the focus of their study changes with the changing times. In the nineteenth century all countries of Europe and America were preoccupied with the origins of national identity, with the need to forge a living past that would give meaning not only to the present but also to the future: Ranke, Macaulay, Michelet, Bancroft and other great historians of the nineteenth century were so preoccupied. As Britain's national identity seemed to be inexorably involved with the evolution of constitutional rights, with liberty, freedom and, particularly, democracy, it is not surprising that an ever growing number of professional historians should devote all their skills and interest to constitutional, legal and political history and that these subjects should dominate university syllabuses when they were first designed in the late nineteenth century.

The First World War, the Great Depression, and the economic disasters which followed gave great impetus to the study both of diplomatic and economic history, the one generally attracting the conservative, the other the radical historians in the 1920s and 1930s. After the Second World War interest in diplomatic history faded first or, rather, transmogrified itself into International Relations and Strategic Studies. Economic history drifted into a professional morass and developed a confused identity – the quantifiers and the econometricians moved in and so did the sociologists, especially American sociologists, hoping to establish an ideology which would refute the Marxist interpretation which had flourished within the realm of economic history.

But the problems of Western industrial society have become much more complex since the Second World War. Fantastic economic growth, and it has been fantastic this last thirty years, has created its own social tensions and, even more important, the very nature of highly industrialized society, apart from its growth, has created new conflicts. Institutions which have lasted for ten thousand years, not only in the West but also in the East, have suddenly seemed to be in jeopardy. In the last two decades there has been a mushrooming of interest amongst historians in the problems of demography, of the nature of the family, of the position of women, children, slaves and servants, of the uses of leisure, of the influence of printing, of the expansion of the arts, of the importance of the images society creates for itself, and of the interpretation of class not in economic but in social terms. A new panorama of social history has spread before the eyes of scholars and led them to subjects which historians of previous generations would have thought of interest only to antiquarians.

Naturally, other forms of history are not dead, even though some of them are corpse-like, but there can be little doubt that the historical imagination, for better or worse, has become intoxicated with social history: for example, the volume of work on death in the last ten years is prodigious and it is matched by the quantity of studies on childhood or marriage.

The danger of social history, which in spite of its present explosion has, in some of its aspects, long roots reaching back through G. M. Trevelyan to Macaulay and Sir Walter Scott, has been the tendency to drift into descriptive history, of how people lived and spent their days with little or no attempt to analyse why their lives, their beliefs, their activities were what they were. Also, the evidence social historians, even very good ones, used in the past was impressionistic – diaries, letters, personal memories, together with material collected from folklorists and antiquarians. Naturally, most of this evidence related to the literate class, always, until very recent times, a modest segment of the nation.

In order to give this material greater rigour, sociological theory, either of Marxist or capitalist bent, has been used and, often, in discussion of death, birth, education of children or the position of women, it has been infused with modern psychological analysis. Although this has given rise to some nonsense, particularly in the history of childhood, it has given the subject, on the whole, greater intellectual weight.

As with economic history, there has also been a powerful movement which has attempted to quantify the evidence of the past in order to give a statistical basis for some of the fundamental questions of social history – average size and nature of the family, whether nuclear or extended; the age of marriage for men and women; death rates and ages at death; even an attempt has been made to quantify literacy. Huge mountains of data have been assembled and computers have hummed away merrily at great expense but the results remain extremely tentative. Before the nineteenth century record-keeping was erratic and its reliability was not easy to test. There is, too, one unknown factor of great importance – how many of the population were never recorded at all, neither their births, marriages, nor deaths? Indeed, most of the results obtained are easy to criticize and must be treated with considerable scepticism. Even so, generalizations about the family and about its size, about marriage, about bastardy, about age of death, all are firmer than they were and, because they are, help us to understand the life of the country in greater depth.

Although statistics may give shadow and depth to the picture, they cannot paint it, and social history still depends upon a great range of records. Formerly, it depended most of all on letters, diaries and imaginative literature but, although these are still of the greatest value, more attention has now been given to artefacts: to the study of houses and gardens, to newspapers, bills and trade cards, to carriages, instruments, games and toys, indeed to everything that may throw a light on the way life was lived or the way it hurried towards its future or clung to its past. By extending its range and its depth, by encompassing a multiplicity of scenes, social history has become a far more complex and intellectually exciting discipline.

Over the last ten years the flow of monographs and articles on the social history of England has increased, mushroomed like an atomic explosion, and the time is more than ripe for an attempt at synthesis.

J. H. Plumb

Preface

Inevitably in a book of this size much gets left out. Let me first stress that my title means what it says: this is a social history of Great Britain not of the United Kingdom of Great Britain and Northern Ireland. Northern Ireland features only where events there affected society on mainland Britain; or, in one case, where the statistics used happen to refer to the entire United Kingdom.

Where I deal with literature, science, philosophy, and the arts, I have not sought to mention every distinguished name. Broadly, my concern has been with interaction with the rest of society, rather than isolated individual achievement, and with individuals who are manifestly part and parcel of society as it developed after 1945; many of those who had made their names in the pre-war years are left out: Bernard Shaw and Somerset Maugham, for instance.

For constructive criticism and helpful guidance on my entire text I am most grateful to the General Editor of the series, Professor Jack Plumb, to Professor Christopher Harvie of Tübingen University, and to my colleagues Tim Benton and Dr Henry Cowper; for specialist advice, my thanks to John Sutherland. My thanks also to Karen Smith, who prepared the typescript in her usual exemplary fashion and to Angi Rutter, who read the proofs.

For permission to quote 'A Tribute to the Founder', from *A Look Around the Estate*, thanks are due to the poet Kingsley Amis and to the publishers Jonathan Cape in London and Harcourt Brace Jovanovich in New York.

Introduction
'How It Was' or 'What Went Wrong?'

Nobody has ever said precisely how many ways there are of skinning a cat. Probably there are about the same number of ways of writing a Social History of Britain since 1945. There are a number of fundamental factors, institutions, and concepts relating to the study of societies, such as population, the family, housing, eating habits, and social class: thus social history can be written as a relatively neutral account of the main changes and developments in these areas. Certainly the basic facts and figures are essential if one is to establish 'How It Was', what it was like to live through these years, and to pin down the nature and extent of social change. However, the British experience since 1945 cries out for a brush more loaded than that.

At first flash, it might seem that the whole experience could be encapsulated within a contrast between the general election of 1945, which, for the first time ever, gave Labour a decisive victory, and the general election of 1979, which brought to power a new Conservative régime avowedly aiming at the reversal of the whole course of post-war economic and social policy. One might wish to say that the country which in 1945 had sought a new future under Labour felt in 1979 that the only salvation from all the problems that had ensued over the three decades lay in the election of a radical Conservative Government under a woman Prime Minister. But the actual voting figures would give one pause. In 1945 47·8 per cent of those actually voting voted Labour; but 39·8 per cent voted Conservative; 20 per cent did not bother to vote at all. In 1979 43·9 per cent of those voting voted Conservative; but 36·9 per cent still voted Labour; nearly 30 per cent did not vote at all. To speak of the electorate doing this, or the country wishing that, is obviously absurd: some people vote one way, others vote another. Elections, certainly, are of crucial significance in political history, the story of critical manoeuvring at the margin; but in social history they reveal rather the continuities within British society. Indeed, there is a danger in speaking at all of '*the* British experience', perfectly respectable and acceptable though that phrase is as a piece of shorthand as long as it is never allowed to obscure the fact that different individuals, different groups, in reality meet with very different experiences.

Still, the general question 'What Went Wrong?' undoubtedly has validity as a central theme since it actually has been a major preoccupation in much recent writing on Britain's immediate past; the question itself has become a very part of the social history of contemporary Britain. Of course, different authors have had different issues in mind: some contrast military victory in the Second World War with economic and political impotence in the eighties; others contrast the high idealism of 1945 with the shoddiness of much of British life in 1981. Discussing Labour's general election victory in 1945, Peter Calvocoressi, in *The British Experience 1945–75*, writes of the electorate hoping and believing 'that the Labour Party would make great strides towards the elimination of absolute poverty and excessive inequality'. His book was to be 'the tale of hopes deflated by failures', the failures being largely the product of economic mismanagement and financial miscalculation together with the two grave weaknesses of 'excessive inequality and excessive secretiveness'. Yet, for Calvocoressi, there were still in 1975 'objective grounds for optimism about the condition of Britain'. Calvocoressi was very much the spokesman of the traditional comfortably off Liberal Left: much had gone wrong, but not irredeemably so. Quite different were the views of those, upper-class former Socialists and lower-class Conservatives, with many shades and positions in between, who formed the new Radical Right at the spearhead of the Conservative Party in the late seventies. Several of them contributed to a volume published in the United States in 1977, its title, *The Future That Doesn't Work*, an awful warning to Americans of what would happen if they imitated British fecklessness, put too much emphasis on sharing out wealth and providing social benefits, and too little on the actual creation of wealth, relied over-confidently on the inevitability of economic growth without bothering to get the basic sums right, gave way too readily to vested interests and pressure groups. For too long, said the Radical Right, Britain had attempted to insulate itself and its people from the true, and corrective, forces of the free market.

But the American volume brought a rejoinder, *Britain: A Future That Works*, from Bernard Nossiter, the *Washington Post*'s man in London. While identifying social, and above all racial, inequalities as grave weaknesses, Nossiter advanced the argument that far from being among the least of the industrialized nations Britain was the foremost in adapting herself contentedly to the realities of post-industrial civilization. Britain, he said, wisely preferred a leisurely pace and a high quality of life to the hectic stresses of working hard, and accepted tourism and 'culture' as the natural trades of a fully adjusted post-industrial society. But the uncomfortable Left would have little of that: inner-city deprivation, high unemployment, continuing squalor, and inequality, all of these, they claimed, had their origins in the failure of the Labour Government in 1945 to seize its opportunity to reconstruct society there and then. Jeremy Seabrook's study, published in 1978, of 'Working People and the Ideals of the Labour Movement' was actually entitled *What Went Wrong?*.

Just as there is no one question 'What Went Wrong?', so there can be no one answer or set of answers. In a way it is a wrong question, because it must immediately imply one defined political point of view, when Britain at all times, to repeat, is made up of many shades of political commitment and political ignorance. Yet I do propose to make that question, albeit in a rather more elaborate form, one of the three central themes of this book. What, it seems to me, must lie at the heart of any social history which is more than a recital of social trends, are the questions of how so many of the high aspirations of 1945 did go sour, and of how, in the years after 1945, leading figures of all political parties came to agree on certain assumptions about the development of British society, which, in the end, turned out to be so seriously wrong. The point really is this: failures were obvious by the later seventies, but not at all so obvious in the previous quarter of a century. The task is to dig among the flowers of optimism and the apparent fruits of success for the roots of longer-term failure.

But social trends go in all directions at once: while the betrayal of high hopes may be one relentlessly developing theme, much else of significance was taking place in British society. For a second theme, I intend to concentrate on the great release from older restraints and controls which took place in the very middle of the period under review. Again, I have nothing political in mind here. Mention commercial television, women's liberation, the Abortion Act, the lowering of the voting age, and the Betting and Gaming Act, and you would probably find people divided for and against on political and moral grounds; but all of these were part of the same movement in which paternalistic Victorian controls were lifted from British society. The upheavals of the 1960s were at least as great as those of the Second World War and have had, I would predict, though it may seem early to do so, an irreversible influence on British society.

My third theme is of a rather different order again. Much has been written of 'stability', or 'tolerance', or 'consensus' in British society. Such words can be mere clichés, begging questions rather than answering them. Yet historians and sociologists have traced a connection between the broad political consensus of the mid twentieth century and the religious tolerance of earlier centuries centred upon an established Anglicanism to which various forms of nonconformity were accommodated without too much fuss. When I spoke on 'Social Change' at the fiftieth anniversary of the admission of Birkbeck College to the University of London in 1970, I introduced the notion of 'secular Anglicanism', noting in England the lack of the extremity of feeling to be found between Catholics and anti-Catholics in France and Italy, among Lutherans and Calvinists in northern European countries, and in the Bible belt of the United States, as also in Ireland and parts of Scotland. Perhaps the phrase is not a very good one; be that as it may, the third theme of this book involves questions about the nature and reality of tolerance and consensus in British society and political culture, including the question of whether consensus (if it existed) contributed to a beneficial stability, or to an unfortunate stagnation.

But surely, I hear many voices muttering, the impact of science and technology on society must be a major theme. It is a commonplace, though also an accurate and significant truth, that economic developments and social conditions in all industrialized countries since 1945 have been mightily affected by scientific and technological change. However, the correlations are not easy to establish; science and technology are best treated as informing, and being informed by, many aspects of social and economic life, rather than as a separate, and perhaps quasi-magic entity somehow having a kind of mechanical 'impact' on an inanimate object, society. Furthermore, it is a purpose of this book to concentrate on what is particular to Britain's social history. All that said, it would be a fool who attempted to write contemporary social history without giving full weight to scientific discovery and technological innovation; I trust that I am not that fool.

It is a long time since 1945. Much in the attitudes and life-styles of people in the later forties seems quite remote from the attitudes and life-styles of people today. It would do no justice at all to the period under review if I were to treat it as one undifferentiated lump of time within which to follow out my three themes, and follow through developments in population, diet, the family, and so on. Thus I have resorted to one of the fundamental technical devices of historical writing, periodization. To stress the way in which change has taken place since the end of the war I have divided the book into three parts, though, it scarcely need be said, there are no real turning points in history – certainly not general elections.

The first period I describe as that of 'Social Consensus', which I take as lasting from 1945 to around 1957. Though, as will quickly become apparent, this period (particularly in its first, highly distinctive few years) was very much dominated by the legacies of the war, 1945, the year in which the war ended and the general election which brought the Labour Government to power took place, is very much as good a starting point as any and probably better than most. The Labour Government's majority was almost destroyed in the general election of 1950, and it fell from office in 1951. However, the point already made about not readily generalizing about the country, or the electorate, voting this way or that way, or choosing this or that, is strongly brought out by the fact that actually more people voted Labour in this election than voted Conservative, and more people voted Labour than had voted Labour in 1945. Since there followed thirteen years of Conservative rule this could not unreasonably be described as a turning point in political history; but as far as social history is concerned it would, in my view, be true to say that the main themes of the late forties continued to be worked out in the early fifties.

In 1954 rationing of most major foodstuffs finally ended; in the same year the Bill introducing commercial television became law. These, certainly, were signs of change. It was in 1955 that the Conservatives were returned with a larger and most convincing majority, led by Sir Anthony Eden now that Churchill had finally left the front line of politics. Yet, if we are to seek a really deep political watershed, then that must lie in the Suez episode of 1956. Some hints of control lasted till 1956; in that sense, as Government statisticians recognize, 1957 was the first year of the new consumer society.

Anyway, I take my second period, described as 'Roads to Freedom', as beginning around this time. The Conservatives regrouped themselves under Harold Macmillan, and went on to win a third election victory, with a yet further increased majority, in 1959. The word 'affluence' began to be bandied around freely. Release came, not just from post-war austerity, but from social controls going back to Victorian times; there was, indeed, something of the air of the eighteenth century about the introduction of premium bonds. There were new critiques of society too: Richard Hoggart's *The Uses of Literacy*, of 1957, and the Boulting Brothers' film *I'm All Right Jack*, of 1959. True, a Labour Government, by the skin of its teeth as it turned out, got back into office in 1964. Not only did it end thirteen continuous years of Conservative rule, but it went on to win a comfortable majority in the general election of 1966. Again, however, from the perspectives of social history the changes seem but surface ones. Despite the serious weakness of sterling, resulting eventually in devaluation, a general spirit of affluence remained, educational and cultural innovation continued, further libertarian measures were enacted, and 'permissiveness' was abroad in the land.

The Labour Government continued till 1970 when, rather narrowly and somewhat unexpectedly, it lost to the Conservatives. Certainly 1968 and 1969 had been troubled by outbreaks of student activism, but in no way can these be compared with the great upheavals which affected France in 1968. Indeed 1968 and its aftermath, including such developments as the lowering of the age of majority to eighteen, marked a continuing progress on the 'roads to freedom'. Whatever the intentions of the new Conservative administration under Edward Heath, it is hard to detect any significant change in life-styles or attitudes before 1973. But then came the first oil crisis, serious industrial disruption, an escalation of violence. The 'Time of Troubles', marked by depression, decline, and cutbacks, had begun; violence in Northern Ireland, which had entered a new crisis phase in 1968, increasingly overshadowed British life. In 1973 Britain joined the European Economic Community, a move confirmed in the referendum held by the Labour Government in 1975. Despite the referendum, it is not easy to generalize about British attitudes towards Europe, but without doubt in the middle seventies there were many manifestations of closer contact with Europe and of a greater cosmopolitanism, allied perhaps with greater insecurity and less insular pride.

Yet, having identified the themes, and the chronology, there remains the problem of what to put in and what to leave out. Apart from tracing out the three themes and establishing a legitimate periodization, my interest is in the nature, extent, and significance of social change. Accordingly, I now define a list of the eleven main groups of inter-related social facts and developments which I take to be most relevant to the history of British society since 1945. These groups (they overlap of course) are: Social Geography (including the physical environment, demography, population, urban and suburban developments, location of industry, etc.); Economic and Technological Change (including innovation in theory as well as techniques and also covering the question of the changing nature of work); Social

Class and Social Structure; Social Cohesion (how far is the nation unified? how far are racial, nationalist, or sex differences pulling it apart?); Social Welfare and Social Policy; Material Conditions; Customs and Behaviour; The Family; Social Deviance and Questions of Law and Order; Intellectual (including Scientific) and Artistic Developments; and, finally, Social and Political Values, Institutions, and Ideas. As can be seen, technology and science feature principally in, respectively, the second group and the second last group; but as will become clear they emerge in other groups as well.

The ebb and flow of society cannot be contained within the limits set by these eleven signposts. In the three separate parts of this book the eleven headings are shuffled and reshuffled, giving different and, I hope, illuminating juxtapositions. But the signposts are there for the reader to use if he wishes, for social history should not be a random assemblage of facts and quotations from the Government papers, still less a swamp of titbits and anecdotes culled from the popular press. Part One, indeed, follows the eleven headings through in the order given: Chapter 1 takes in Social Geography *and* Economic and Technological Change; Chapter 2 concentrates on Social Class *and* Social Cohesion; Chapter 3 is limited to Social Welfare and Social Policy; Chapter 4 covers Material Conditions, Customs, the Family and Social Deviance; Chapter 5 sticks to Intellectual and Artistic Developments; while Chapter 6 uses the topic of 'Values' to assess the period as a whole. The pattern is radically altered in Part Two; then, though the allocation to chapters is different, returns to its original shape in Part Three.

But enough of structure. This book seeks to inform, but it aims also to appeal to the general reader. Of all the books I have written, it is the one I have most enjoyed writing. I hope readers will share some of that enjoyment.

Part One

Social Consensus
1945–57

1. *British Journey*

On 24 August 1945, J. L. Hodson, a prosperous and well-connected journalist, wrote in his diary:

The war is over; the conditions of war in some respects continue. You need only make a long railway journey in England to become aware of it. I travelled last Sunday to Newcastle on Tyne. The journey which in peace-time took four hours now took eight and a quarter. No food on the train. No cup of tea to be got at the stops because the queues for this remarkable beverage masquerading as tea were impossibly long. At Newcastle an army artillery captain and I got hold of a truck and wheeled our bags along a platform almost impassable through luggage and merchandise waiting to be shifted. No taxi to be got. My hotel towel is about the size of a pocket handkerchief, the soap tablet is worn to the thinness of paper, my bed sheets are torn.

Many of the conditions of war were indeed to continue until early 1950, with rationing and controls enduring still longer. Yet the war itself cracked many of the conventions of British society, so that idealists could genuinely welcome the peace as heralding a new dawn. Between 1945 and 1950, then, the country lay in a crepuscular zone with the shadows of night as firm upon the landscape as the heartening hints of the rising sun. None the less I have taken the full dozen years of 1945 to 1957 as one period because it was only in the later years that certain consequences of the war were clarified, certain continuities of British society re-established, and certain assumptions which were to determine the future course of British society fully worked out.

Life in these dozen years was dominated by the consequences of the war, both negative and positive, though at the same time it largely conformed to patterns of behaviour established earlier in the century. Over 70 per cent of the nation's dwellings dated back to the late nineteenth or early twentieth century, or earlier;

most of the remainder belonged to the various types of more or less 'traditional' housing estates built in the inter-war period. Parking spaces abounded; but then that was because so few people had cars. Sound film and sound broadcasting, both creations of the inter-war years, enjoyed their last golden age. Those just reaching adulthood had spent their formative childhood years in a time when, without doubt, living standards were rising, but when, also, much of the country was affected by severe economic depression. Those already reaching middle-age had lived out the best years of their lives in such conditions.

In waging war Britain had acquired debts of £3,000 million, had allowed domestic capital to deteriorate by around the same amount, had used up overseas investments to the extent of £1,000 million, and had had to let exports fall to one third of their pre-war level. Britain had been able to keep going during the war because of the Lend-Lease agreements with the United States; these, however, were brought to a sudden end with the defeat of Japan. North American loans were secured, but on the condition that the pound should be restored to full convertibility as quickly as possible: when convertibility was restored in the autumn of 1947 it created the first of the sterling crises which were to be the fiscal mark of the new era.

With re-building going on everywhere in the world, many materials and foodstuffs were even scarcer than they had been during the war. The coal-mining areas had been shamefully mistreated during the Depression, then conjured into flurried, though not usually very productive, activity during the war. In 1945 coal production was again down at the very low level of 175 million tons and output remained low during the post-war years, matching the pre-war level only in 1950. With the war barely over, there came in the winter of 1946–7 the most serious blizzards and the greatest freeze-up for over a century, followed in turn by floods, though there was a fine summer. During the worst of the cold spell power supplies were cut, creating a wave of temporary unemployment which reached a peak of 800,000 in 1947.

If we survey Britain as it was in the late forties and early fifties, the furthest reaches of mountain and valley, of island and fishing village, as well as the towns and cities and the plumper farming lands, we can identify a number of major forces shaping life within the geographical diversities. In the thirties had come the first halting attempts to control depression and unemployment through diversification and the introduction of new industries into the hardest-hit areas; these policies had scarcely got very far by the time of the outbreak of war, but the idea of diversification and the direction of industry was very much in the minds of Government planners after the war. The war itself had had an enormous direct influence in stimulating all kinds of expanded or new industrial development often in areas remote from the attentions of German bombers. For all that, the traditions, and the hard contours of bricks and mortar, products of a century and a half of industrialization, could not suddenly be wished away.

Planning, direction of the economy, and social engineering in general, it was hoped, would be achieved through nationalization of the major industries, the Distribution of Industry Act (1945), and the channelling of new investment to 'development areas' through the building of new towns, and, on another plane, through the establishment of national parks under the provisions of the National Parks and Access to the Countryside Act (1949). 'Green belts' were to be preserved round London and the major conurbations. Demand after the restrictions of the war years was high, while, at the same time, building materials were in short supply, and, anyway, were deliberately controlled by the Government. Furthermore, it was absolutely vital that Britain achieve its salvation in the post-war world by maximizing exports and, therefore, domestic production. Trends, therefore, were favourable to economic expansion; given the shortages, those areas which had had their industrial capacity extended during the war were at a special advantage. Overall, despite the frustration and austerity of the immediate post-war years, there was modest prosperity, and the bulk of wage and salary earners did reasonably well. There was something of a recession in 1952–3, which served to sort out the areas which were genuinely embarked upon prosperity from the ones where post-war Sellotape and plaster had not fully served to conceal deeper industrial wounds.

The war had had a great influence, also, on the exploitation of science and technology. The Second World War is sometimes called 'the physicists' war', and many of the developments inspired by purely military objectives were to have social repercussions, often rather unexpected ones. The adaptation of nuclear power to the generation of energy for civilian purposes was obvious enough, as was the application of radar to commercial air transport; but radio isotopes, a by-product of the nuclear industry, proved to have important applications in medicine, while the infra-red devices developed during the war for detecting the enemy in the hours of darkness proved invaluable in the scanning techniques developed in medical physics. Penicillin was a pre-war discovery, but it was only exploited in wartime. The successful search for new antibiotics (mainly carried out by American scientists) revolutionized medicine in the post-war years. Within chemicals generally there was a whole range of important developments, including plastics, artificial fibres, fertilizers, and pesticides, and a broad shift from 'light' chemicals to 'heavy' chemicals (detergents are an important example). Out of the war experience came two new, or almost new, science-based industries: electronics and optics; while an older industry was expanded and transformed, engineering. For even more traditional industries, new possibilities opened up: the use of oxygen in the continuous strip-mill made possible the rapid production of high-quality thin sheets.

The relationship between the war, science and technology, and post-war British society is rather similar to that between the war, economic and social planning, and post-war society. Many of the great scientific and technological developments could scarcely be attributed to conscious decision-making. Thus, though there was great enthusiasm for, and much talk about, the importance of science and technology to Britain's social regeneration, there was a good deal less understanding of how to set about harnessing science and technology in the most effective manner. As there was to be a hit-and-miss quality about post-war social engineering, so there was to be something of the same quality about the nation's exploitation of science and technology.

For such a small island – 750 miles long, and, at its widest point, 375 miles across – Britain is a very diverse country. The war had been a national and, within limits, a universalizing experience, in much greater degree than had the depression of the inter-war years. The tangible effects of the war, however, were distributed unevenly as if by some ferocious, but casual, wizardry. Tracts of London, Merseyside, the Midlands, Plymouth, Clydeside, and many historic towns besides, lay desolate; in other areas, new factories, new roads, new bridges, gave an air of bustle and prosperity which had been lacking for a generation.

When J. B. Priestley, at the height of the Depression in 1933, was collecting material for his *English Journey*, he discovered three Englands: the old England of the guidebooks; nineteenth-century industrial England; and twentieth-century England of bypasses and suburbia: much of nineteenth-century England had in fact become a fourth England, England of the dole. Probably there had been more Englands than that: rural outposts, for example, mostly enduring hard times; and, outside of England, the remote highlands of Wales and Scotland, the specially deprived industrial areas of these two countries, and the 'Scotland and Wales of the guidebooks'. Priestley's taxonomy had certainly already been partially overturned by the war, yet it continued to have meaning for the post-war years. Indeed there is no completely satisfactory categorization which combines physical and human geography. So let us simply start at the top of the country and work our way steadily down to the bottom.

The Highlands and Islands of Scotland, peopled sparsely with crofters and fishermen, had continued to decay in the inter-war years. Though it was actually in the Orkneys that the first loss of life occurred as a result of an enemy air-raid, this region was hardly affected by the bombing war. But it suffered a renewed outflow of population as young women went, or were directed – a major grievance of the Scottish Nationalists, this – to factories in England. However, the wide spaces and sheltered inlets of the Highlands could be exploited for military training grounds, airfields, and port facilities. An attack was made on the long-neglected problem of communications, new roads being built in the Orkneys, the Shetlands, and on the islands of Lewis,

Benbecula, and South Uist, the last two being joined together by the completion of the South Ford Viaduct. New piers were constructed at such shipping ports as Wick, Thurso, Tarbert, and Ullapool. Furthermore, a new hospital for 640 patients was built at Raigmore, Inverness. These were not unmixed blessings, but they served to breathe some semblance of life back into areas which much needed it. More important was the Government's campaign to increase home-produced food supplies. Highland farmers benefited, and even prospered moderately, from grants under the marginal agricultural production scheme and from subsidies for hill sheep and hill cattle.

Hydro-electric schemes had been launched in the inter-war years. During the war, thanks in large measure to the energetic policies of Scotland's Socialist Secretary of State in the wartime coalition, Tom Johnston, had come the establishment of the North of Scotland Hydro-electricity Board. The building of new hydro-electric schemes continued at a rapid pace in the post-war years. Again this meant new life and new amenities for the Highlands. New construction sites provided opportunities for unskilled labourers to make high earnings, so long as they were prepared to live in unattractive temporary accommodation. The Highland economy was not saved, and not all of the changes were welcome ones. But a stop had been put to the absolute decline of pre-war years.

Probably the area of Scotland which benefited most from the war and post-war years was that of the Southern Uplands, the Border Country, where both arable and pasture farming prospered in meeting new demands. In between lies the industrial area of Central Scotland stretching from Glasgow and the Clydeside in the west, with its shipbuilding and heavy engineering industries, to Edinburgh in the east, with its more traditional industries, such as printing and brewing, and its high middle-class professional element, but surrounded, none the less, by coalfields, and northwards through the Fife coalfields, the linoleum factories of Kirkcaldy, to the port town of Dundee, whose staple industry had been jute.

Industrial Scotland, though Edinburgh least of all, had been deep in distress throughout the thirties. Something of a revival seemed to be heralded by the locating of a number of Royal Ordnance factories, as well as other industrial developments, in this area. A Ministry of Supply clothing depot at Motherwell became, in the post-war years, a Metropolitan Vickers engineering factory. A wartime Rolls-Royce factory at Hillington, just outside Glasgow, was the precursor of other factories in what, in the post-war years, became a new industrial estate. Garelochhead acquired a Metal Industries Ltd depot, Falkirk an aluminium rolling mill, and Edinburgh an important Ferranti electronics complex. Government policy deliberately aimed to bring industry to Scotland; and until the early fifties, at least, a new level of prosperity was attained, even if, from the point of view of the national economy, Scotland was not always the most sensible place in which to site new industry. The real basis of prosperity, in any case, lay in the recovery of the traditional heavy industries.

Many of the complications and contradictions involved in the heritage of the war, and the Labour Government's determination to engineer prosperity out of it, show up well in the North-East of England. Coal, iron and steel, and ships, were all in great demand during the war, so the North-East, which had been in the deepest depression in the thirties, prospered. Again wartime Royal Ordnance factories provided the bases for the development of post-war industrial estates. A new urban pattern emerged very clearly. Whereas older industries had been located along the rivers with copious provision of railway sidings, the new industrial estates developed on the outskirts of towns, and depended upon the roads. The Royal Ordnance filling factory at Aycliffe became the focal point for the new town of Newton Aycliffe. A site chosen for wartime purposes was scarcely the best choice for a post-war new town, particularly since it was so close to the substantial town of Darlington.

In general, the brave new world tended to be built to contours shaped by the war, or even along lines determined by the bad old industrial world. One of the most striking sights in the North-East is the Consett ironworks, rising starkly from a hilly moorland landscape. Unfortunately, judged rationally, this remote spot is scarcely the ideal one for a major ironworks. However, the aim after 1945 was to pump prosperity into the former depressed areas, not to carry out a complete rationalization of industry. Hence, under the Labour Government, the Consett ironworks were developed and expanded. But the largest post-war developments in the North-East took place on Teesside, major developments being the establishment of a vast new ICI nylon polymer plant at Wilton and the building of the Lackenby steel smelting shop, which came into production in 1953. As part of its policy of diffusing jobs, and of curbing office development in the South-East, the Government located its new Ministry of National Insurance in Newcastle.

Cumbria, on the other side of the Pennines, has a wilder landscape, and a higher proportion of the population working on the land. Again the small industrial area had suffered greatly during the Depression. Better times were signalled with the establishment at the beginning of the war of the special steel-works at Distington. In the post-war years this became an iron foundry and general engineering works, which, in turn, pro-vided a market for the output from the long-established Workington steelworks. Further employment opportunities were created by the war-generated growth of Vickers at Barrow. But Cumbria was also touched by the greatest of all the technological spin-offs from the war. Already in 1946 work was going ahead on a nuclear plant at Windscale; nearby, at Calder Hall, Britain's first nuclear power station, which began producing electricity in May 1956, was built.

Continuing down the west side of the country, we come first to rural Lancashire, then to the holiday resorts and to the cotton towns heavily stricken during the Depression, for which there was to be no long-term recovery; then to the South-East Lancashire conurbation centring on Manchester, and west, past the old chemical towns of Warrington and Widnes to the great port of Liverpool, which prospered with the post-war producti-vity drive. New industries, based mainly on synthetics, had been fostered during the war, and the county had been given an injection of metropolitan middle-class life-styles by the settle-ment of certain civil service departments in the resort towns of Lytham St Annes and Blackpool. The big changes in the chemicals industry brought a new prosperity to Warrington, Widnes, and their vicinity.

Back across the Pennines there was no real recovery for

the woollen mills. It was in West Yorkshire that the post-war policies of the Labour Government, aimed at the distribution of industry, were at their most unsuccessful. New industries were excluded, and even established textile firms were encouraged to expand in areas whose need was felt to be greater, for example the North-East. Thus, although the West Riding conurbation itself, mainly through the growth of the service trades, continued to develop, with suburbia filling in the gaps between such main towns as Leeds and Bradford, West Yorkshire was on the way to becoming more a museum than a hive of industry. Yorkshire was a very varied county, of course: the rural areas did well, and the coal-mining regions to the south prospered as a consequence of the wartime and post-war demand for coal. There were important coal-burning electrical power stations in such places as Ferry Bridge. Rather out on a limb was the region of Humberside where modest prosperity came to the main town of Hull, and to such fishing ports as Grimsby which re-established themselves after the disruption of war.

The coal seams of South Yorkshire practically merge into those of the East Midlands. Here, around Nottingham and Derby, we are in D. H. Lawrence country. The coal mines had done moderately well in the Depression, and they did even better in the post-war years. There was considerable growth of light industry in both Nottingham and Derby. Nottingham had its famous Raleigh bicycle works, and Derby had its Rolls-Royce, Midland Railway, and British Celanese factories. Again, we must not take counties or regions as homogeneous. Where the Pennines come to an end in Derbyshire is one of the most famous and popular beauty areas in Britain: in 1949 the Peak District was designated Britain's first national park.

The most striking success story of the war and post-war years was that of the West Midlands. The Black Country, to the north and west of Birmingham, original home of the Midland coal mines and ironworks, certainly had a somewhat desolate air at the end of the war. But Coventry, to the south-east of Birmingham, although blitzed in November 1940, already by the end of the war stood out for its prosperity resulting from the boom in engineering, motor manufacturing, and other light industry; it was to benefit further from the deliberate attempts to stimulate technological innovation after 1945, as also from the pent-up demand for cars. The West Midlands conurbation can be taken as the most successful example of post-war suburban growth. The potteries of North Staffordshire to the north were always of a rather different character. During the war, 37,000 pottery jobs disappeared here; on the other hand two important Royal Ordnance factories were established which continued, though on a reduced scale, after 1945 and wartime shadow factories located in the potteries were taken up by Rists, A E I, and Simplex. Furthermore pent-up demand, and the general terms of trade, did bring something of a revival in both pottery and coal mining and by 1951 both industries were re-established at almost pre-war employment levels. Development policies perhaps benefited the West Midlands more than strict assessment of need might have suggested: one eighth of the area was declared to be 'development land' and was steadily built on and filled in. When the stop–go came in 1952–3, it had only relatively mild effects on this region, and unemployment always remained at around half the national level.

West of the industrial areas, going towards Wales, lies what has often been described as the cradle of the Industrial Revolution, centred on Ironbridge. This is beautiful countryside, more and more so as one moves towards the heights of South-West Shropshire. These, more sung about than made use of in former years, were reclaimed for pasture farming during the war and in the post-war years, through the exploitation of advanced agricultural technology, continued to yield a good profit as a centre of cattle-rearing.

Central and North Wales met with fewer direct incursions from the war than did the Highlands and Islands of Scotland. Again there was a drive to bring marginal land under cultivation, and on the whole the farming communities of North Wales did well. Industrial South Wales, upon which most attention is usually fixed, is little more than a coastal strip with knotted fingers poking up the valleys as far north as the once-mighty town of Merthyr Tydfil. If the West Midlands can be taken as a paradigm of relatively successful industrial Britain in the first decades after 1945, South Wales, in many ways, forms

the paradigm of relatively, though by no means totally, unsuccessful industrial Britain. At the end of the war, South
Wales still very much fell within J. B. Priestley's 'nineteenth-
century' category, for collapse in demand for coal and steel had
made South Wales a scrap-heap in the inter-war period. Because
of wartime needs, these two industries again dominated in 1945.
As Graham Humphrys (*South Wales*, 1972) has so well put it:

> Individual industries still wore their nineteenth-century forms. Steel
> sheets were still being hand-dipped in molten tin to make tin-plate
> in small scattered works. Colliers still picked coal by hand from
> two-foot seams and afterwards went home to wash in a tin bath in
> front of the fire. Many of the hospitals were condemned, and in many
> places things like bread, milk and coal were still being delivered by
> horse and cart.

Working their effects upon this traditional background as the
post-war decade advanced, was the familiar mix of ideas
mooted (and to some extent practised) in the thirties, the forced
changes of the war, and the good intentions of politicians and
planners. Apart from expansion in the coal and steel industries,
munition factories were built at Bridgend, Hirwaun, Glascoed,
and Pembrey, together with servicing and stores depots, and a
new aluminium works was established. The Treforest Industrial Estate, near Pontypridd, was a brave, if tiny, thirties
initiative: after war broke out new factories were set up to
produce a range of strategic goods from optical lenses to
parachutes.

During the war, and immediately after, a number of amalga-
mations took place within the steel industry, so that by the late
forties it was largely dominated by Richard Thomas and
Baldwins (formed in 1944), the Steel Company of Wales
(formed in 1946) and Guest Keen and Nettlefolds. Guest Keen
and Baldwins were responsible for re-building three blast-
furnaces during the period 1943–6. In comparison with these
private initiatives, the question of the nationalization of the iron
and steel industry, which generated so much political fury, was
of little real relevance.

The great symbol of the post-war reconstruction of the iron
and steel industry was the building, between 1947 and 1951, of

the Port Talbot works at a total cost of £73 million. Its importance is encapsulated in the local nickname given to it of Treasure Island. But as with the expansion of the Consett ironworks, the location of this new massive plant was determined more by tradition and the immediate past, than by any careful analysis of future trends. The Port Talbot site was chosen essentially with tin-plate in mind rather than uncoated sheet-steel and, as David W. Heal has written, it 'represents a prime example of a location which was chosen in the context of one trade, but which has been required to serve another'. The governing factor was the internal development already undertaken by Guest Keen and by Baldwins.

Wartime factories were there to hand for eager industrialists. Deliberate Government policy encouraged the building of the new type of one-storey factories located in open fields outside the towns. The Government sponsored 112 of the 179 new factories (or substantial factory extensions) which were built in South Wales between the end of the war and 1949. Unemployment dropped to 2·8 per cent compared with 20 per cent in the thirties. Prosperity continued right through to the later fifties so that, not unnaturally, the development area policies were relaxed. But, in the longer term, they were perhaps not as satisfactory as they appeared: diversification was the great panacea, while close attention was not always given to the needs either of the world or even of the national market.

The steel industry had performed competently during the war, and its industrialists, vigorously supported by the Conservative Party in Parliament, were able to delay nationalization. The record, long-term as well as short-term, of the coal industry was very different, and nationalization was carried through in 1946. Much needed investment was channelled largely into the bigger collieries, though the smaller ones lasted till the late 1950s. South Wales in this period, then, was a mixture of refurbished nineteenth-century industry, together with enthusiastically developed new industry with all its accoutrements. It, too, had its new town, Cwmbran, designated in 1948.

Across the Bristol Channel lies the West Country, with Cornwall at the extremity rather barren, Devon much less so,

and Somerset joining the other lush counties in stretching east-
wards into the heartland of pre-industrial England. Bristol itself
did well: out of the war experience burst the growth industries
of light engineering, aviation, and electronics; nail-biting civilian demand in a time of austerity created a boom in the
age-encrusted tobacco trade. The historic port of Plymouth, its
town centre blitzed to the ground, had to embark immediately
on an intensive re-building programme. However, it was the
whole varied region, both to the north and the south of the
Thames, which profited most from the expansion in arable land
promoted by the war. This was the area which embraced most
enthusiastically new farming methods, and which achieved new
levels of prosperity whether in dairy farming or in the fast
developing industry of market gardening. In the upper Thames
valley such major centres as Reading and Oxford were doing
nicely, as were the slightly smaller towns of Banbury and New-
bury, already developing as substantial industrial centres.

So we come to London and the South-East, which, in the
plottings of planners then, as in the plots of playwrights both
before and since, commanded the lion's share of attention. And,
although the Industrial Revolution began in the provinces,
there can be no gainsaying the special place occupied by London
in both history and geography. The war had focused attention
on the noisome nature of London's slums, while at the
same time destroying numbers of them. Overspill, rehousing,
and the establishment of the green belt were key notions. At
the same time, the Labour Government sought to restrict office
building in Central London. The overall picture was of a movement outwards to new suburban estates, and further afield to the
new towns of which London's periphery had a disproportionate
number: Basildon, Bracknell, Hemel Hempstead, Hatfield, Ste-
venage, Harlow, and Crawley, together with the older Welwyn
Garden City. By 1956 each of these was expanding at a rate
of 9,000 houses a year. Overspill could go yet further afield
and in 1952 the first Londoners arrived in Bletchley, a town
lying on the frontiers of the Home Counties and the South
Midlands, which had itself undergone some transformations
during the war due largely to the siting there of large numbers

of civil servants and the establishment of the Military Intelligence unit in Bletchley Park.

Whatever the planners' intentions, the Greater London conurbation expanded at a rate comparable with that of the West Midlands. That unique wash of brick-built terrace houses, brightened by little high street shopping centres, which spread across such inner London suburbs as Kentish Town, Islington, Leyton, Hackney, Fulham, and Camberwell, asserted a special charm. It was already clear by the early fifties that there was no rush whatsoever to leave these terraces and that, indeed, they were rising in value as London continued to parade its age-old attractions.

Last we come to East Anglia, often treated as least, since it does not fit easily into any broad taxonomy of British social geography. Still in the forties and early fifties East Anglia retained something of its remote quality, though change was fast breaking in. Predominantly a region of arable farming, it had been in steep decline in the period from 1870 to 1939. As with other areas the war brought new prosperity. The amount of land under arable was actually increased while, in addition to this, there were also increments in livestock farming. By the early fifties there were trading estates at Haverhill and Thetford; more crucially, modest prosperity in other parts, particularly London, intensified tourism on the Broads and round the coasts so that villages and towns were being prodded out of the romantic isolation hymned to every middle-class child in the days of Arthur Ransome and Coot Club.

One characteristic of the depressed industrial areas in the inter-war years had been their loss of population. Over the country as a whole, the birth-rate had been declining in the inter-war years, and was down to sixteen births per year per thousand of the population on the eve of war. However, in 1942 there occurred the first rise in the birth-rate since 1880. This developed into the post-war 'baby boom' which culminated in 1947 with a birth-rate of 20·7 per thousand. However, this appeared to be a purely war phenomenon, for the birth-rate fell again thereafter, causing something of the same concern as there had been in the thirties that Britain was moving towards having a declining population: hence the setting-up of the Royal Commission on Population at the end of the forties.

In the development areas population at least seemed to be stabilized, no longer in decline. There was a definite drift towards the West Midlands and towards London and the South-East; and there was a general drift from country to town. The Highlands of Scotland remained a place apart in that this region continued to suffer a serious loss of population, but for Britain as a whole a new stable prosperity seemed to be recognized when the 1951 census revealed for the first time a net gain by migration of half a million: England and Wales gained three quarters of a million from Scotland, Ireland, and overseas, while Scotland lost a quarter of a million. Britain in the late forties and early fifties, then, was a densely populated country (though with areas of very sparse population), exceeded in population density only by Japan, Belgium, and the Netherlands. Four fifths of the population were living in towns, and half of these town dwellers were to be found in Greater London or in the six provincial conurbations of the West Midlands, South-East Lancashire, Merseyside, West Riding, Tyneside, and Clydeside.

Yet there was still a slightly archaic quality to transport and communications. The expanding sector, certainly, was that of road transport – meaning, however, transport by bus and coach not by private car. Rail passenger transport remained pretty static, whereas in 1950 passenger mileage by bus and coach had risen to 50·2 thousand million passenger miles (as against 19·4 in 1938), accounting for nearly one half of the total market compared with less than one third before the war; road transport as a whole now accounted for about 75 per cent of all mileage travelled. In the towns, buses were taking over from trolley-bus and tram: by 1952 bus passenger miles within the cities and towns amounted to 14·5 thousand million, as against 2·9 thousand million clocked up by trolley-buses, and 1·8 thousand million taken by trams.

The great expansion in private car ownership began only in the very last years of the period under review. In 1938 there had been just under 2 million private cars and vans on the roads; in 1948 there were just over 2 million, and in 1950 between 2·25 million and 2·5 million. In 1955 the figure rose steeply to over 3·6 million, though that was still a mild foretaste of things yet to come. Roads were poor, and still served local needs rather than those of national travel. Although dual carriageways had been built near large towns, trunk roads on the whole were narrow and winding. It took a whole day to drive from London to Edinburgh; if going further north, you went up-river to the Kincardine Bridge, or queued for a ferry as medieval citizens had done in the days when Queensferry got its name. To get to South Wales it was necessary to go through Gloucester. Only in 1955 was it announced that Britain's first motorway (planned in the forties) would be built; but the word itself was as yet scarcely known to the wider public, certainly not as a term of abuse. For those with eyes to see it was clear that, compared, say, with Germany, France, and Italy, the British motor industry had taken the soft option of catering to home demand, failing to develop a strong orientation towards exports; while the road transport system, likewise, was inadequate for the needs of the modern world.

However, there were many successes. Britain spent far more on research and development than any of the European countries. The heaviest spending was channelled into aircraft manufacture, telecommunications, precision engineering, and chemicals. By the early fifties a considerable reorientation of Britain's exports had taken place, so that two thirds were drawn from the new science-based and technological industries. But scientific discovery and technological innovation, by their very nature, are international in their consequences. Britain derived much from American pioneering; but other countries took much from Britain. Scientific and technological innovation alone would not keep Britain in the position which, precariously, she still occupied in Europe in the later fifties.

2. *That Topic All-Absorbing: Class*

Nobody would disagree that it makes sense to divide Britain up geographically into different regions, though there might be a good deal of disagreement as to how these regions should be defined: is there such an entity as East Anglia? Should Scotland be divided into three? Should one be guided by political history, or by physical geography, or by basic occupational activity? Probably there would be about as much agreement that Britain in the late forties and early fifties could be divided up into a number of social classes, though there would also be much disagreement about how and where lines should be drawn.

If we study the popular vocabulary of the time we find widespread and quite precise use of the phrase 'working class' or 'working classes' – the phrases are really synonymous, for the latter one was not intended to indicate several distinct classes but rather the variety of occupations and income levels within the one class; we find a rather more varied and less precise use of 'middle class' and 'middle classes' as well as 'lower-middle class' and 'upper-middle class' (journalists and academic writers might also speak of a 'middle-middle class' but that phrase had no standing in ordinary colloquial English). While the broad notion of there being a working class and a middle class, however divided up, was well established, there was less agreement over the use of the term 'upper class': many of those who might be thought, by objective criteria, to have belonged to such a class preferred to refer to themselves, and were often described by others, as 'upper-middle class'. This usage postulated the continuing, if somewhat etiolated, existence of an 'aristocracy', the real upper class.

The essential difficulty in studying class is that while one can directly recognize the existence of women, of blacks, of the Catholic Church, or of council housing estates, one cannot directly apprehend the existence of classes. All one can do then (unless one has some *a priori* theory, such as Marxism) is agree that class exists when people themselves, explicitly or implicitly, recognize its existence and behave in ways which reflect its existence. Three elements make up class as it actually is. First of all, class is shaped by history. It originates with the Industrial Revolution, which steadily replaced an older society of estates and orders by one made up of the more fluid and imprecise social classes. Industrialization proceeded at different speeds in different parts of the country. Political events, traditions, national characteristics, and the more recent upheavals of war all affected the forms of class as they were after 1945.

Second, class has a very strong subjective element. It is by studying what people say and write about class, by studying, that is, 'images' of class, that we are best able to map out a social structure which conforms with life as actually lived in the period under review, as distinct from merely being an abstract tool of analysis. Thirdly, we can quite unequivocally perceive areas of inequality in modern society: in power, authority, wealth, income, job situation, material conditions, and culture and lifestyles. Once the subjective contours of class have been sketched out, it becomes clear that they do tend to coincide with the major social inequalities.

Was there, then, an upper class in post-war Britain? Long before the Industrial Revolution successful men of business, politics, and the professions had become part of the aristocracy and, within a very short space of time, they and their descendants were behaving as to the manor born. No revolution overthrew this aristocracy which continually renewed itself from below. There used to be much loose talk of 'the rise of the middle class' and of the middle class taking over from the aristocracy with the passing of the Great Reform Act of 1832. In fact the great commercial families, like the Peels and Gladstones, did not overthrow the aristocracy, they joined it, leaving the vast mass of middlingly successful business and professional people to continue occupying a middling station in life.

As the nineteenth century advanced, a new composite upper class emerged consisting of the older aristocracy (many of whose members, anyway, were, a generation or two further back, products of commercial wealth) and a greatly increased number of recruits from commerce, industry, government, and the higher professions. It was still possible, of course, to make a fine distinction between 'aristocrats' on one side, and the 'upper-middle class' (by one definition) on the other. Here we come up against one of the many confusing features of class. When it is a question of fine distinctions, as opposed to the broad historically significant categories, we find that much depends on the class position of the individual observer. If you belong to the upper class yourself you may well be very aware of the distinction between a true landed aristocrat and a successful industrialist; if you belong to the classes below the distinction may not even be apparent let alone real. Thus, just before the war, Lord Londonderry could refer to Britain's then Prime Minister, Neville Chamberlain, as 'a Birmingham tradesman' while most of Chamberlain's fellow countrymen may well have been more struck by his projection of the upper-class manner and life-style. For, in the nineteenth century, the upper class elaborated on older traditions in evolving a distinctive ethos inculcated through the major public schools and, in lesser degree, Oxford and Cambridge universities. There was created an upper-class 'box' of attitudes and life-styles into which newcomers could be socialized.

We have to recognize, then, that there is ambiguity in the usage of the phrase 'upper-middle class'. For myself, I prefer the simple phrase 'upper class' to describe what Sir Ian Fraser (in a private letter written in the 1930s) shrewdly defined as that 're-servoir of persons economically free and accustomed to responsibility from an early age' who, as a matter of objective fact, turn out to exercise a dominance in the spheres of power, authority, wealth, and income totally disproportionate to their numbers, and who have a distinctive culture and life-style of their own. I would estimate this class as making up about 2 per cent of the population in the years after 1945. The phrase 'upper-middle class' is then better applied to the upper segment of the class below, a class without this disproportionate dominance of wealth and power. Still, the ambiguity does exist and indeed has a real significance. It was part of the very upper-class ethos that one should be reticent in speaking of class: hence many upper-class people preferred the softer camouflage of the description 'upper-middle-class'; but more than this – 'everybody loves a lord', and there was a very deep vein of snobbishness making for the continued elaboration of a distinction between those truly aristocratic and those who, for lack of a better phrase, must be distinguished as 'upper-middle-class'. Finally, there was the problem of that wretched foreign word *bourgeois*, often translated into English as 'middle-class'. Those who believed that the bourgeoisie now ruled the country thus sometimes confusingly termed the upper class the 'middle class' or the 'upper-middle class'. (In fact the bourgeoisie – the urban élite whose wealth was based on commerce and trade – had been invading the aristocracy since the sixteenth century.)

There was little ambiguity about the composition of the working class. Of the total employed population, well over 60 per cent did manual work of one sort or another, ranging from unskilled roadwork to the craftsmanship of the engine driver or mechanic. Manual workers and their families formed the working class, with which would usually be included small shopkeepers and publicans in working-class areas. Foremen and floor managers occupied an ambiguous position on the fringes, as did the technicians in many of the newer industries. If we mark off the upper class and the working class, we are left with the middle class, or middle classes, in between, amounting to well over 30 per cent of the population. Setting aside all the subtle shades of distinction which exist within all social classes there remains quite an important, though far from rigid, line between the lower-middle class of, essentially, clerical and other types of white-collar worker, and the upper-middle class of local businessmen and the more prestigious professionals.

According to classical Marxist sociology, classes in the modern era are becoming polarized, an upper class of the owners of capital on one side, and a proletariat on the other, with the 'transitional' middle class steadily being forced down into the latter. Increasing polarization, inevitably, means increasing likelihood of class conflict. Conservative sociologists, on the other hand, have presented a thesis of the 'disintegration' of classes, producing a long continuous range of status groups, in place of a small number of discrete social classes.

The growth of large-scale industrial organization and the so-called 'managerial revolution' has, it was argued, replaced old-style capitalists with salaried managers. This analysis was at least as superficial as the polarization thesis: owners of capital in the forties and fifties were often also managers; successful managers often acquired capital. Thus there was in fact quite a clear class distinction between major businessmen on the one side, who, combining managerial power with capital ownership, formed part of the upper class, and mere managers on the other, who were part of the middle class.

The disruptions of war had not been without effect on class and relationships between classes. The most important single development was the change in status and bargaining power of the working class. Resorting as necessary to strikes, the workers were able to exploit the very high demand for labour engendered by the necessities of war to push their real earnings up by well over 50 per cent. The much vaunted 'mixing' of social classes during the war was more in spirit than substance, but undoubtedly there was a new upper-class and middle-class concern that, having played so crucial a role in the war effort, the workers should not be plunged back into the economic depression of the inter-war years. The egalitarian policies mooted during the war and, in large degree, carried out by the Labour Government after the war did not, as many hoped (or feared), alter the basic social structure, but in general they favoured the working class. High taxation during and after the war hit the upper-middle class hardest, lowering the barriers between it and the lower-middle class. Overall, the war strengthened the solidarity and self-awareness of the working class. Thus there was both disintegration of class boundaries and consolidation within classes.

The advent of a Labour Government in 1945 did not mean that the upper class necessarily relinquished power. Of Labour leaders, Hugh Dalton, Sir Stafford Cripps, and John Strachey could scarcely be described as anything other than upper-class; Clement Attlee, the new Prime Minister, undoubtedly thought of himself as middle-class and was usually perceived as such by political opponents; but as the product of a prosperous family of solicitors, who had been educated at the fairly prestigious public school, Haileybury, and at Oxford, he could more reasonably be placed as first-generation upper-class. The Haileybury school magazine in November 1945 was able to congratulate itself on the election of only one Conservative old boy, but of four Labour old boys and its first ever Prime Minister, to whom it extended congratulations, 'proud that he is a son of Haileybury, and confident that he will not fail his high trust'.

In any case, the Conservatives were back in power after 1951, by which time, however, there had been a slight shift in the balance of forces within the party: there were more small businessmen and fewer big businessmen, and more representatives of such new growth areas as investment trusts, insurance, property development, advertising and public relations, entertainment, and communications. Whatever party was in office, the higher civil service continued to be dominated by the upper class; of the successful candidates for open entry to the administrative class in 1949–52, 74 per cent came from Oxbridge. Nationalization changed little: in many cases the former private owners and managers simply because the managers and directors of the state enterprises; in others the directorate was filled with established figures from the army, politics, and the civil service, social revolution being represented by a handful of trade unionists.

Rationing, controls, and shortages might have been expected to have had a crippling effect on traditional upper-class lifestyles. A quick survey of the sources shows that many within the upper-class fold were able to lead a life of considerable amplitude in the age of austerity. Already in 1946 'Chips' Channon was celebrating the fact that life was back to 'normal' and that the fashionable Carcano–Ednam wedding of that year was a suitably lavish affair. Channon was American-born: his career in high society, charted in his diaries, clearly demonstrates the existence of the upper-class 'box' into which a wealthy outsider, prepared to adopt the appropriate life-style and mannerisms, could readily be absorbed. Harold Nicolson, his family, his wife's family (the Sackvilles), and their associates were not noticeably thrown by rationing either. The Nicolson diaries contain many classic presentations of the upper-class self-image:

for example, 'I do believe, as I have always believed, that Social Democracy is the only possible antidote to communism. But I do not like the Labour Party. I am a mixture of an aristocrat and a Bohemian. The bedintness ['a Sackville expression, denoting the attitudes and manners of the lower-middle class,' explains Nigel Nicolson] of the Labour people is as repugnant to me as is their gentility.'

But Harold Nicolson could scarcely match the boisterous élitism of Labour's own Chancellor of the Exchequer, Hugh Dalton, recording in his diary the personal triumph of an old King's man back on the familiar ground of the Cambridge Union:

I scored the first Labour victory of the term by 180 to 170 odd, which was very gratifying. Two points which I think turned votes were:
(i) my declaration that we were spending, and would continue to spend, substantial sums on the Universities, and
(ii) a new declaration of Government policy which I made on the Olympics. I said that I had been informed by the President of the C.U.B.C. [Cambridge University Boat Club] who had the good sense to belong to my old college, that in the Olympics the Boat crews would have to row in old British boats with old British oars against foreign crews in new British-built boats with new British-built oars ... I was, however, very glad to inform them that that very day, before leaving London, I had been in touch with the Admiralty as well as with the Secretary of State for Air who was not only an old King's man and an old President of the Union, but also an old Olympic Captain, and I was able now to say that the Admiralty would give special consideration to providing, as a most exceptional case, suitable boats and oars for the British crews in the Olympics. 'After that declaration of Government policy,' I cried, 'I am confident that no rowing man will vote for this ridiculous resolution.'

If, instead of flicking through the diaries of the rich, we turn to the meticulous social survey conducted by Professor Margaret Stacey between 1948 and 1951 in the Oxfordshire town of Banbury, we encounter the considered verdict that 'it was impossible to ignore the existence of upper-class people'. Furthermore, 'in so far as this class sets the standards and aspirations of traditional social class attitudes ... it is important out of all proportion to its size'. Finally, 'members of the traditional upper class in the Banbury district were all educated at one of the major public schools'.

High politics was a traditional occupation for the denizens of Sir Ian Fraser's 'reservoir'; otherwise the city, the diplomatic corps, or the higher civil service. But in a new age, upper-class figures were moving into other jobs as well. After Eton and Balliol, the Hon. John Godley (later Lord Kilbracken) joined the *Daily Mirror*, 'in preference to becoming a diplomat'. By the mid-fifties journalism, publishing, films, radio, television and advertising had become classic refuges for the upper class. More: on the eve of coal nationalization J. L. Hodson visited three up-to-date collieries in the North-East: 'The first surprise was to discover that the chairman of directors, managing director and chief engineer are the sort of men one meets as officers in the Guards or Royal Navy: men in their thirties or forties, beautifully turned out, quietly spoken, with accents traditional to the South.'

Perhaps these men were upper-middle-class rather than upper-class – that much is suggested by their quiet speech, definitely not an upper-class characteristic. Some insecurity over where the borders of the upper class lay might be suggested by Nancy Mitford's infamous article in *Encounter* (September 1955) defining the distinctions between upper-class usage ('U') and non-upper-class usage ('non-U'). In fact a basic point of the article was to assert that the significant barrier lay between aristocracy and upper-middle class on one side, and middle class and the rest on the other.

The middle-class self-image comes through clearly in some unpublished Mass Observation material dating from 1949. A woman civil servant clearly envisaged a three-class society, with herself in the middle, or lower-middle:

I definitely think of myself as middle-class. It is difficult to say why. I had a typical middle-class education (small private school and secondary school). I have a middle-class job and I live in a middle-class district. But none of these things would make me middle-class in themselves. If I had been clever enough to get a higher post or profession, or rebellious enough to choose a more attractive manual job, I should not thereby have changed my class. Nor should I change it by living in a different district. Besides, my education and job and residence (to a certain extent) were determined by the fact that my parents were middle-class so it is like the old riddle of the hen and the egg. Income has something to do with it but is not in itself a deciding factor nowadays as many working-class people get higher pay than the lower middle-class, and many upper-class 'new poor' get less.

A prosperous housewife gave her reasons for allocating herself and her husband to 'the Upper-Middle Classes'. These were 'Financial' – her husband earned a good income and they now lived on the interest from investments; 'Genealogical' – their fathers were respectively architect and headmaster; 'Occupation and Educational' – her husband was an MA of Cambridge and had been Director of Agricultural Research in the Sudan; 'Sartorial' – 'We know what is correct wear even though we may have to make do with our old clothes'; 'Cultural' – they enjoyed good music, books, plays, etc.; 'Conventional' – 'We eat in the dining room and use the conventional speech. We speak grammatical English in accepted pronunciation.'

Another woman, the wife of a production manager in an engineering firm, in declaring herself to be 'lower-middle-class', placed the emphasis on contrasting their position with those below:

... our education is of a higher standard than most working-class people. This has produced a standard of tastes in music, art and literature different from those of working-class people. (There are exceptions of course.) Our speech is different than most working-class people in this district, having a particular dialect and a larger vocabulary. Our circle of friends is mainly of the same type of person as ourselves as with two or three exceptions they do not coincide with those of working-class acquaintances. Do not think I am a snob. Can mix easily with working-class people, and do so in church and Parents' Association activities. But as friends, I find them unsatisfying and in conversation limited in subject common to both.

A fourth housewife chose to describe herself simply as of 'professional' status because: 'I can hardly say "middle class" now, though I was brought up in it. Our threadbare conditions seem at variance with the comfortable plumpness one associates with the term "middle class".'

Margaret Stacey found that a common educational background was not a specific middle-class characteristic. This makes sense: the middle class recruited from all sections of society. On the other hand, Professor Stacey found, 'the majority of the working class have received only an elementary education while a much higher proportion of the middle class received a secondary education'

Historians have argued that, for the late nineteenth and early twentieth century, the distinction between 'respectable' working class and 'rough' working class was at least as significant as that between the working class and the lower-middle class. After 1945 this does not appear to be the case; there were still 'roughs', it is true, but on the whole the working class presents a homogeneous appearance, and a self-confident one, with little aspiration after middle-class values. None the less, it is true that Reginald Bevins, a Conservative Minister in the sixties, wrote in his autobiography, *The Greasy Pole* (1965): 'My mother and sisters dominated the family and, like many women who came from working-class families and have seen the effects of insecurity, her main ambition was that her children should be secure'; but he also recorded that 'she had a positive horror of politics (she would not even vote) which she regarded as an exclusive aristocratic pursuit and, for a shopkeeper, an invitation to bankruptcy'. The new sense of security of the post-war generation was boldly articulated by a plumber (interviewed in 1951): 'There is now so much work to be done and so little unemployment so if the boss rattles at you or threatens you with the sack you can just up and leave ... The working people are better off and the bosses have lost a lot of their grip.' Above 'the bosses', incidentally, he recognized a 'snob class, the high-ups, senior civil servants, directors and such'. In 1949 a leader of the Transport and General Workers had declared: 'Let there be no mistake about it, we have made substantial progress in working-class conditions during the life-time of this government.'

For all that, the basic fact remained: to be working-class meant performing manual work, most usually under arduous, uncongenial, or just plain boring circumstances. Conditions of work still demanded special working clothes, and still often left definite physical marks – calloused hands, for instance. When it came to 'life chances' members of the working class were still at a disadvantage compared with all of the rest of society. Individual members might move upwards, but conditions within the working class, not excluding working-class attitudes themselves, discouraged educational aspiration.

Class is a difficult and messy subject, but indisputably neither the upheavals of the Second World War nor the programme of the Labour Government abolished it. Technological change, certainly, brought new obfuscations and subtleties. Margaret Stacey reckoned that alongside the clearly marked traditional three-tier class structure, there also existed 'non-traditionalists' whose mobility through the technocratic sectors of society was such that they could scarcely be placed in any definite class. This is a useful concept, though, personally, I prefer to take it with a pinch of salt. When a representative sample of the British public was polled in 1948 there was little hesitation over opting for appropriate class labels, even if there was an evident tendency for some manual workers to put themselves in the middle class: asked, without prompting, to allocate themselves to a social class, 2 per cent said 'upper', 6 per cent said 'upper-middle', 28 per cent said 'middle', 13 per cent said 'lower-middle', 46 per cent said 'working', and only 5 per cent recorded 'no reply'.

If we are to compare the significance of class with that of other sources of distinction and inequality, such as age, sex, nationality, race, or religious community, class stands out as a key factor in such matters as wealth, political power, educational opportunity, and style of life. The social facts of post-war Britain cannot be *explained* solely by reference to class, but they certainly cannot be fully *understood* without reference to class.

3. The Welfare State

The phrase 'welfare state' (actually coined by Professor Alfred Zimmern in the 1930s) came into widespread use during the war to point a sharp contrast with Hitler's 'warfare state'. The phrase has since been used in a variety of rather loose ways, but essentially it means the totality of schemes and services through which the central Government together with the local authorities assumed a major responsibility for dealing with all the different types of social problems which beset individual citizens.

Most fundamental of these problems is that of income or *social* security: people can fail to have enough to live on through being unemployed, through being unemployable, through being too old, through having too many children, through being injured, through being pregnant, and through being ill. But if people are ill, they do not just need an income while they are out of work, they need treatment: the second problem is that of the provision of *medical services*. Sickness, in the past, had often been engendered by bad housing; good housing for everyone, in any case, was the mark of a civilized society. *Housing*, then, was the third problem to be dealt with by the welfare state. If individuals were to participate fully in a civilized society they should also have a decent *education* – the fourth problem. But what point in having national insurance benefits, free medical care, proper housing, and wise schooling, if there were no jobs? It was a fundamental assumption of the war and post-war period that all of the different pieces of welfare state legislation would be backed up by an economic policy deliberately designed to create jobs and *avoid unemployment*. Finally, there were other areas of social life which a government, determined to hoover into spotlessness the Britain of the slums and Woolworth's spectacles, could also suck up: the arts, the environment generally, the care of children.

Whatever Government had come into power in 1945, undoubtedly legislation would had been passed to deal with these various issues. The great symbolic statement of British objectives, one which had been quoted round the world, was the Beveridge Report of December 1942. A vain and difficult man, very much, as a top civil servant and head of an Oxford college, a member of the upper class, Beveridge had deployed much Victorian fustian in his report, borrowing indeed from the language of *A Tale of Two Cities* when he pinned down the problems discussed above as five 'giants': 'want', 'sickness', 'squalor', 'ignorance', and 'idleness'. The report which, formally, was on the rather boring topic of 'social insurance and allied services' recommended a universal social security system covering everyone in the country; but it stressed as 'assumptions' that there should be a national health service, an economic policy directed towards avoidance of mass unemployment, and, more tenuously, an attack on the other 'giants'. Despite recent (erroneous) claims by Margaret Thatcher to the contrary, the Beveridge Report was in fact attacked by many Conservatives, and also by many other vested interests. Churchill, in his 1945 election campaign, emphasized (and who would now say he was totally wrong?) the country's serious economic position and the difficulties in the way of quickly establishing all the social provisions which the Labour Party, in its campaign, promised.

Social security provision, of a sort, went back half a century. Workmen's Compensation dated back to 1893, old-age pensions to 1908, with a more elaborate scheme introduced in 1928, unemployment insurance and health insurance to 1911 (implemented in 1913).

The Labour Government's legislation was in part intended to mark a break with the past, but it was also, on the one hand, constrained by the legislative framework evolved in the past, and, on the other hand, coloured by memories of that same past. Broadly, Labour policies were hitched to the star of 'universality'; the Conservatives would probably have aimed lower at 'selectivity'. Every Labour politician knew of the bitterness of the unemployed man thrown off unemployment insurance once his claim on the system was exhausted; the 'means test' which had to be undergone before unemployment assistance was forthcoming sounded in Labour ears as once the phrase 'Spanish inquisition' had sounded in the ears of Protestant zealots; and the humiliation was still deeply felt over the way in which 'panel patients' got one standard of service from their doctors, while the private patients got another. The Labour idea, then, in stressing the principle of universality was two-fold: only by making the state services open to all could it be ensured that the highest standards would be available to all; only by having a universal service could the stigma be removed from those who had to make use of state services.

Actually, the first piece of new social security legislation was carried through by the Conservative 'caretaker' Government, which held office briefly in the period between the resigna-tion of the wartime coalition, and the assumption of office of the newly elected Labour Government. The most significant point about family allowances, payable in respect of second and later children in all income groups, was that they were payable to the mother, a very rudimentary sign of feminist influence on social legislation, which recognized women's rôle as child-rearers, and was designed to prevent husbands from spending the money on drink or horses.

Family allowances, in a rather small way, embodied a social philosophy adhered to by many members of the Labour Party: not only did they apply to the whole community, but they were financed by general taxation, and they were, furthermore, themselves subject to taxation; in other words, a need in respect of having two or more children was automatically recognized; the rich in general contributed more and got back less, and yet there was no public distinction between the poor (who in prac-tical terms did best) and the rich. But when it came to the central element in the maintenance of income, the National Insurance scheme as promulgated by the National Insurance Act of 1946, other philosophies prevailed. In the past there had been much Labour hostility to the principle of contributory insurance, but an even stronger hatred from the recent past was of anything that could be presented as a 'dole' or unearned hand-out. Thus the new concept of universality was simply grafted on to the older tradition of National Insurance.

In the Beveridge plan it had been intended that benefits, to be paid at one flat rate, should be sufficient for the maintenance of a basic minimum subsistence standard (Beveridge expected individuals to top this up with private insurance schemes); introducing the National Insurance Bill, the Minister, James Griffiths, formerly a Welsh miner, declared that it marked the introduction of 'the principle of a National Minimum Standard'. Actually, at forty-two shillings (£2.10), the benefits were already falling behind the cost of living, and continued to fall ever further behind. The consequence of the National Insurance scheme, therefore, was that 'every person who on or after the appointed day, being over school-leaving age and under pensionable age, is in Great Britain, and fulfils such conditions as may be prescribed as to residence in Great Britain' would have a National Insurance card upon which weekly National Insurance stamps would have to be stuck; but for many of the well-off, whose earnings often continued anyway even if they were off work, the scheme would be of little real relevance, while for those whose incomes did cease with sickness or unemployment, and who had indeed to go through the whole business of securing sickness notes, the benefits were actually quite inadequate. Although the qualification and requalification conditions were elaborately spelled out, the scheme could never come anywhere near to being an authentic piece of self-financing insurance, since old-age pensions, which were soon taking up two thirds of all expenditure on National Insurance, were to be paid immediately at the full rate. At the same time the scheme could be considered neglectful of the interests of the self-employed, who were not provided with any cover against unemployment.

Yet, since the scheme was theoretically an insurance scheme, there would have to be a further means of providing for those who, in one way or another, failed to meet the qualification conditions. Thus, although the 1948 National Assistance Act formally abolished the old Poor Law, it did retain in new form the autonomous body which had begun life as the ill-famed Unemployment Assistance Board of 1934 and had been continued in 1940 as the Assistance Board. In practice this National Assistance Board had to cope also with those who received insurance benefits but found them inadequate to their needs. Save in emergencies, National Assistance would only be paid out after a personal needs test; it later transpired that many in need were in fact deterred by this from applying for it. The failure was one of misunderstanding how ordinary, bemused, ill-educated people react, rather than one of deliberate harshness; it was, indeed, a failure very much in keeping with the consensus which had developed during the war between upper-class politicians, upper-class civil servants, and self-educated working-class representatives of lofty vision. Compared with the ministerial documents and handouts of the 1930s, those of this new era were genuinely friendly and unbureaucratic and pervaded with the spirit of social democracy and welfare for all; yet the probability is that they never got through to those who most needed help.

Still, in one sense, income security, through National Insurance and National Assistance, was a relatively simple matter. All it needed was cash, and that could be raised through National Insurance contributions and through general taxation. With a slight expansion in the lower civil service it could be administered through institutions which in essence already existed. Dealing with the nation's medical problems was not so easy. The range of services required for the maintenance of health is large; the services have to be provided by qualified practitioners, often in specially designed and expensive accommodation, such as hospitals; although medical science yields new means of prevention and treatment, these means tend to be ever more costly. Medical provision before the war depended upon a primitively unstable mixture of class prejudice, commercial self-interest, professional altruism, vested interest, and demarcation disputes. For the rich there was a personal service backed up by private nursing homes, with the substantial fees earned by the doctors to some extent dependent on observing the whims of their patients. Hospitals, in origin, had been for the poor only. By the thirties there were two major types of hospital, both now taking, and charging, middle-class patients, while continuing to treat poor patients free, but bitterly divided against each other. The one thousand or so voluntary hospitals ranged from the tiniest cottage hospitals, where operations were carried out by the local general practitioner, to the great teaching hospitals, which had high-quality specialist services; surgeons made their reputations by working for nothing in the most important of these hospitals, and their incomes by ministering to rich patients. The voluntary hospitals preferred to accept only the more interesting and acute cases; the chronically sick tended to be dumped on the other type of hospital, the local authority hospitals, of which there were about 1,750. The emergencies of war brought a more rational organization, with both types being merged into the Emergency Hospital Scheme organized on a regional basis, though the destruction and disruption of war reduced still further the actual amount of reasonable hospital accommodation available over much of Britain.

The National Health Insurance scheme, administered through private companies known as the 'approved societies', permitted the insured worker to have free medical service from his 'panel' doctor and occasionally, depending on the efficiency of the approved society, to have additional benefits, such as help towards purchasing spectacles. But there was no free medical service for the families of the insured workers, and many others were excluded from the scheme. For these groups doctors provided private services, charging what fees they could, sometimes having to employ professional debt collectors, and always being limited in what they could prescribe by the patients' ability to pay.

Dental care and ophthalmic care were luxuries for the middle and upper classes. The worker went to the dentist only in the last agony of toothache, and then only to have teeth pulled out. Glasses, he obtained direct from Woolworth's or other department stores. For the well-to-do, the private midwife and the nursery nurse supplemented the ante-natal, post-natal, and infant care provided by the general practitioner. For the generality of the nation's mothers one blessing at least of the First World War, much neglected by historians, had been the Maternity and Child Welfare Act of 1918: through the provisions of this Act a separate, inferior, but not inefficient service was provided by health visitors, midwives, and doctors working for the local health authority. Finally, the last tattered elements in this rag-bag of medical provision were to be found in the compulsory inspection and treatment of school children at the state schools, imposed by the Education Act of 1918, and in the distribution of milk and welfare foods developed during the war. The one major piece of social legislation actually enacted by Churchill's National Government was the Education Act of 1944 (pressed on with, in part, in order to divert attention from the costlier and more controversial issues of social security and national health): this Act continued the policy of local authority responsibility for the health care of school children while, in keeping with the tenor of the times, it abolished all charges made to parents.

In planning a national health service the responsible Minister (Aneurin Bevan, like James Griffiths a former Welsh coalminer, though of distinctly patrician tastes) had the advantages of the nationalized hospital system which had in all but name been operated during the war and of the strong current of opinion in favour of radical reform. His major problems concerned the shortage of resources and the (real or perceived) conflicts of interest within the medical profession, and between the profession and the local authorities, and the fact that the British local government system, established in the late nineteenth century, was now seriously out-of-date.

The National Health Service Act passed into law in the autumn of 1946; but the new National Health Service was not to come into being until 'the appointed day', 5 July 1948. In between, many tense battles had still to be fought out. In broad outline the proposed National Health Service was a monumental expression of the principle of universality. Although a proportion of the income from National Insurance stamps was to be devoted to the Health Service, treatment in no way depended upon insurance contributions: it was entirely open to everyone, and, save in the case of certain specified extra services, it was, at the point of service, entirely free; that is to say, there was no question of having to pay first then recovering the payment later, as was to be the case with health provision in certain other countries. Most important, there was now a firm separation between the question of income need (dealt with by National Insurance and National Assistance) and health need, which had no connection with these schemes.

The biggest innovation was the nationalization of the hospitals, opposed by the Conservatives, though in fact the way had been well prepared by the war experience. No one was to be forced to join the service, whether as doctor or patient. Private pay beds would be allowed to exist within the hospitals, and general practitioners would be able to carry on their own private practice if they so wished. The senior consultants knew that they would be able to go on earning large fees, and they also had the satisfaction of knowing that the special position of the big teaching hospitals would be safeguarded; junior hospital doctors were quite happy to settle for a salaried service; but how the general practitioners were to be paid was not defined in the Act. In fact, these doctors resisted the infringement of their traditional professional status which they believed to be involved in the acceptance of a completely salaried service and held out for a scheme resembling that of the old panel system whereby they received a capitation fee for each patient on their list. Thus, though industrious or popular doctors might be particularly well rewarded, there was no real incentive to good practice.

The establishment of the National Health Service has been widely seen, both at the time and since, as the most significant and successful social innovation of the period. Much of any subsequent criticism was directed towards the failure to achieve a unified administration; it became something of a cliché to inveigh against the 'tripartite' structure though, as a commission of inquiry was to note in the fifties, this bore 'the imprint of the historical circumstances from which it sprang'. Many of the better services upon which the poor had been able to draw in the past were those provided by the local authorities. So it was not altogether unreasonable that important community health services should be left firmly in the hands of the larger local authorities (the smaller authorities were deprived of their health functions): these services included midwifery, maternity and child welfare, health visiting, home nursing, domestic help, vaccination and immunization, local mental health services, ambulance transport, and the provision of health centres (though in Scotland the last two were the responsibility of the Secretary of State for Scotland). The bulk of the medical profession was not, however, prepared to be placed under the authority of local government when, after all, matters of specialized professional judgement would be involved. Thus for administering the family practitioner services a separate structure of, in England and Wales, 138 executive councils (in all but eight cases responsible for areas coterminous with counties or county boroughs), on which twelve out of twenty-five members were to be representatives of local professional interests, was established; while in Scotland, twenty-five executive councils were established on the same broad principles, though they generally covered areas larger than those of any local authority. These executive councils administered family doctor services, pharmaceutical services, dental services, and ophthalmic services.

To administer the new hospital organization, there were, in England and Wales, fourteen regional hospital boards, each centred on the medical faculty of a university, and appointed by the Minister of Health. Management committees for the 388 hospitals within the system were to be appointed by the regional boards, but the thirty-six teaching hospitals were given a special autonomy in that their boards of governors were to be appointed directly by the Minister. In Scotland, five regional hospital boards were established, four based on universities, and the fifth based on Inverness, and eighty-four hospital boards of management.

Under the National Health Service, the sale of practices was abolished. Though there was no direction of labour, doctors would be refused permission to establish themselves in wealthy areas which already had an excess of doctors, and incentives were offered to induce doctors to settle in poorer areas which were short of doctors. No such restrictions were placed on dentists; here, as was to be expected in the light of the woeful dental history of the 1930s, there simply was an absolute shortage of dentists. The scale of fees devised for dentists in order to yield an 'average' income encouraged speed rather than quality.

In the first five years of the new National Health Service economic circumstances precluded the building of any new hospitals; existing hospitals simply had to be patched and adapted. The demand for attention, for dentures, for spectacles, and for medicines of all types proved to be enormous. The more passionate enthusiasts for the new system declared that this demand simply encompassed the terrible backlog which in itself condemned the appalling neglect of the pre-war system. However, by the early 1950s it was clear that there were no finite limits on the amount of health provision that the inhabitants, even of the new Jerusalem, could consume. In 1951 (when, additionally, Labour's Chancellor, Hugh Gaitskell, was looking for money to finance Britain's contribution to the Korean War) charges were introduced in respect of spectacles, and in 1952 a basic charge was imposed for all prescriptions, and charges were made both for the supply of dentures and for dental treatment.

As public opinion polls revealed, housing was the issue on which people felt most strongly in 1945. People had endured crowded, low-standard housing in the 1930s; during the war they had been bombed out, shunted around, doubled up: now, couples looked forward most of all to a home of their own. Housing is also the area of social policy to which it is most difficult to apply a universalist philosophy. While the actual basic cost of a particular piece of medical treatment does not really vary much, land prices, house prices, the standards accepted as normal by different social classes, vary enormously; different geographical districts tend to assume distinctive class characteristics.

Existing housing legislation was quite explicitly selective: housing Acts were housing Acts 'for the working classes' as were the subsidized council housing estates which resulted from them. Formally, the housing legislation of 1946 made no departure from established principles, though both Bevan, in introducing the English Act, and Joseph Westwood, in introducing the Scottish one, explained that the phrase 'working classes' would be interpreted as meaning 'all sections of the working population'. Bevan expressed a wish to re-create the classless villages of the seventeenth and eighteenth centuries. He hoped to achieve this by raising the standard size of subsidized housing and ensuring that all houses were provided with all the conveniences of modern living.

Understandably enough, given the complexities in both

cases, the Government nationalized neither the land nor the house-building industry. Thus council housing continued to be financed in the traditional way: local authorities borrowed the money with which to build the houses, then repaid the loans partly out of an annual Government subsidy, partly out of money it was authorized to raise from the rates, and partly from the rents paid by tenants. Yet, while helpful to those in a position to invest in local government bonds, the Act offered no support whatsoever to private house building. The balance between private landlord and tenant was also kept firmly in favour of the latter by the Rent Control Acts of 1946 and 1949.

The Housing Act of 1949 did, at last, drop the phrase 'for the working classes', and at the same time made subsidies available for conversions and renovations. However, although the rents charged in the new council houses were higher than could be afforded by the lowest-paid workers, those members of the middle class who had any opportunity at all of raising a private mortgage showed no wish to live in them either. The building industry was in disarray, materials were in very short supply: in the upshot only 806,000 houses were built between 1945 and 1950; for the less fortunate there were the 157,000 pre-fabricated houses which were erected in the same period. The Conservatives in opposition spoke of 'a property-owning democracy' which, as a concept, was at least as defensible as Labour's rigid yet confused policies. In 1950 and 1951 local authorities were allowed to authorize only one privately built house for every four they built themselves. With the return of the Conservatives, private houses could be built up to the same quantity as local authority houses, and from January 1953 local authorities were empowered to license smaller private houses without question, and larger ones on their merits. In 1954, 28·5 per cent of all houses completed were constructed by private builders.

Educational policy in the post-war era was governed by the major Act passed in 1944, and, at times more important, the *interpretations* placed upon it. The major strength of the Act was that it ensured that all pupils would, around the age of eleven or twelve, move on to a form of secondary education which would, at the least, be continued till the age of fifteen. As implemented by almost all local authorities this entailed an 'eleven-plus' examination whose results would determine whether the pupil went on to a grammar school or to a secondary modern school. The route to better jobs and to higher education was through the grammar schools; the secondary modern school was the route to the traditional working-class occupations. It also became apparent that middle-class children were far more likely to do well in the eleven-plus than working-class ones who came from a background where academic pursuits were not encouraged. Apart from the non-fee-paying state schools, there continued in existence an older and higher class of grammar schools, charging fees, but also supported by a direct grant from the Government (as distinct from a subsidy paid through the local authority). And the expensive and exclusive public schools remained untouched. Thus, although the potential for mobility through the educational system was greater than it had been in the 1930s – rather more working-class children did now get through the eleven-plus into grammar schools – the whole system still very much replicated the division of the social structure into working, lower-middle, upper-middle, and upper classes.

Shortages of accommodation, equipment, and teachers made difficult the achievement of anything more than a bare implementation of the provisions of the 1944 Act. In the 1950s modest advances became possible. By January 1955 the number of pupils throughout the kingdom remaining at school till the age of seventeen and beyond was twice what it had been in pre-war years, although, expressed as a percentage of the total age group, the figures were far from impressive: 7·9 per cent in England and Wales and 9·1 per cent in Scotland. While the Conservatives ruled, the Labour-controlled London County Council opened the first three specially designed comprehensive schools which sought to overcome the eleven-plus segregation between grammar and secondary modern education; other areas, including Leicestershire and Anglesey, followed.

Where significant developments did take place, though affecting only small sections of the population, was in university education. The Labour Government adumbrated the new policy by extending the terms of reference of the University

Grants Committee in 1946; the Conservatives carried it out by raising the central grants payable to the universities. By 1956-7 almost 70 per cent of university income was coming direct from the State. Owing to the presence of ex-servicemen, the university population reached a peak of 85,421 in 1949; by 1956-7 it was up to 89,833. At this time over three quarters of all students in England were receiving public grants, with the proportion rather higher in Scotland and Wales. Thus the proportion of students drawn from 'the lower occupational categories' was higher than ever before; but the odds were still heavily weighted against a university education for a working-class child.

While it is not always easy to see just what social philosophies, if any, lay behind policy in the four obvious areas of income security, health, housing, and education, there can be no doubt that both Labour and Conservative Governments were fully committed to a philosophy of the avoidance of mass unemployment. How far their policies, as distinct from world circumstances beyond their control, were directly effective is less easy to establish. There were mild recessions in 1953-4 and 1956-7, but Governments were not really pushed to go beyond the broadly Keynesian macro-economic policies which they were pursuing. Questions of employment protection, industrial re-training, and so forth had scarcely yet surfaced in this period.

Perhaps greatest vision was shown in the realm of environmental planning though, as we saw in our tour around Britain, escape from the legacies of the past was never simple. The Town and Country Planning Act of 1947 placed a firm obligation on the larger local authorities to prepare comprehensive plans for their entire areas, for which purpose they were given extended powers of compulsory purchase and grants from the Government. A development charge was levied on any increase in land values brought about by development or projected development; this innovation, however, though recommended by the wartime Uthwatt Report, was abolished by the Conservatives in 1955. It was the Conservatives, on the other hand, who were mainly responsible for the practical carrying-out of the provisions of the New Towns Act of 1946. In 1949 came the National Parks and Access to the Countryside Act.

The flurry of legislation carried through by the Labour

Government was completed by a number of less well-known Acts which can, perhaps, be seen as adding further dimensions to the concept of the Welfare State. The wartime Council for the Encouragement of Music and the Arts was renamed the Arts Council and given a positive rôle as the Government's official agent for the support of the arts. The Local Government Act of 1948 empowered local authorities to raise a penny rate purely for the support of the arts. The Children Act of 1948 defined the responsibilities of local authorities towards homeless children. The Legal Aid and Advice Act of 1949 provided legal aid for those too poor to pay for it.

There are two further areas which did not figure at all prominently in contemporary debates over the establishment of the Welfare State but which would usually be considered relevant to any discussion of welfare policies today. These areas concern other mechanisms for the redistribution of income apart from the obvious National Insurance and National Assistance schemes; and the question of the rôle of the social worker. The post-war era was certainly one of high progressive taxation, moderated however by a system of tax allowances going back to an earlier period. Tax relief on contributions to private pension schemes, on mortgages, and on bank loans were perhaps concessions to the better-off, though, of course, allowances in respect of dependants very much had an egalitarian basis. Food subsidies could also be seen as having a redistributive effect.

Many of the ancillary provisions of the major Welfare State legislation created a new need for trained social workers, though the great explosion in that profession was not to come till a later period. Apart from its main provisions, the National Assistance Act compelled local authorities to provide domiciliary and residential care for the physically handicapped, the elderly, and the homeless. Here few trained social workers in fact were available, and most social work continued to be undertaken by voluntary agencies operating side-by-side with the statutory services. Community care of the mentally disordered was a further responsibility placed upon the local authorities, this time by the National Health Service Act. To begin with, most staff came from a voluntary body, the Central Association for Mental Welfare. A further need for social workers was created within the local authority children's departments set up under the 1948 Children Act. In this connection the Home Office had, with the help of social work departments at certain universities, embarked on training courses. The new regional hospital boards, too, required medical and psychiatric social workers. The great burst of post-war legislation pointed the way, though it was some years before the corps of trained social workers were to become an integral part of what was understood by the Welfare State.

Politicians liked to speak of the 'mosaic' of the Welfare State; in reality it was more of a crazy paving. What was done – and it was a lot – was the result of truly noble vision, but inevitably circumscribed by the country's economic situation, by the continuing barriers and preoccupations of class, by the nature of traditional welfare institutions, and by the perceptions planners had at the time of major social issues, perceptions clouded by a knowledge of life as it had been, rather than by an understanding of life as it would be. The foundation was laid for a more professional approach within a more caring society; at the same time a new vested interest, even if determinedly disinterested, was created.

4. *Hearth, Home, and Street Corner*

We can allocate people to different social classes, we can allocate them to different regions of the country, but fundamentally life was everywhere lived as a member of a family.

The war had, in many instances, disrupted marriages and family life. Divorces reached a peak of 60,000 in 1947, ten times the pre-war figure. The passing of the Legal Aid Act two years later opened the possibility of divorce to many who had previously been deterred by the expense. By the middle fifties there were about 25,000 divorces a year. Yet there could be absolutely no doubt as to the continued popularity of marriage as a social institution. Even of those divorced, three quarters remarried. The more important historical trend can be seen in the figures relating to women in the twenty to thirty-nine age group: in 1911 only 552 out of every thousand women in this age group were married; in 1951 731 of them were married.

There was a brief 'baby boom' in the immediate post-war years, with the birth-rate reaching a peak of 20·5 per thousand in 1947. Thereafter, the birth-rate levelled off again, and it became apparent that in almost all sections of society deliberate policies of family limitation were being followed. Over the whole country in the mid-fifties the average family size (to give the figure in the absurd way in which averages always come out) was 2·3; the lowest unskilled workers and the very poor tended still to have the larger families, but in a reversal of the trend of the previous half-century, most working-class families were having the smallest number of children, whereas middle-class and upper-class parents were beginning to have slightly larger families. Of all children born in 1955, 5 per cent were illegitimate.

It was a commonplace of American sociology at the time that urbanization everywhere was converting the extended family of earlier times into isolated nuclear units. More locally, the Welfare State could be seen to be having effects in the same direction. If the State was tiding people over bouts of illness and unemployment and offering free medical advice and treatment, perhaps there was less need to call in a grandmother or raise a loan from a more fortunate uncle. Post-war housing policies offered homes in new housing estates, often many miles from the older communities in which grandparents and other relatives lived. In fact, detailed social investigation showed that, much as the family was changing, it was far too soon to write off the extended family. It was in certain sections of the middle class that the movement towards the nuclear family had gone furthest. Professional men, more than any other group, had to go where the job took them; thus professional households could become detached from the network of family relationships. At the same time, professional families were quite likely to have the resources to make possible the transport, or at least the tele-phones, by which contact could in fact be maintained. The maintenance of family connections was a facet of the upper-class ethos in any case; and upper-class people had greatest freedom of choice in place of occupation and greatest freedom of movement.

Change, and its accompanying stress, was most marked in the working class. But if surveys of the new housing estates revealed the difficulty of keeping up the old family relationships, when grandparents, particularly on the mother's side, would fre-quently live close at hand, they also revealed a strong will to keep such relationships in being. By the later fifties we are still in a transitional period. Not many working-class families had cars, and only a few had telephones: but at least the prospect was in view of being able to overcome some of the problems of geographical separation. In 1956, too, though re-housing and slum clearance programmes were well under way, many of the old working-class communities still existed virtually intact.

Even if the social services had diminished the rôle of the extended family, there were many traditional functions which were scarcely likely to disappear. Social assumptions, moral attitudes, and everyday behaviour are first learned at home. While various sorts of welfare and various kinds of schooling

might be on offer, the choices actually made could depend
heavily on parental attitudes: working-class children, as we have
noted, most often had their educational progress brought to a
premature halt. Margaret Stacey's inquiries indicated that on
political and religious issues families presented a pretty united
front: in 83 per cent of cases husbands and wives had the same
politics and 80 per cent of couples shared the same religious
affiliation. Religion, even if not actively practised, continued to
be very much a family affair. Politics, too, were often a matter
of family loyalty: working-class Conservative voters often had
Conservative parents and middle-class Labour supporters often
had Labour parents. A good case in point is the later Conservative Minister, Peter Walker, whose father, at the end of
the war, was a factory worker in the HMV factory in South
Harrow and had regularly done voluntary work for the Conservative Party during election campaigns.

In a time of serious housing shortage (there was a shortfall
of about a million and a half dwellings in 1951) many couples
had to begin married life in the home of one or other parent,
more usually the wife's parents. The wife's mother, in fact,
continued to have a key rôle. Often it was the mother who
checked out the possibility of any houses becoming vacant in
the locality. Two remarks recorded by Michael Young and
Peter Willmott say it all: 'We got it through my mother's agent.
We had to agree to do it up though and we had to give him
a bit of a dropsy' and 'Her Mum lived in Bethnal Green and
she spoke to the landlord for us. She told him we'd pay ten
quid if we could get in there.' As families moved, often unwil-
lingly, from private accommodation condemned as slums to
council housing, the opportunities for such quiet, personal
corruption diminished drastically. Here, indeed, was a clear
token of the Welfare State taking over from the extended
family: councils awarded houses on the basis of need, those from
the worst slums or with the largest families being given priority.
But the welfare authorities did not have it all their own way,
especially when it came to the ancient mysteries of childbirth
and child-rearing: 'I take more notice of my Mum than I do
of the welfare. She's had eight and we're all right. Experience
speaks for itself, more or less, doesn't it? If you're living near

your mother, you don't really need that advice. You've got more confidence in your mother than you would have in the advice they'd give you.' Maternal influence shows itself, too, in the continuance of the old custom of churching, even among the irreligious majority, after the birth of a child. When one young woman explained the custom to Young and Willmott, saying, 'It's after you've had the baby. You go and give thanks to God that you're safe and all that. It's just a matter of form, really,' her husband broke in to remark, 'Because your mother done it, you mean.' Nevertheless, out of the forty-five wives in the Bethnal Green marriage sample, all except four were churched after the birth of their most recent child.

It is perhaps slightly less easy to single out quite such a distinctive rôle for mothers in middle-class families, though no doubt it existed there as well. Certainly, Margaret Stacey in her survey of Banbury found that middle-class parents together played a critical rôle in determining what schools their children should be sent to. The special functions of the upper-class family scarcely need stressing: the putting-down at birth of the son's name for the father's public school; the ensuring of the son's succession to the appropriate Oxford or Cambridge college; and, of course, the whole apparatus of debutante balls designed to ensure that a daughter's marriage was to a properly eligible young man.

Once the family had been important as an economic unit. More and more, especially in the freer economy of the 1950s, it was becoming important as a centre of consumption. Advertisements would be directed at wives and at children as much as, or more than, at principal wage-earners. Grandparents, too, sometimes assumed a new rôle: buying insurance or creating trusts for children's education, devices which were also useful for tax deduction.

The position of women in society, and therefore to some degree within the family, had been changing since the beginning of the century, and the changes had been greatly accelerated by the Second World War. However, the basic principle of a differentiation of rôles as between husband and wife prevailed, with a wife's tasks clustering round her function as homemaker and child-rearer, just as a husband's clustered around his function as principal breadwinner. The most rigid segregation of rôles was perhaps to be found in the more isolated industrial areas, mining communities in particular. One investigation in a Yorkshire mining village described the family there as 'a system of relationships torn by a major contradiction at its heart; husband and wife live separate, and in a sense, secret lives'; wives, said the report, were placed 'in a position which although they accept it, is more demanding and smacks of inferiority'. This was a situation of tension and potential conflict, which frequently broke out into domestic rows. Middle-class folklore had it that everywhere working-class husbands lorded it over their wives, treating them with brutality and violence.

In our own age of very proper concern for the plight of the battered wife it is important to remember that violence had always featured in a proportion of marriages in all stations of life, and that it had been very prevalent in poorer working-class areas before the First World War, where poverty, bad housing, frustration, and drink produced a vicious combination. Social surveys conducted in the early 1950s found that, while, of course, traditional male attitudes persisted, there were examples in working-class homes of husbands sharing in duties formerly thought of as the wife's alone, and, above all, an acceptance that questions of family size were a matter for joint decision, not a matter of the husband's will alone. Women were having fewer children, earlier, and then often going out to work: some husbands, at least, accepted that if their wives did go out to work then they had a responsibility to help in the home.

One leading authority (Elizabeth Bott) argued that the question of whether husbands' and wives' duties were rigidly segregated or not had nothing to do with social class, but that it was in families where the family network itself, and the network of relationships with friends and neighbours, were most extensive that segregation of rôles was most marked; where the family came closest to the isolated, nuclear model, there was greatest likelihood of sharing of jobs between wife and husband. This makes sense; but it should be taken in conjunction with the fact that it was in older working-class communities that networks through the extended family and beyond were most extensive, and among middle-class professional families that they were of least significance. Thus there is much truth in the stereotype that it is in middle-class professional families that husbands would be most likely to share domestic chores with their wives. One must tread carefully, though, in this era long before the advent of women's liberation. Clearly, middle-class professional husbands, dedicated to success in their careers, depended very heavily upon their wives providing them with the comforts and security of domesticity. If we move into the upper class, we can at once see a very clear sense of rôle separation. The young man, hoping to become a Conservative MP, would find his wife inspected as well as himself; she would have a defined supportive and subordinate rôle: the constituency party, as has been said, would be counting on getting 'two for the price of one'. In the upper class, more than in any other social milieu in Britain, women were expected to be ornaments and foils to their menfolk, with the further task of maintaining the status of the family.

The most thorough study of British attitudes to marriage, courtship, and sex in this era was contained in the survey conducted by Geoffrey Gorer in January 1951 through the *People* newspaper (and published in book form as *Exploring English Character*). Asked 'Do you think English people fall in love the way you see Americans doing it on the films?' more than three quarters of his respondents said 'no', with a mere 7 per cent saying 'yes'. Two thirds of the married men and half the married women claimed they had never seriously considered marrying anyone else; 27 per cent of the men and 44 per cent of the women had – but the majority of these women belonged to the prosperous middle class of the South of England. Gorer summed up English courtship patterns as follows:

A young man meets a young woman, becomes attracted to her, courts her for between one and two years, and then may have an engagement lasting less than a further year. If the young man is a working lad from the Northern regions his future wife is likely to be the first girl by whom he was seriously attracted; if the girl is of the middle classes and from the big cities or the Southern regions she is more likely to have considered other young men before allowing herself to become seriously attached. There is little here of whirlwind romance, or of playing around before finding Miss or Mr Right; there is also little of the in-group marriage of old acquaintances which characterizes some settled communities.

Gorer further offered the generalization that 'what English men most value in their wives is the possession of the appropriate feminine skills, whereas what English women most value in their husbands is an agreeable character'; 'beauty or strength, good looks or good figure,' he concluded, 'are very seldom mentioned, and then chiefly by the single'.

Expressed attitudes towards sex are notoriously hard to disentangle from actual sexual behaviour. Loudmouths may be the shortest in actual performance; the discreet may be quietly living it up. Just over half the men and nearly two thirds of the women interviewed by Gorer expressed disapproval of sex before marriage; 43 per cent of his total sample admitted to having had a sexual relationship before or outside of marriage, while 47 per cent gave an emphatic denial. Differences both in attitudes and in actual experience (or enjoyment) of sex were apparent as between men and women. It was mainly men who declared sex to be 'very important' in marriage, and mainly women who disagreed with the statement that 'women really enjoy the physical side of sex just as much as men'; 65 per cent of men *agreed* with this statement, and 51 per cent of women. Yet the 'double standard' in sexual morality appeared to be approved more by women than by men. In support of this contention Gorer quoted a sixteen- or seventeen-year-old Liverpool girl, asked first if a man should have sexual experience before marriage: 'I think yes because until a man has such an experience he really cannot define LOVE as anything particular, because men fall victims to their emotions much more easily than women'; but women should not have such experience, 'because although I am a woman and believe in Equality of the sexes, I am still old-fashioned enough to believe a woman should be perfectly pure before she enters into matrimony'.

Lest one such example should deceive, let us balance that emancipated, yet consciously 'old-fashioned' girl against the case history of 'Miss T.' presented by Rowntree and Lavers also in 1951:

Miss T. is aged 24 and is a shop girl. She lives alone in lodgings, but frequently spends her weekends with her parents who 'have been married thirty years and are still in love'.

Miss T. is popular with men as she is very attractive (without being particularly good-looking) and she leads an active sexual life. She is quite open on the subject and says 'I don't see any harm in it. I always have one steady lover and it doesn't hurt him if I have an occasional fellow besides.'

Miss T. bets on horses if she gets a good tip, but 'cannot be bothered' with pools or greyhounds. She smokes heavily and drinks a good deal for a girl – mostly gin and lime. She was in the Land Army during the war and liked the life, except that it was too lonely. She is not happy as a shop girl and her superior is always rebuking her for laziness.

She is not interested in religion, and her sole knowledge of the Christian doctrine is that 'at school we used to read aloud from the Bible – one verse each in turn round the class. I once went to church with my friend, but it was all bobbing up and down, and I couldn't find the place in the book.'

She says her hobbies are dancing and 'going round the shops'.

Rowntree and Lavers clearly disapproved of 'Miss T.'. The 'double standard' lived. In fact, there were many evident inequalities between men and women. It is not always easy, however, to distinguish inequalities imposed by social custom (such as unequal pay for perfectly equal work) from those more deeply rooted in biology. Child-bearing and child-rearing, menstruation, lesser physical strength (balanced though by greater dexterity and, often, greater endurance) are facts. Differential ageing is probably a fact too: girls mature more quickly than boys, women last better into old age than do men, but also pass more rapidly into middle age. Where, though, do we place the custom whereby (despite Gorer's verdict on what people value in marital partners) women tended much more universally to be judged on the basis of looks alone than did men? A later generation of women were to fight against all of these, facts, fictions, and customs. For the moment we are still in an age when many old traditions governed the rôles and rewards of men and women.

If the fundamental relationship of man and wife had not really changed since the beginning of the century, the relationship of children to parents had changed considerably. Two comments from the Bethnal Green survey placed the difference in the context of the changing generations. First a young mother: 'Dad used to be very strict with us, we are different with our boy. We make more of a mate of him. When I was a kid Dad always had the best of everything. Now it's the children who get the best of it. If there's one pork chop left, the kiddie gets it'; and a young father: 'There's certainly been a change. I whack mine now, but not the beatings like we used to have. When I was a boy most of us feared our fathers more than we liked them. I know I feared mine and I had plenty of reason to.' Geoffrey Gorer found a general belief among parents that toilet training should begin early: within six months of birth, or at most within a year. There was little belief in the innocence or innate goodness of children; 68 per cent of his sample considered that children needed more discipline. 'At least some English parents,' Gorer concluded, 'find pleasure without conscious guilt in inflicting severe pain on children as punishment. The majority disapprove of such behaviour, but the emphasis with which such disapproval is voiced suggests the possibility that there is an unconscious temptation against which such defences have to be erected.'

In general, probably, changing attitudes within the working class were a little behind those in the middle and upper classes. The change is related to the limitation of family size, so that instead of being a depressing succession of squalling mouths to be fed, children could be enjoyed, and this was reinforced by the better living standards and job security of the post-war years. Finally, the war, with the evacuation of children and the separation of families, and the destruction of young lives in the bomber raids, seems to have put a new premium on the importance of children and the need to provide them with loving care. Female children were treated differently from male children, of course. The basic assumption in all classes was that girls would become wives and mothers, and should therefore be treated accordingly. Middle-class families might often be willing to send a daughter to a private school, while sending sons to the state schools; but while a son would be encouraged to fight his way on up through the system to university, the daughter's education would usually be terminated much sooner.

Where, in traditional working-class communities, extended family relationships were closest, so too, generally, were relationships with neighbours. Typically, the more isolated middle-class family would have closer associations with 'friends' rather than with 'neighbours'. Much depended on actual geographical and living conditions. To a monied squire in rural Oxfordshire, a neighbour could mean the nearest landowner, several miles away.

In the realm of working-class housing this was a time of rapid transition. The worst conditions of all were in the decaying tenements of industrial Scotland, in the workers' flats that had often been the creation of English philanthropic impulses of an earlier era, and in those larger houses in what had formerly been inner suburbs in London and the big towns, now divided into a multiplicity of, often, one-room flats: in this kind of accommodation primitive facilities were shared by several families – one lavatory on a landing, with, near it, one gas cooker on which several harried housewives had to prepare their meals. The notorious back-to-back was perhaps, by a degree, not quite so appalling: external, shared, lavatories, a rear wall which was also the rear wall of the house on the other side, and so a great shortage of light. The standard working-class house (though with infinite local variations), left intact by the slum clearance drives of the thirties, was the 'two-up two-down': two bedrooms on the first floor, two rooms on the ground floor, with a tiny scullery at the back, opening on to the yard containing the lavatory. The variable incidence of damp, dilapidation, and vermin could render the intolerable beyond description, and the tolerable degrading. None of these types of houses had baths, a condition shared by one third of all houses in Britain in 1951.

Rents were kept low by legislation, so there was no incentive for private landlords to carry out improvements. In general, local authorities cleared out the multiple-occupancy buildings first. Some families had had a taste of uncongested life outside the cities through the wartime evacuation experience and were glad to go; others were very reluctant to go: all found the local authority rents in the new estates three times as high as what they had been paying before. Husbands, therefore, having less to spend in the pubs, had to spend more time with their families. It was not always easy for middle-class couples to secure housing, at least until the acceleration of private building in the fifties; but they were used to the ethos in which money was saved in order to acquire a mortgage.

Whether life was lived in an overcrowded slum, in a new council house, on a private estate, in a Victorian semi-detached, or in a luxury flat, material conditions for everyone were somewhat different from what they had been in the 1930s. For all the harassment of rationing, shortages, and austerity, the nation as a whole was healthier and fitter in 1951 than it had ever been before. From 1948 onwards around 98 per cent of the country's school children were each drinking one third of a pint of free milk daily. Children in all sections of the community were taller and heavier than in 1936. In 1950, for the first time, infant mortality fell below thirty per thousand.

In the first post-war years almost everything was rationed, with basic foodstuffs on 'coupons', clothing on 'clothing coupons', tinned foods and dried fruits on one kind of 'points', and chocolate and sweets on another, more popularly known as 'sweetie coupons'. Rations fluctuated, but in 1948 they worked out at a weekly allowance per person of 13 oz. of meat, 1½ oz. of cheese, 6 oz. of butter and margarine, 1 oz. of cooking fat, 8 oz. of sugar, 2 pts of milk, and one egg. Between July 1946 and July 1948 even bread was rationed. Officially meals in restaurants were restricted to three courses not costing more than five shillings (the majority of British people did not, in any case, at this time eat meals on that scale in restaurants; the minority who did, though irritated by the restrictions, often were able to find ways round them). Clothes rationing, which did not end till March 1949, was a special bane. J. L. Hodson remarked that the rich were distinguished by their ability to bring a bit of colour into their clothing. A special feature of the autumn of 1946, before the icy winter set in, was that of the 'squatters', homeless families who moved in on army camps (not all of them unoccupied) and empty private mansions. Controls were greatly reduced in 1948 and again in 1950. After the abolition of clothes rationing, milk rationing followed in

January 1950, points and the restrictions on restaurant meals in May 1950; in the autumn controls were removed from flour, eggs, and soap. In one of their interview sessions in Bethnal Green, Young and Willmott encountered the father of the family eating his tea: a chop with boiled potatoes and peas. This was a far cry from the late forties, when the weekly meat ration was down as low as half a pound. For the housewife there were indeed specially serious problems in the first five post-war years in coping with shortages and juggling with points and coupons.

In a very real sense these austerity years were a threshold to the whole first post-war era: rock-hard and grey, whitened maybe by dedication and labour, but opening on the warmer times within. As the war ended, there was a great and immediate resurgence of the leisure activities characteristic of the inter-war years. Blackpool, Scarborough, the Isle of Man boomed. Cinema attendances reached a peak in 1946 (when one third of the population were going once a week, 13 per cent twice a week) and remained high; football enjoyed a golden age of large crowds. Slowly, from being a lower-middle-class preserve, the holiday camps were taken over by working-class holidaymakers. These activities drew the family in different directions. Football, and football pools, which embarked on a new lease of life after the war, were largely a male preserve. Cinema attendances divided the family by generation – young people going with other young people most frequently, parents slightly less frequently. Holidays, on the other hand, were a family matter. The more aristocratic sporting venues, Ascot and Henley for instance, provided the perfect opportunity for upper-class women, elegantly attired, to act as foils to their husbands.

The war had given children certain freedoms; economic conditions after the war fostered their independence. Gangs of adolescent, and even younger children, were nothing new; but the post-war years provided a jagged, brittle world, with the sanctions of war removed. In the forties the grown-up generation provided the semi-outcast figure who shocked the respectable and outwitted the sluggish Government: the spiv. With the early 1950s there came the first nationally recognized figure representative of youth's detachment from the rest of society and representative also of the fact that for the first time working-class youth could take the initiative: the Teddy boy.

The name derived from the Edwardian form of dress which, actually, had briefly been assumed by some bright young men of the upper class in the late forties. The family, and all its activities, still rooted in tradition, was being more and more affected by national influences; changing circumstances seemed to be pushing working-class families into middle-class attitudes, but working-class youth was preparing to take initiatives of its own. National influences were reflected in the names with which children were christened. It had been a working-class tradition to name son like father, daughter like mother. Now, in the post-war years, there was a special fashion for names like Len, Garry, Steven, Nicholas, Christopher, Graham, Adrian, Kevin, and for Maureen, Marilyn, Carol, Jacqueline, Janet, June, Susan, Gloria, Lana, and Linda.

One particular national institution served as a fundamental influence on the lives of all young males, National Service. Under the terms of the National Service Act of 1948 something around 160,000 young men were each year called up to undergo basic military training and military service for a period of two years, sometimes in such hot spots as Malaya or Korea. For most men National Service implied boredom and waste, though few denied to it any personal benefit at all. A young factory worker whose personal experience is given in the collection *Called Up* (1955), edited by Peter Chambers and Amy Landreth, noted: 'When I was back in Civvy Street and looked back on all the good times I'd had with my friends, my National Service didn't seem so bad after all. But I do think that a lot of time is wasted in the Army just hanging around.' While it is probably true that once a Teddy boy had been called up he probably ceased for ever to be a Teddy boy, it is hard to say whether National Service really served as a force for social control (as latter-day right-wing advocates of its restoration have maintained) or whether, by breaking family links, disrupting apprenticeships, opening new horizons, imposing new, and sometimes brutal, stresses it was a potential agent of social disruption. The editors of *Called Up* found it difficult to estimate to what extent National Servicemen take advantage of the freedom from parental control to gain sexual experience. Certainly a young man unversed in the 'facts of life' will very soon learn the repertoire of sexual possibilities from the conversation of his comrades. If he is posted abroad, he may visit a brothel for the first time in his life, but that does not mean he will avail himself of the opportunities provided by the establishment ... On the other hand, the moral climate of Service life tends to impel the soldier towards sexual adventures, and if he leaves the Army unexperienced in this field, then it is likely to be for moral or psychological reasons, not for lack of opportunity.

Probably National Service did help to preserve that slightly archaic quality which one finds in British life in the post-war era. Its abolition in 1960 very much fitted into the exuberance and libertarianism of the new age described in Part Two of this book.

5. *The Culture of Austerity*

'Culture' is a word with many meanings. This chapter is about the intellectual and imaginative life of Britain in the late forties and early fifties. It will include films and radio and television. It might have included football and holidays. Arguably the knowledgeable football fan exercises greater powers of intellect and imagination while at a football match than he does stretched supinely in front of some television parlour game. However, basic leisure activities were included in the previous chapter; this chapter is oriented towards what the quality newspapers of the time would have called 'the arts and entertainment'; it also deals with all forms of reading, as well as all forms of listening and viewing.

It is important to keep in mind the distinction between traditional 'high art', of concern only to a small (and usually wealthy) minority, and the leisure pursuits of the many, sometimes described as 'mass culture' or, more precariously, 'popular culture'. Another distinction was later popularized by C. P. Snow: when he spoke (in the late fifties) of 'the two cultures', he meant 'the sciences' on one side, 'the humanities' on the other. Applied science and technology were touched on in Chapter 1 as elements in the general economic and geographical context; here scientific discovery will feature as one of the important pursuits of the academic minority. Questions of religious belief concern both the minority, and also the wider society, though the community of believers was itself steadily shrinking.

This chapter addresses itself to various questions which are more than usually difficult to answer. I take it for granted that just as it is important to ask about the effectiveness of the country's social services, or about the genuineness of its concept of political democracy, so also is it important to ask both about the quality of the highest art produced by that society, and about the accessibility of that art to the majority of the people. One is, in other words, asking questions about what is now often termed 'the quality of life'. Further, in what ways, if any, was artistic and cultural change related to the other social changes already discussed? What light, if any, do the arts throw on the nature of British society in this period? Theories have been put forward accounting for both high art and popular culture as products of the hegemony established over society by the upper class; simpler souls have often talked of art as 'reflecting' society. I adhere to neither position, but hope simply to suggest most tentatively one or two connections between the matters discussed in this chapter and the matters discussed elsewhere in this book. Necessarily, I shall be pronouncing qualitative judgements on particular artists and writers, and on particular works of art; but the purpose is not to award plaudits here, and deduct penalty points there – it is, rather, to establish broadly whether we are talking about high art and minority culture, or about general leisure and popular culture, or about a sort of 'middle-brow' culture in between, or, on occasion, about a mixture of all of these.

Two developments which have already been mentioned expressed the Labour Government's own commitment to the idea that the Welfare State was scarcely complete if provision was not also made for the imaginative and intellectual side of life. The wartime Council for the Encouragement of Music and the Arts, which had done an immense amount to bring forms of high culture to places where they had hitherto been unknown, was in 1946 converted into the Arts Council, with a modest Government grant of £235,000 to dispense. The 1948 Local Government Act made it possible for local authorities to levy up to sixpence on the rates for the support of the arts. Not many did, but the Government commitment was there clearly enough.

For a hundred years the most accessible cultural form had been the novel, consistently priced at about one tenth of the average weekly wage. In the late forties, the audience for the novel was still basically a middle-class one. Most novels made no great profits for their publishers, but publishers expected every now and again to cash in on a bestseller. Chain stores and even quite small shops had circulating libraries from which books were lent out for a penny or two a week. Publishers would hope particularly to do well from the larger circulating libraries: Smith's, the Times Library, Harrods, Mudie's, and Boots. The 'paperback revolution' had not yet materially affected the fiction trade, even though Penguins had been in existence since the 1930s publishing, apart from their serious non-fiction works, a number of contemporary British authors as well as such international giants as Ernest Hemingway.

It is, no doubt, something of a commonplace that the novel had reached its last great apogee in the 1920s, and that there were few, if any, writers after 1945 who could compare with D. H. Lawrence or James Joyce or Virginia Woolf. Though it would be unwise to press the point too far, it could reasonably be said that in the forties and early fifties British political and social thought was inward-looking, concentrating, for instance, on the Welfare State, on the British vision of the brave new world. So the novels of the time, too, perhaps have a national, even parochial, quality.

Evelyn Waugh's war trilogy *Sword of Honour* (*Men at Arms*, 1952; *Officers and Gentlemen*, 1955; and *Unconditional Surrender*, 1961) has been unfavourably compared with the great First World War 'Tietjens' sequence by Ford Madox Ford. Waugh certainly got some important points about the war right:

'Take cover,' said the voice.
A crescent scream immediately, it seemed, over their heads, a thud which raised the paving-stones under their feet; a tremendous incandescence just north of Piccadilly; a pentecostal wind; the remaining panes of glass above them scattered in lethal splinters about the street.
'You know, I think he's right. We had better leave this to the civilians.'

But Waugh was very much a man of the inter-war years, a brilliant satirist of upper-class manners and morals. There is social significance in the fact that he could continue well through the post-war years still focusing on this particular social class (as did a lesser-known writer from the thirties, Anthony Powell, who in 1951 launched a long sequence, *The Music of Time*, which essentially dealt with the life-styles of the upper-class world, beginning with *A Question of Upbringing*, 1951; *A Buyer's Market*, 1952; *The Acceptance World*, 1955; and *At Lady Molly's*, 1957). With special testiness Waugh recorded the problems some members of this class encountered in a changing world: the irascible Gilbert Pinfold in *The Ordeal of Gilbert Pinfold* (1957) abhorred everything 'that happened in his own lifetime'.

The two most consistently lauded writers, also before the public in the 1930s, were Joyce Cary and Graham Greene. Both wrote within a distinctive variation of the traditional English novel. In his wartime trilogy, *Herself Surprised* (1941), *To Be a Pilgrim* (1942), and *The Horse's Mouth* (1944), Joyce Cary, around the splendid characters of the outrageous painter, Gully Jimson, and the shrewd, immoral, Sara, deliberately wrote a panorama of certain aspects of English history over the previous sixty years. His post-war trilogy *A Prisoner of Grace* (1952), *Except the Lord* (1953), and *Not Honour More* (1955) dealt more explicitly with political life in the era before, during, and after the First World War. In turn, we see the main characters from the inside. According to the famous Cambridge literary critic F. R. Leavis, the great English novels are 'moral fables'; Cary's books definitely fall into this category.

The agenda for Graham Greene was not the recent past, but the immediate present; sometimes, indeed, he seemed, with the insight of the crack journalist, to anticipate public events. Greene had been a Marxist in the early thirties, then became a Catholic convert: he thus, as we shall see later in this chapter, represented an important social and intellectual phenomenon. Apart from the tortured wrestling over the relationships between God and Man, Greene's novels are probably most celebrated for their power, based on all the devices of style and metaphor at the novelist's disposal, to evoke a particular period and a particular place. Thus for the social historian *The Heart of the Matter* (1948) tells much about a West African colony as British colonialism, mortally wounded by the war, is coming to an end, *The End of the Affair* (1951) evokes the blitz and wartime London in a far more direct way than Waugh's books, and *The Quiet American* (1955) adds its special dimension to the unfolding of the Indo-China tragedy in the Cold War era.

Corporate violence, very much the background to everyone's experience in this period, is ever-present in the novels of Graham Greene. Personal violence and menace, characteristic at this time only of the less well-known and less well-received talents, featured in the highly individualistic novels of Ivy Compton-Burnett. Her mannered, deliberately non-naturalistic novels such as *Parents and Children* (1941) or *Darkness and Day* (1951), set amidst the Edwardian upper class, attracted a cult following. To say that this was in keeping with the rather insular character of much of British minority culture at this time is in no way to deny the high literary repute she enjoyed. The most famous of all commentaries upon the grimness of the times, in which the nightmare of fascist dictatorship had scarcely faded and that of Stalinist oppression was ever-present, was George Orwell's vision of a not-too-distant totalitarian future, *Nineteen Eighty-four* (1948).

With C. P. Snow we return to the mainstream of the British novel. Snow himself described the purpose of his 'Strangers and Brothers' sequence which began in 1940 with the book of that title, and continued with *The Light and the Dark* (1947), *Time of Hope* (1949), *The Masters* (1951), *The New Men* (1954), *Homecomings* (1956), and *The Conscience of the Rich* (1958), as to give insights into British society over the period 1920–50 and to follow the *moral* (my italics) growth of Lewis Eliot, the narrator of the series. Snow, it would be widely agreed, could neither present all of his main characters in the round and from the inside, as could Joyce Cary, nor could he evoke the richness and subtlety of atmosphere of a Graham Greene. The novels, too often, seem much too consciously social and political documents; in many ways, since Snow himself moved in the scientific and governmental circles he describes, this makes them of greater interest to the historian. Here we light on a banal fact: it is often the lesser novels which more consciously and directly tell us about social attitudes and social change. Post-war society, muses Lewis Eliot in *Homecomings*, 'had become more rigid, not less, since our youths'.

A minor novel which hilariously satirized the implications of political consensus was Edward Hyams's *Gentian Violet* (1953). James Blundell was a working-class lad who, like many real-life figures (Edward Heath for instance), had ascended the social scale by means of a distinguished war career. Though as James Blundell he retained his contacts with his humble origins, in upper-class circles he became known as James Stewart-Blundell. Thus he contrived to be elected to Parliament both as a Conservative MP for a rural constituency and as a Labour MP for an industrial one. Any fears he might have of exposure in the House of Commons proved to be groundless:

Nobody noticed anybody else ... A member might be on his feet talking away yet boring nobody, as nobody was obliged to listen ... it reduced the most ambitious and domineering public men to the status of mere prefects, with certain privileges, like putting their feet on the table . . If democracy was to be found anywhere, Jim felt, it was here in the House of Commons.

And Jim soon began to be very proud of being two members of it.

Among middle-brow readers the most popular genre was that of the detective story. Agatha Christie, the leading practitioner, even had the endorsement of Labour's middle-brow Prime Minister, Clement Attlee. And Agatha Christie largely set the tone: her stories were cunning crossword puzzles filled out to book length, without sex and without gratuitous violence.

Poetry had lost the central position it held in the days of Tennyson or Kipling: it was not now usually expected to make money and appeared mainly in non-commercial 'little magazines'. Among those who (apart from the long-established T. S. Eliot) enjoyed modest commercial sales were Dylan Thomas, John Betjeman, Laurence Durrell, and Roy Fuller. Thomas, a rumbustious Welshman with a gift for magical incantation, formed the centre of a somewhat self-indulgent romantic bohemia; he died in 1953 at the age of thirty-nine. Betjeman wrote appealing satires on the Welfare State and conjured up nostalgia for an older England. On the whole, literary historians have seen the post-war years as a leaden age for British poetry: Fuller and Durrell, it is said, did better work earlier, and their best work later. Any parallels with international events must be utterly suspect; however, it may be noted that just as America was assuming a primacy in the world of art, so American poetry at this time was eclipsing British. In the middle fifties a number of younger poets, somewhat vaguely described as 'the Movement', joined in attacking the cult, as they saw it, of post-war neo-romantic poetry and its exclusive bohemian trimmings. One of them, Kingsley Amis, declared: 'Nobody wants any more poems about philosophers or paintings or novelists or art galleries or mythology or foreign cities or other poems. At least I hope nobody wants them.' The Movement included almost all of the best-known of recent British poets: Donald Davie, Philip Larkin, Tom Gunn, and Ted Hughes. Many of those who came to dominate poetry (and literary criticism), Raymond Las Vergnas has pointed out, were (or, more accurately perhaps, became) university teachers: 'The result is a kind of enlightened literary class dealing with average beings; of a poetical *élite* preoccupied with the trivialities of daily life.'

War conditions, and especially long nights in the air-raid shelter, encouraged the reading of novels; bombs destroyed theatres, or at least placed them under threat. The same novels could be read all over the country, but drama, before the Second World War, was very much centred on London. Plays aimed at commercial success were put on in the West End theatres, where audiences were predominantly middle-class and upper-class; a few theatres consciously aimed to put on avant-garde plays for a minority within that same audience. The main theatres in the provincial centres were essentially touring theatres receiving repertory companies, usually London-based, doing standard works, and also West End productions before or after their London run. The war destroyed or badly damaged one fifth of London theatres, and fostered the growth of monopoly in theatrical ownership: yet it also helped to stimulate the beginnings of a theatrical revival in the provinces. In 1942 Prince Littler began to buy up derelict London theatres; by the end of the forties the Prince Littler Consolidated Trust owned eighteen out of forty-two West End theatres and nearly three quarters of the main provincial touring theatres. But in 1943 a group of citizens joined together to save the historic Bristol Old Vic Theatre, and in 1946 it became a part of the London Old Vic Theatre; the establishment of the Coventry Municipal Theatre at the end of the war was essentially a response to the destruction of war and to the desire to build a richer life in the post-war world. Regional repertory companies began to flourish as never before, and in 1948 Basil Dean staged a season of provincial productions at the St James's Theatre calling forth a certain measure of praise from the London critics. At the same time, theatre folk, like everyone else, suffered the restraints and burdens of austerity: 10 per cent of gross receipts was whipped away in entertainments tax.

Anyway, older traditions persisted. The dominance of the consortium, known as 'The Group', in which Prince Littler was a key figure, meant that on the whole commercial considerations were paramount. The actor-manager principle was still very much alive: Sir Donald Wolfit gave a season at the Bedford, Camden Town, in 1949; Sir Laurence Olivier gave two seasons at the St James's in 1950 and 1951; and Sir John Gielgud gave a season at the Haymarket in 1954–5. For serious theatre-goer, and serious producer alike, most opportunities were confined to the classics, and 'the classics' almost always meant Shakespeare. It was in *Measure For Measure* that one of what was to prove a new breed of theatrical producers, Peter Brook, established himself. Above all, perhaps, the rather limited theatrical world of the late forties and the early fifties provided a particular kind of golden age for actors working within a strict convention. Kenneth Tynan, the dynamic critic who burst on the public scene in 1951, looking back from the sixties, put it this way: 'I claim no intrinsic superiority for the actors of the immediate post-war period over those of today. What is undeniable, however, is that the equivalent actor of today spends far less of his time on the stage than his predecessors did. We may see their like again, but we shall not see the like of their theatrical careers.'

Three names, perhaps, encapsulate the main theatrical fare of the first post-war decade: T. S. Eliot (with, however, only two plays in this period: *The Cocktail Party*, 1949, and *The Confidential Clerk*, 1954), Christopher Fry, and Terence Rattigan. Like Eliot, Fry wrote rich stuff for a time of austerity – *A Phoenix Too Frequent* (1946), *The Lady's Not for Burning* (1949), *A Sleep of Prisoners* (1951) – which sounded like theatre (though it did not always look like it), and struck a fine poetic note (though C. S. Lewis commented that 'Eliot's stage verse imitates prose, with remarkable success'). Terence Rattigan offered 'well-made plays', comfortably upper-class or upper-middle-class British in content: *The Winslow Boy* (1946) centred on a successful barrister's defence of the naval cadet son of a prosperous family, and *The Browning Version* (1948) centred on a public school and its classics master.

In 1954 one of the poets of the Movement, stooping to what he saw as a less important art form, published a novel. *Lucky Jim*, by Kingsley Amis, was a bestseller. A few months earlier John Wain had published *Hurry On Down*, which was also very successful. In 1956 the English Stage Company, with George Devine as artistic director, was established at the Royal Court Theatre in London. In that same year it presented *Look Back in Anger* by John Osborne: only the enormous success of this production kept the company from going bankrupt. In 1957 came John Braine's novel *Room at the Top*, set in the post-war era but cynical about the professed ideals of the then Labour Government: 'the top' was to be achieved not through socialism, but by ruthless individual self-advancement. In one way or another, these works had provincial settings, but they were certainly not working-class. The press lumped their authors together as 'angry young men'. All cocked a snook at the comfortable and flowery conventions of the post-war literary scene and also at the comfortable platitudes of consensus politics; they provided an interesting commentary on aspects of social change, on educational opportunity which yet brought no real opportunity, for example. In the wider perspective they can be seen as forerunners of the 'cultural revolution' which erupted in the sixties.

There was no cocking of snooks in the world of music, where the point of change, in so far as there was one, was definitely the Second World War. During the war the Sadler's Wells Opera and the Sadler's Wells Ballet were forced out on tour through the benighted provinces. At the end of the war the Sadler's Wells Theatre was reopened as the home exclusively of English-language opera, while the Sadler's Wells Ballet transferred to the Royal Opera House, Covent Garden. Covent Garden had been the home of opera on the international scale, and in January 1947 a reassembled Covent Garden Opera gave its first performance: the opera was *Carmen*, by the

Frenchman Bizet, just as the gala opening performance of ballet had been of *The Sleeping Beauty*, by the Russian Tchaikovsky. Music at least was not parochial, though it might be argued that a neglect of British composers was a parochial British characteristic.

Opera, self-evidently, commanded a smaller audience than drama; on the whole, it was an audience drawn from higher up the social scale. Covent Garden, at least in its more expensive seats, was a social focus for the upper class and upper-middle class. Sadler's Wells, with its opera in translation, was much more a resort for the middle class and lower-middle class. Since 1934 there had existed what was almost a paradigmatic upper-class institution, the Glyndebourne Opera House in the Sussex Downs.

In the realm of music, as in other spheres, the war had brought destruction and affirmation. The Queen's Hall in London was destroyed forever; the Free Trade Hall, home of Manchester's famous Hallé Orchestra, was not fit for reoccupation until 1951. The Royal Liverpool Philharmonic and the Hallé became full-time permanent orchestras for the first time in 1942 and 1943 respectively. In 1944 the City of Birmingham Orchestra was re-formed; and at the end of the war the four major London orchestras: the Royal Philharmonic (brought together again in 1946 under the direction of Sir Thomas Beecham), the London Symphony, the London Philharmonic, and the Philharmonia were re-established as self-governing institutions. Developments in the post-war years were the reorganization of the Scottish Orchestra into the permanent Scottish National Orchestra in 1950, and the expansion under Charles Groves of the Bournemouth Symphony Orchestra in 1954. But without doubt the major force in British music was the BBC – through its own Symphony Orchestra, through its regional orchestras, through its broadcasts on its new post-war Third Programme, through its sponsorship each summer of the Royal Albert Hall Promenade Concerts (the Proms), and through the valuable subventions it offered each time it broadcast a concert or music festival.

That creative individuals genuinely aspired to make the new dawn of 1945 a rich and life-enhancing one is best evidenced by the festivals established in the first post-war years. That such aspirations were not confined to individuals alone is evidenced by the success of these festivals. The grandest venture of all was the Edinburgh International Festival of Music and Drama, instituted in 1947 to plans conceived by Rudolph Byng, General Manager of the Glyndebourne Opera, Harvey Wood, Director of the British Council in Scotland, and Sir John Falconer, Lord Provost of Edinburgh. In 1948, under the inspiration of Benjamin Britten, the Aldeburgh Festival on the Suffolk coast was founded.

While the theatres played Shakespeare, Fry and Rattigan, the big orchestras played Mozart, Beethoven, and the nineteenth-century classics. However, the omens for native British music were probably more auspicious than ever they had been (since the seventeenth century at any rate). Vaughan Williams still bestrode the musical scene like a colossus: he had, as Percy Young has written, 'demonstrated how a new mode of expression could be discovered by bypassing the Romantics, though by no means missing out on Romanticism'. But the composer who was universally recognized at home and abroad as being the one to carry on the torch rekindled by Elgar was Benjamin Britten, whose entire achievements are bound in with the whole deliberate attempt to sponsor a renaissance of the imagination in the post-war years. It was his opera *Peter Grimes* which reopened the Sadler's Wells Theatre on 7 June 1945.

Next only to Britten in critical acclaim was Michael Tippett. Through these composers, and their younger successors, a genuinely English tradition of music-making was maintained and developed, while the composers, at the same time, sought to come to terms with the modes and preoccupations of the mid twentieth century. Thus the more private works tended to be inaccessible to the vast majority of potential listeners. But there could be a real involvement with the wider society as well. One outstanding instance of the serious composer's involvement in the writing of film music was Vaughan Williams's score for *Scott of the Antarctic* which then formed the basis of his *Sinfonia Antartica*.

New works in the visual and plastic arts (in plain English,

painting and sculpture) normally reached their rather limited upper-class and upper-middle-class public through the private commercial galleries. For the wider middle-class public, prepared to view but not to purchase, there were municipal galleries in most towns and cities, and the major galleries in London. These, naturally, mainly exhibited works from the great European tradition, showing in greater or lesser degree examples of recent and contemporary British art. Many private art galleries, of course, derived their main income from the buying and selling of 'old masters'. Thus while the indisputable quantitative evidence that art sales boomed during the war certainly supports the thesis that amid the catastrophe of war there is a turning of minds towards the precious elements of civilization, it does not necessarily suggest that native British artists were doing particularly well. Still, I think it would be a valid conclusion that the sponsorship of war artists, the concentration on the specific British heritage, and the general disruption of normal modes of looking at things in the war did serve as a stimulus to British art.

Most firmly within the idiom of the artist pushed by the war into a deeper celebration of Britishness was John Piper, war artist to the Ministries of Information and of War, with a special commission to record bomb damage, and also a member of the Recording Britain Project financed by the Pilgrim Trust. Piper's expressive and romantic renderings of British buildings gained, through the medium of reproductions, quite a wide currency. He provided his own definition of romanticism as pertaining to 'a vision that can see in things something significant beyond ordinary significance: something that for a moment seems to contain the whole world; and, when the moment is past, carries over some comment on life or experience besides the comment on appearances'. Human beings do not intrude upon Piper's buildings, yet, as Robert Melville put it in introducing Piper's 1964 retrospective exhibition, Piper has 'salvaged the Humanist scale and undepicted man remains in his work the measure of all things'. An older British painter who continued to operate within a very restricted British, indeed provincial, perspective was L. S. Lowry. If one mark of the true artist is that his work has an utterly distinctive personal quality, then this distinction certainly attaches to Lowry's Lancashire factory scenes.

For the majority of the better-known British artists, however, though the war might be a minor influence – 'liberating', says Sir John Rothenstein, in the case of Graham Sutherland, 'ambivalent', he says in regard to Ceri Richards – the major influences came from the great European painters of the early twentieth century. Post-war exhibitions of the work of Picasso and Braque, and of Van Gogh, both showed the great appetite for art among the middle class (20,000 a day attended the 1948 Van Gogh exhibition) and also provided a great stimulus to British painters. Victor Pasmore confessed to being 'very much moved' by the work of Picasso, 'even though I didn't like it'; but by 1947 he had reached the position that 'abstraction is the logical culmination of painting since the Renaissance' – or, as he later put it, 'the solid and spacial world of traditional naturalism ... could no longer serve as an objective foundation. Having reached this point the painter was confronted with an abyss from which he had either to retreat or leap over and start on a new plane. The new plane is "abstract art".' Yet for some artists, patronage, rather than theory, could still be a critical influence. For Graham Sutherland there came traditional commissions both ecclesiastical and lay. For St Matthew's Church, Northampton, he painted a crucifixion, and for the new Coventry Cathedral, between 1954 and 1957 he designed the tapestry, 'Christ in Glory in the Tetramorph'; for Somerset Maugham, Lord Beaverbrook, and the Honourable Edward Sackville-West he painted what were to become well-known portraits.

In these scattered fragments there can be no thesis about the artist and society; but let us for a moment look at the social origins, and ultimate careers, of three important figures. Henry Moore was born in 1898, the son of a former miner who had established himself as a mining engineer; Francis Bacon was born in 1909, the son of a well-connected family of the Anglo-Irish ascendancy (he was a collateral descendant of his illustrious Elizabethan namesake); Robert Colquhoun was born in 1914, the son of an engineering worker in the west of Scotland.

Moore had already arrived at his distinctive style as a sculptor by the 1930s, though his reputation was still a limited one. During the war he produced a famous series of drawings of people sheltering in the London Tube, drawings which, apart from anything else, showed a somewhat detached and distanced attitude towards suffering humanity around him. In the postwar years Moore emerged as one of the recognized international figures on the British art scene.

Completely untrained, Francis Bacon had made sporadic attempts to set himself up as a painter. An exhibition at the Lefevre Gallery in April 1945, which contained works by such better-known British artists as Matthew Smith and Henry Moore himself, also included a large triptych by Bacon entitled 'Three Figures at the Base of a Crucifixion': this contained those ingredients by which Bacon was eventually to become well-known, malignant, ominous, twisted figures, part-human, part-animal. From most critics the response was one of outrage and ridicule. But the sheer power of his work – Bacon spoke of making 'the paint speak louder than the story' – quickly brought paintings first attacked as being obsessive, ferocious distortions into the front line of critical acclaim. Robert Colquhoun, whose work was more obviously in the tradition of Picasso and Braque, had already found acceptance in the bohemian cultural world of Second World War London. Reaching a peak of success in 1945–6, Colquhoun thereafter steadily drank himself to death. Somehow, even in the world of the arts, workers' sons (and Celts) seemed to be more vulnerable than sons of the middle or upper classes.

The personal vision of individual artists, the whims of the coteries within which they worked, may appear quite detached from the social context. Architecture, on the other hand, as is often remarked, is the most socially determined of the plastic arts. Yet, in a way, architecture is the most élitist of all art forms. The public could ignore Moore or Colquhoun; what the major architects decided was often forced upon it. Wartime planning and socialist vision offered architects a key rôle in rebuilding the post-war Britain, and the young modernists of the thirties (Frederick Gibberd, Denys Lasdun, Maxwell Fry, and others) were given opportunities denied their counterparts in

Italy and France where the Old Guard remained in control. The main emphasis till the early 1950s was on building houses and schools. The first generation new towns, started in the 1940s, catered to the traditional taste for low-rise housing set in reasonable space, while at the same time adopting some of the tenets of the international functionalist style. Harlow (planned by Gibberd) has been widely praised, though it also encountered early on a problem which became endemic in post-war architecture: the smart white terraces in the international style by Maxwell Fry and Jane Drew simply wore much less well than some of the more traditional brick-built neighbour-hoods. In the big cities local authorities made a start on building massive high-rise housing estates. Denys Lasdun, for example, was involved in the Wholefield Estate, Paddington, in West London; while the LCC Architects Department's realization of Le Corbusier's vision of a high-rise city set in parkland at Roehampton in south-west London was in its day (1952–9) lauded as one of the great achievements of British architecture. Industrial techniques for building schools were pioneered in Hertfordshire, then, in 1948, taken up by the Ministry of Educa-tion. Many of these schools, for instance the Henry Hartland Grammar School at Worksop, a secondary modern school at Wokingham, a primary school at Amersham, and a village school at Finmere in Oxfordshire, all light and airy, not specially impressive from the outside, but extremely well-designed in their use of space inside, won international reputations.

The first great break from the needs of home, family, and children towards the needs of public spectacle came with the preparation of the bombed-out South Bank site for the 1951 Festival of Britain. Here was a remarkable opportunity to present the British public with a concentrated dose of modern architecture. The entire exhibition area, designed by Sir Hugh Casson, presented the contemporary idea of architecture as a single concept linking together spaces and buildings. The most impressive building was Robert Matthew's Royal Festival Hall, though two temporary constructions, the Skylon and the Dome of Discovery, conveyed even more strongly the feel of a new age.

Many of the new housing estates of the post-war years – and

most of the occupants were probably very glad of it – were very traditional in style. How the houses were furnished depended on a number of factors. Wartime necessity had led to the creation of 'utility' furniture; one nationwide economical style. Wartime aspiration had led to the creation of the Council for Industrial Design. Both of those upper-class socialists, Hugh Dalton, President of the Board of Trade during the war, and Sir Stafford Cripps, his successor in the Labour Government after 1945, were enthusiastic supporters of good design. Cripps played an important part in the presentation of the 1946 Design Exhibition at the Victoria and Albert Museum, 'Britain Can Make It'. A million and a half people visited this exhibition of simple, unfussy, rational products, each a tribute to the best in modern functionalism. Unfortunately, few were available for general sale, so that the exhibition was quickly nicknamed 'Britain Can't Have It'.

In 1948 reform was carried through at the Royal College of Art: the theories were those of the great German centre of rational design of the 1920s, the Bauhaus, but the practice was very much that of the progressive element in the British upper class, as in so many of the other experiments of the post-1945 period. The Council for Industrial Design worked hard to cash in on the popularization of good contemporary design achieved by the Festival of Britain. In 1956 the Design Centre was opened in Haymarket, London, and a year later the Design Centre awards began. Gradually manufacturers were persuaded that it was worth trying to attain the label 'Design Centre approved'. Yet, as Fiona MacCarthy has remarked – and how typical this is of the entire British cultural scene: 'Design was still in many ways an amiable clique. Identical professors seemed forever giving prizes to their own RCA students, identical designers were forever smiling thanks to the Duke of Edinburgh.' Much British design was in fact highly derivative, with Scandinavian influences heavily in evidence in the 1950s. Speaking of the Council of Industrial Design, Fiona MacCarthy adds that: 'Through the fifties, its activities were altogether cosy and low-key, with lunch meetings at Overseas House (sample topic: *Design Starvation in the Public Schools*); with musical evenings at the Geffrye Museum; with little exhibitions in Charing Cross

Station, "Register Your Choice" and later "Make or Mar".'

Creative work in the realms of the intellect and imagination was carried on in a number of different interlinked groups, each of them a tiny minority within society as a whole, but each of them rooted, however feebly, in the social compost. The least utilitarian items (like philosophy and literary criticism) and the most capital-intensive (science) tend to find their home in the universities. Despite the fact that they form the tiniest of minorities within the minority, British philosophers betrayed an isolationism at least as marked as that of British literature. Leading British philosophers, such as Gilbert Ryle or John Austin, eschewed big metaphysical issues and, under the influence of the great mathematical logician (and, incidentally, publicist of libertarian causes), Bertrand Russell, and of the Austrian-born Cambridge philosopher Wittgenstein, concentrated instead on what many continentals saw as the tedious triviality of 'linguistic philosophy'. Neither in history, which was replacing philosophy and classics as the staple academic subject, nor in sociology, still regarded as a slightly suspect subject in many British universities, was the British achievement marked by any great innovation in content, though history did achieve a new popular appeal, first in the forties through the work of G. M. Trevelyan, then in the fifties through the Pelican History of England series. By 1954 Arnold Toynbee had completed the tenth and final volume of his massive universal history *A Study of History*, begun in the 1930s. Yet, though based on immense knowledge both in classical civilizations and the contemporary world, this was a work of poetic inspiration – particularly as a kind of religious transcendentalism more and more coloured the post-war volumes – rather than a work of methodological innovation or analytical rigour. It won readers round the world but created no great new British school of scholarship.

It was in the most international, and most rapidly changing intellectual universe that British academics did best, science. The physicist Professor G. H. A. Cole (in *The Twentieth Century Mind*, vol. 3) has written: 'Pre-war physics was fun for those lucky enough to be involved with it, but it scarcely affected anyone else; postwar physics was still fun for those lucky enough to be involved in it, but the general world community now could not stand back uncaring.' Much of the pioneering pre-war British work in nuclear physics was now locked up in the United States, but such new sciences as geophysics, medical physics, and molecular biology advanced. In great secret, the British Government proceeded with the development of a British nuclear weapon, principally at the research establishment at Harwell and at the nuclear pile at Windscale. On 3 October 1952 Britain exploded her own test atomic bomb, thus becoming, after America and Russia, the third nuclear power. British physicists, and British finance, played an important rôle in the setting-up of CERN, the European Centre of Nuclear Research, at Geneva in 1952. For nuclear fission, enormous amounts of energy were required. The major work by J. D. Cockcroft and Ernest Walton in developing a 'voltage multiplier' had been done in Rutherford's Cambridge laboratory before the war; but it was in 1951 that they received the Nobel Prize. Throughout the entire period covered by this book British scientists were to notch up a total of Nobel Prizes second only to that achieved by American scientists.

Developments in radio-astronomy, in which at this time Britain was very much in the lead, again owed much to the war, when it was discovered that signals sent out by the sun in the microwave region were interfering with radar. It soon became clear that the stars also transmitted radio signals. The world's first large-scale radio telescope was built at Jodrell Bank under the supervision of Sir Bernard Lovell. British astronomers played a leading rôle in debates over the nature and origins of the universe: was it expanding, contracting, oscillating, or remaining in a steady state of continuous creation? W. B. Bonnor was a proponent of the oscillating universe, while Hermann Bondi and Thomas Gold put forward the theory in 1948 of steady state or continuous creation, a theory which was to be greatly developed in the 1960s by Fred Hoyle.

An enormous range of discoveries made by scientists of many nationalities greatly influenced medical science. From the original discovery by Alexander Fleming in 1929, penicillin was developed in the United States by the Australian-born scientist Howard Florey and his German-born associate Ernst Chain; in 1945 Fleming, Florey, and Chain were jointly awarded the

Nobel Prize in medicine and physiology. The search for other antibiotics (the word was coined in 1942 by the American bacteriologist Waksman) was on. Thanks to Waksman's discovery of streptomycin, tuberculosis in post-war Britain was no longer the scourge it had been in the inter-war years. The next great advance in pharmaceuticals was the development, based on earlier work carried out at the Harvard Medical School, of the Salk vaccine; it did not, however, come into general use in Britain in the attack on polio till the 1960s. The widespread use in medicine of radioactive tracers also depended heavily upon work carried out in the United States. However, it was the British chemist R. G. Westall who, in 1952, marked an important stage in the attack upon deficiencies of the metabolism by isolating the compound 'porphobilinogen'. In connection with the treatment of pernicious anaemia, the isolation of a pure sample of Vitamin B12 by Ernest Lester Smith in Britain in 1948 was important. The complex molecular structure of Vitamin B12 was eventually determined by the British chemist Dorothy Hodgkin; in carrying through the enormous calculations involved she had to make use of an American advanced electronic computer. She gained her Nobel Prize for Chemistry in 1964. Another great sphere for international medical research concerned the development of various defences against the viruses which attack the human body. It was a group of British bacteriologists, led by Alick Isaacs who, in 1957, isolated the protein 'interferon' which was to prove in many respects more effective than the older antibiotics.

In April 1953 it was announced that Francis Crick and James D. Watson at Cambridge had discovered that the molecule of deoxyribonucleic acid (DNA), the carrier of genetic inheritance, was in the shape of a double helix. The final discovery was only possible because of the mass of work by scientists in different countries deploying a range of expensive specialist equipment, yet the achievement of the donnish Cambridge biophysicist Crick and the bouncy American viro-chemist Watson, then only twenty-five years old, has much of the romance of a piece of individualistic freebooting in which personal ambition seemed at least as strong a motive as disinterested pursuit of scientific knowledge. The charming human frailties of science, the moods of triumph, the worries over the rival activities of the famous American structural chemist Linus Pauling, the visits to the pub, come through grippingly in Watson's own description of the days after the final breakthrough had been made.

Francis's preoccupation with DNA quickly became full time ... Constantly he would pop up from his chair, worriedly look at the cardboard models, fiddle with other combinations, and then, the period of momentary uncertainty over, look satisfied and tell me how important our work was. I enjoyed Francis's words, even though they lacked the casual sense of understatement known to be the correct way to behave in Cambridge. It seemed almost unbelievable that the DNA structure was solved, that the answer was incredibly exciting, and that our names would be associated with the double helix as Pauling's was with the alpha helix.

When the Eagle opened at six, I went over with Francis to talk about what must be done in the next few days. Francis wanted no time lost in seeing whether a satisfactory three-dimensional model could be built ... Though I was equally anxious to build the complete model, I thought more about Linus and the possibility that he might stumble upon the base pairs before we told him the answer.

That night, however, we could not finally establish the double helix. Until the metal bases were on hand, any model building would be too sloppy to be convincing. I went back to Pop's to tell Elizabeth and Bertrand that Francis and I had probably beaten Pauling to the gate and that the answer would revolutionise biology. Both were genuinely pleased, Elizabeth with sisterly pride, Bertrand with the idea that he could report back to International Society that he had a friend who would win a Nobel Prize ...

The following morning I felt marvellously alive when I awoke. On my way to the Whim I slowly walked towards Clare Bridge, staring up at the gothic pinnacles of King's College Chapel that stood out sharply against the spring sky. I briefly stopped and looked over at the perfect Georgian features of the recently cleaned Gibbs Building, thinking that much of our success was due to the long uneventful periods when we walked among the colleges or unobtrusively read the new books that came into Heffers book store. After contentedly pouring over *The Times*, I wandered into the lab to see Francis, un-characteristically early, flipping the cardboard base pairs about an imaginary line. As far as a compass and ruler could tell him, both sets of base pairs neatly fitted into the backbone configuration. As the morning wore on, Max and John successively came by to see if we still thought we had it. Each got a quick, concise lecture from Francis, during the second of which I wandered down to see if the shop could be speeded up to produce the purines and pyrimidines later that afternoon.

Actually, the discovery was ignored by the popular press. Acclaim came only in the sixties when, something the popular press *could* understand, Crick and Watson won their Nobel Prize.

The divide between scientists and the rest of society, or rather between scientists and other academics and intellectuals, was the subject of C. P. Snow's first analysis of 'The Two Cultures', published in the *New Statesman* on 6 October 1956. In theory politicians had recognized the immense significance of science in a wartime and post-war world. In the Cabinet, the Lord President of the Council was supposed to act as a kind of Science Minister, and in January 1947 the Advisory Council on Scientific Policy was set up. According to the official statement the appointment of the Council 'marked a further step in the development of close relations between science and the central government'. The reality, echoing, as has already been suggested, the differences between the theory and practice of social planning after the war, was slightly different: as Professor J. G. Crowther has put it (in *Science in Modern Society*) the Advisory Council served more as 'a commentator on' rather than 'a leader of' scientific policy. At the top, British scientific achievements were considerable; there was an impressive reorientation of industry and of medicine towards the new technologies: but there was little effective communication of the significance of science to the wider society, whether by Government agencies, or through the press.

Times, indeed, were hard yet cosy for the British press in the post-war years. With papers little more than flimsy fly-sheets there was more than enough advertising to go round, especially since, relative to population, the British were greater newspaper readers than any other nation in the world. In 1950 the total circulation of all the national daily papers reached just under seventeen million; thereafter there was a slight drop, but circulation none the less remained over sixteen million throughout the 1950s. At this point, three press barons dominated the newspaper world: Beaverbrook, Rothermere, and Kemsley Daily Mirror Newspapers Ltd, with Cecil King as Chairman, emerged in 1951, and in 1953 Roy Thomson, a Canadian millionaire, bought up Scotsman Publications in Edinburgh; but the great upheavals in ownership did not come till the very end of the fifties. As restrictions lifted in the fifties it became clearer that the sharp division in the British press was between the 'quality' papers, *The Times, Manchester Guardian, Daily Telegraph, Observer,* and *Sunday Times* on the one side, and the popular press on the other. The quality press took about two million of the total daily circulation, and was actually expanding in size. It was the in-between papers, in particular the *News Chronicle,* which found conditions hardest, while what remained of the independent provincial press steadily withered away.

Because of a certain repute and authenticity in their presentation of the news the quality papers appealed to upper-middle-class and upper-class readers; they thus could attract advertising at expensive rates. The popular press sought to retain large readerships through presenting sensational, entertaining, and often trivial material rather than hard news and serious comment; in this way they too could attract the advertising necessary for survival.

The one form of communication totally untainted by commercial considerations was the BBC. At the end of the war the radio services were reorganized into three: the Light Programme, the Home Service Programme, and the Third Programme. The audience research which the BBC had pioneered shortly before the war treated the audiences for these three services as synonymous with working-class, middle-class, and upper-middle and upper-class, respectively. Few challenged the validity of the BBC's position or the power of what Lord Reith, first Director General of the BBC, had described as 'the brute force of monopoly' to act for the preservation of certain social and cultural standards.

In reality the BBC was a very upper-class institution. The most successful radio soap opera of all time was 'Mrs Dale's Diary', set in a distinctly upper-middle-class milieu. There was a strong feeling within the BBC, dating back to the early years of the war, that an outlet ought to be provided for genuinely working-class aspirations and that something equivalent to a working-class Mrs Dale's Diary ought to be put on the air. Little success attended these efforts and the working-class Mrs Dale's Diary was never discovered. The Third Programme played an important part in the musical renaissance after 1945; but many of its serious talks were characterized by a mannered pedantry and a distinctive academic parochialism. The war had brought an end to television broadcasting only in its swaddling clothes at the end of the thirties; it grew again only slowly in the post-war years though by the early fifties there were five million television viewers. In order that television might not become an addiction nor distract children from their studies nor adults from their duties, television broadcasting was confined to a limited number of hours per day – also very much in keeping with the BBC ethic. The first serious debate over the BBC's position took place in 1954 when, in fact, the Act was passed which made possible the setting-up of a separate commercial television channel.

The means of communication which were fully developed and ready to hand got a great boost from the war: paperback books, radio, and also films. There had been individual British films of considerable merit in the 1930s, but on the whole it could be said that the war provided the necessary stimulus, and also opportunity to the more progressive film-makers, to establish a consistent output of high-level films of a distinctive British character. It was in the war that Ealing Studios came to the fore, making films on definite, but low-key, patriotic themes. Ealing went from strength to strength in the post-war years with a series of instantly recognizable British genre films both serious and comic. Undoubtedly Hollywood imports continued to be most popular with British audiences, but Government import restrictions gave a helpful encouragement to British film-makers. Few British films attempted grand themes but within their limited aims they were, thanks to workmanlike direction, competent scripts, usually derived from theatrical or literary sources, and an extremely high level of character acting, artistic successes; usually aiming at gently satirical comment on British ways they often succeeded unintentionally in revealing a great deal more about fundamental British social assumptions. The golden age of Ealing petered out around 1951 when *His Excellency* was generally treated as but a poor successor to *Passport to Pimlico* (1949), *Kind Hearts and Coronets* (1949), and *The Man in the White Suit* (1951). The Government-sponsored Group Three had one great achievement in *The Brave Don't Cry* (1952) which, most unusually, treated, with great sensitivity, an industrial working-class community, a Scottish mining village; but after that, just as a second television channel was on the way, British films relapsed into mediocrity.

In absolute terms there was expansion at all levels of society in opportunities for entertainment, for intellectual stimulus, and for refreshment of the spirit. All of that could not but continue to hasten the decline of traditional religious observance. At the beginning of the fifties under 10 per cent of the population were regular churchgoers. Within the small circle of those who were active and concerned believers there were as yet no very exciting developments. The Catholic Church continued to gain adherents; the non-conformist persuasions continued to do worst. On the whole old positions were held to and sectarian rivalries continued.

In the arts and entertainment, in concern for the environment, in the accessibility of the best to the most, Britain was in a healthier state than it had ever been: if drama was stereotyped, the novel fading, poetry flagging, art was imaginative, architecture positive, music inspiring, and opera and ballet on a more secure basis than they had ever been. Yet in all spheres there was a sense of dominance by established in-groups, a feeling of following the current cult. In all spheres British thought and artistic endeavour were inward-looking, seemingly unconcerned with the great issues which racked continental intellectuals: existentialism and social commitment, the challenge to Marxist faith presented by Stalinist tyranny, the possibilities of a Catholicism attuned to the needs of the modern world. The many British literary works which bring in the Second World War seem somehow to treat it as a little local affair, without epochal significance, when compared, say, with American novels dealing with the same war, or with British literary reactions to the First World War.

6. Consensus Re-examined

Before 1945 Labour had twice formed shaky minority Governments, the second of which collapsed ignominiously in 1931. Never before had Labour had a secure majority. In 1945 the majority in Parliament was a crushing one: Labour had 393 seats to 210 for the Conservatives and their various 'National' allies, with the Liberals having twelve, the Communists two, and various others twenty-three. For those who took the trouble to look, the portents of a Labour victory had been clear enough (the Gallup poll in the *News Chronicle* had forecast a Labour victory, though by a much narrower majority): yet conventional wisdom had firmly predicted a victory for Churchill, 'the man who won the war'.

Shortly after the results were known, a middle-class lady wrote in a private letter: 'We were certainly staggered by the election result especially as I live and work in a very Conservative atmosphere – the end of the world would have occasioned only a little more alarm.' An upper-class one declared: 'But this is terrible – *they've* elected a Labour Government, and the *country* will never stand for that.' An alarmed and disgusted Conservative Member of Parliament described the Labour members flooding over the Government benches as 'just like a crowd of damned constituents'. All the worst fears seemed confirmed when these crowded benches rose to sing 'The Red Flag'. However, it was clear that many Labour men did not actually know the words, and traditional urbanity was restored when the newly re-elected speaker, the Conservative Colonel Clifton-Brown, remarked that he hoped he had been elected Speaker of the House of Commons and not director of some musical chorus.

It was 'a good sign', noted 'Chips' Channon, who was in an excellent position to assess the possibilities of continuing upper-class political dominance, 'that the Labour Party have decided to elect a Conservative Speaker unanimously'. On the Labour MPs themselves he was firmly dismissive: 'Never have I seen such a dreary lot of people.' Channon probably had a clearer perception of what was really going on than Sir Hartley Shaw-cross, one of Labour's recent upper-middle-class recruits, who on 2 April 1946, as the Government was pushing through its Trades Disputes Bill, designed to restore to the trade unions the legal powers they had enjoyed before the 1926 General Strike, declared: 'We are the masters at the moment – and not only for the moment, but for a very long time to come.'

Of votes actually cast, the Conservatives and their allies had received 39·6 per cent, Labour 48 per cent: the country was actually more evenly divided than the House of Commons figures suggested. However, Labour continued to do well in the country, increasing its majorities in the first few by-elections, all in Labour-held seats, and doing very well in the first round of local government elections. In the 1950 election Labour still secured 46·1 per cent of all votes cast, to 43·5 per cent for the Conservatives; and in the 1951 election Labour's share actually went to the highest ever at 48·8 per cent, which was 0·8 per cent ahead of the Conservatives, though, thanks to the single-member-constituency system, the Conservatives actually won a parliamentary majority.

If we concentrate upon the charmed circle of parliamentary politics it is perfectly reasonable to speak of a quick restoration of political consensus. Churchillian thunder pealed more and more distantly as he, and the entrenched right-wingers, became increasingly isolated from the main body of the Conservative Party, whose younger leadership, notably Eden and Butler, de-liberately set out to adapt Conservative policy to meet the assumptions of the Welfare State and the full-employment society. But conventional notions of a general consensus receive a jolt if one studies the popular right-wing press, particularly Beaverbrook's *Express* and Rothermere's *Mail*. These kept up an abusive campaign against the Government and all its works, coining a loaded language of their own, such as 'grab' for nationalization, and, of course, always referring to Labour as 'the socialists'. They also coined some witty slogans such as, at

the time of the fuel and bread crises, 'Shiver with Shinwell and
Starve with Strachey'. Ribbing of the Government, both
sharply pointed and more gentle, was to be found in other
forms of mass media: the film *The Blue Lamp* (1950), the first
to feature a new folk hero, PC George Dixon (he was
actually killed in the film, but that did not stop him being
revived for innumerable future television series), managed to
bring in a bitter criticism of the Government's rationing
policies; *Passport to Pimlico* more gently mocked Government
bureaucracy.

Parliamentary consensus should not be overstated either. The
Conservatives did divide the House on the third reading of the
National Health Service Bill. While early nationalization
measures went through fairly easily, the Conservatives mounted
a powerful and sustained campaign against the nationalization of
iron and steel, and indeed used their permanent majority in the
House of Lords to frustrate the Government's intentions.
Nationalization was very much a major issue between the two
parties in the general election campaigns of 1950 and 1951.

Parliamentary consensus was most evident after the return of
the Conservatives to power in 1951. Steel, which had not really
been nationalized anyway, was denationalized; the practical
effects of this political game, as suggested in Chapter 1, were
not particularly significant either way in any case. Parts of the
road haulage industry were also returned to private ownership.
Despite Conservative mutterings over Labour's Trades Disputes
Act, trade-union law was not altered, and the Conservative
Minister of Labour, Walter Monckton, was noted for his con-
ciliatory policies. 'Butskellism' was the word coined in the early
fifties to represent the continuity of economic policy as between
the outgoing Labour Chancellor of the Exchequer, Hugh Gaitskell, and the new Conservative one, R. A. Butler. A much
publicized political divide did exist between the majority of the
parliamentary Labour Party and the left-wing group led by
Aneurin Bevan, who had resigned from the Labour administration over the rearmament policy (which, among other things,
involved the imposition of health service prescription charges)
adopted because of the outbreak of the Korean War. Though a

minority in Parliament, the Bevanites had the support of many party activists at constituency level.

Political consensus appeared to be shattered by the Suez Crisis of 1956. But the really significant point with regard to British political attitudes and values is the speed with which passions cooled: Suez was scarcely mentioned in the general election campaign of 1959, despite the fact that the then Conservative leader, Harold Macmillan, had been closely associated with the disastrous policies of Sir Anthony Eden. In collusion with the French and the Israelis, Britain waged war for one week against Egypt in pursuit of Eden's delusion that Colonel Nasser was another Hitler, and vain hope that the Egyptian President could thus be removed from power. Eden's 'armed conflict' lasted just long enough to demonstrate that Britain no longer had the logistic power to mount an efficient sea-borne operation in the Middle East, and for Britain to be branded by the United Nations as an aggressor, before American opposition, Russian threats, and the inevitable run on the pound brought an ignoble venture to a humiliating conclusion. In the early stages of the episode it appeared that Government and opposition and much of the public were united in xenophobic hostility to Nasser. But once the Labour opposition had decided on outright denunciation of government policy, public opinion divided very much along party lines. Opinion polls did not support the widely held contention that many Labour supporters found their patriotism agreeably stirred by Eden's venture in gunboat diplomacy. Only one Labour MP, Stanley Evans, supported the Government, and he was shortly forced to resign by his constituency party. On the other side Conservative dissidents were treated with similar roughness by their local organizations. That most Labour voters opposed the Suez venture does not necessarily imply, however, that the entire working class, many of whom voted Conservative in any case, did so.

Public attitudes towards defence policy generally can also be studied through the opinion polls. In January 1949 50 per cent of those interviewed agreed that conscription should be continued in peacetime, while 33 per cent wished it to be discontinued; in November of the same year the percentages were

53 and 38 respectively. In September 1950, before the official
announcement that in response to the Korean situation length of
service would be increased from eighteen months to two years,
55 per cent gave advance endorsement of this move, while 33
per cent disapproved. Two and a half years later 45 per cent
of those polled favoured continuing the two-year term, 45 per
cent favoured a reduction to eighteen months. A year later
(May 1954), when Churchill's name was introduced into the
pollsters' question as a believer in the necessity of Britain's
retaining two-year conscription, 49 per cent agreed with
Churchill, 35 per cent disagreed. But after the Government
had announced in October 1955 that it proposed to cut
National Service the majority of those polled echoed the change
in policy: 47 per cent favoured cutting the two-year period,
34 per cent thought such a cut would be unwise. In September
1956 44 per cent were in favour of abolishing National Service,
38 per cent were against such abolition.

Reactions over defence expenditure were very similar:
majority support (58 per cent in February 1952) for the steady
increase in defence expenditure to 1953; a slightly less decisive
majority support for cutting defence expenditure after 1956.
After the testing of the first British hydrogen bomb in 1955 a
more crucial issue stole the scene. Throughout the second half
of the fifties opinion polls indicated that between one quarter
and one third of the British public favoured Britain's unilater-
ally renouncing nuclear weapons.

How far, and at what point, a majority of the British
people had digested the fact that Britain was no longer a
major world power is difficult to determine: probably not till
the 1960s, though, objectively, Suez is the watershed. In the
imagery of newsreel, press, radio, and television, Britain continued to be presented, along with France, as a 'big' country;
the Netherlands, Belgium, Switzerland, and Denmark, though
already beginning to demonstrate considerable economic
power, were 'small' countries. Undoubtedly a pervasive sentiment was 'we won the war'. While the frequent attribution of
low productivity in the pits to the desire of the miners to enjoy
the fruits of peace ignored the much more debilitating effects of
a long history of appalling industrial relations, it is true that at

no level in British society was there a deep commitment to the notion that the continued survival of the nation would depend on a prolongation of the heroic efforts of wartime. In the austerity conditions of the post-war years there were constant exhortations to support the 'export drive', and, indeed, by 1950 immediate export targets had been achieved. But in the fifties, as terms of trade improved, and the economic gloom lightened, very much there was a sense that the British people now had entered into their just inheritance. The consumer market expanded and the pressure to fight for export markets lessened.

Newsreels in the later forties had made something of a fuss over the granting of independence to India, quite possibly because Churchill took a belligerent stand on this issue (not that Britain really had any choice anyway). There has been much theorizing about the impact 'the loss of empire' ought to have had on the British psyche; the empirical evidence is that it really had very little. The most notable consequences were felt by members of the upper and upper-middle classes who no longer had the Raj as a territory in which to exploit their natural gifts of leadership. Apart from a few Victorian regrets over India the official line was one of self-congratulation that Britain once more was leading the way in granting independence to former colonial peoples.

In the formal sense, Britain in the post-war years approached more closely to being a full democracy. Until 1948, businessmen could vote twice, once in their home constituency, and once in the constituency in which their business was situated; at the same time the separate university constituencies, which had provided university graduates with a second vote, were abolished The non-elective, hereditary, House of Lords had been able to frustrate the nationalization of iron and steel, though from 1948 its power to delay legislation was reduced to one year Yet many aspects of British political culture remained profoundly undemocratic. At parliamentary level individual MPs had few powers to initiate legislation or even to bring Cabinet and senior civil servants under serious scrutiny; there was little in the way of participatory democracy. Politics was left very much to the politicians, apart from the purely temporary excitements of general elections – the turn-out in

1950 and 1951, 83·9 per cent and 82·6 per cent respectively, was impressively high, comparing with 72·7 per cent in 1945, 76·8 per cent in 1955, and 78·7 per cent in 1959.

In one sense industrial relations had been totally transformed by the war; in another sense they had scarcely been changed at all. After 1945 the bargaining power of Labour was far stronger than it had ever been in the inter-war years, and this power was maintained by high demand and consequent full employment. Yet, although some attention was given both during and after the war by the TUC to the question of 'industrial democracy' and worker participation in management, traditional attitudes remained very strong here on both sides. It became clear that the TUC was only interested in worker participation in management in respect of the nationalized industries; in private industry management should remain in the hands of the bosses while trade unions continued to uphold their members' interests in the old ways. Sir Stafford Cripps was speaking both as a member of the upper class and of the Labour Government when he stated that workers simply did not have the necessary skills to participate in management. In general, managements went as far as they thought necessary to appease and conciliate their workforce; but in essence the line between was as firmly defined as it had ever been.

By the late fifties it was clear that one central feature of British values was a strong loyalty to the institution of monarchy. The evidence suggested that monarchism was least strong in the immediate post-war period of severe austerity, but that it strengthened as social and economic circumstances improved in the fifties. In the abstract, luke-warm and even hostile sentiments towards the monarchy could be found; but as the great monarchical events, funerals and coronations, focused attention, royalist sentiment strengthened. Overall, monarchist views were expressed most strongly in London, where the great pageants took place, least strongly in the remoter provinces.

In May 1947 George VI and Queen Elizabeth set out on what could well appear a lavish tour of Southern Africa. A majority of those having any defined opinion on the tour at all, 32 per cent of those polled, disapproved of the tour because of the contrast it presented with austere conditions at home; 29 per cent approved of the tour, usually on the grounds that it would strengthen the bonds of Empire. However, the announcement later that year of the engagement between Princess Elizabeth and Prince Philip revealed enormous warmth towards the monarchy, even if there was a widespread view, as Philip Ziegler puts it, 'that the Prince was amiable but dim' – 'a nice enough man even if not over-bright', said one housewife. Yet, in July, 40 per cent of those polled were unenthusiastic about the expenditure involved in the wedding preparations, though 40 per cent also actively approved. But by October those actively approving had risen to 60 per cent, and in November, a fortnight before the wedding, only 29 per cent felt that the arrangements were too costly. The wedding itself, when it came, undoubtedly monopolized attention, with news-papers quickly sold out as the public sought pictures of the royal couple. People interviewed offered various explanations for their enthusiasm: the need for colour and spectacle, the emphasis on the institution of the family, but, above all, a pride in having something in which the British stood out from other countries: 'I expect that some of the royal visitors would feel jealous and wonder whether they would get the same kind of greeting in their own countries,' one man from south-east London commented.

During the night of 5–6 February 1952, George VI died. Again, there was quite evidently a widespread sense of loss and shock, quite different from anything experienced over a civilian leader, even, as it was later to transpire, one as eminent as Churchill himself. Still, the death of one monarch meant the coronation of another one. The nearer the coronation of Queen Elizabeth II came, the more public opinion polls showed enthusiasm for, and interest in, that event. At least two million people turned out in the streets to watch the coronation procession; but the new twist was that almost twenty-and-a-half million people, 56 per cent of the adult population, could watch, and did watch, the entire proceedings on television; a further 32 per cent, 11·7 million, listened on radio. From survey material, it does seem that the coronation was associated in many people's minds, however vaguely, with the idea of a new

Elizabethan age in which, through the Commonwealth, if not
through the Empire, Britain would still retain a glorious place
in the world. The coronation established not so much a peak,
but much more a plateau of popular sentiment favourable
towards the monarchy: though there were fluctuations in individual polls, it could be said that outright republicans seldom
numbered more than about 11 per cent of the population.

Civic loyalty to the established order of things was perhaps
even more powerfully demonstrated by attitudes towards the
police. Geoffrey Gorer found that 73 per cent of the men and
74 per cent of the women in his sample thought highly of the
police. Though 18 per cent were prepared to voice critical
opinions, this was over individual police activities, not of the
police as an institution. On the other hand, religious observance was undoubtedly in decline – though even here vestiges
of traditional loyalties remained strong. At the beginning of the
fifties 26 per cent of men and 18 per cent of women admitted
to no religious affiliation at all. The figures for regular church-
going were even lower: 11 per cent of women and 7 per cent
of men; 45 per cent of the population could be described as in-
termittent churchgoers, that is to say they went to church once
or twice a year, 40 per cent of the population did not attend
church at all, but, and it is an interesting but, all except 7 per
cent did expect to attend church for weddings or funerals,
furthermore 50 per cent of all parents still sent their children
to Sunday school.

In the late fifties commentators of both major political
persuasions were ready to argue that the British had done
marvellously in the war, had with sense and restraint accepted
difficult post-war circumstances, and were now in the fifties
reaping the fruits of compromise between collectivist welfare,
sponsored by Labour and accepted by Conservatives, and the
element of free enterprise and respect for the consumer fostered
by the Conservatives. Britain still evoked the admiration of
European commentators: 'A progressive social revolution is
being sketched out, peaceful and silent,' wrote a French
sociologist, Pierre Laroque, in 1955, 'which is apparent to those
who after an interval of several months or several years return
to England, and take note of the profound transformation

taking place there.' An indigenous commentator, writing in the early sixties, was to be much less respectful· 'Far from introducing a "social revolution" the overwhelming Labour victory of 1945 brought about the greatest restoration of traditional social values since 1660.' The words were those of the left-wing, public-school and Oxford-educated journalist, Anthony Howard.

Complacency, parochialism. lack of serious structural change, these are sustainable charges. Did the fault lie with an absence of political leadership? The first two post-war Prime Ministers, Attlee and Churchill, were certainly not weak men, though Churchill was way past his best by the time he returned to office. Political leaders, really, were prisoners of the consensus. If faults have to be looked for, they probably have to be sought at a rather deeper level than that of the actions and thoughts of individual politicians. Consensus was laudable in respect of maintaining social harmony and providing the opportunity for post-war reforms to be worked out. But in some respects, at least, the mixed economy presented the wrong mix. Conservative leaders, mostly upper-class, could join with Labour leaders, mostly a mixture of upper-class and working-class, in supporting the large unit: Labour preferred the State, the Conservatives in certain circumstances preferred large-scale private industry. Both showed little interest in the small businessman, offering little encouragement to true private enterprise

Part Two

Roads to Freedom
1957–72

7. Affluence, Appliances, and Work

Technology had been a growing force in the shaping of society since the end of the eighteenth century; nevertheless in the sixties there evolved a technological civilization of a sort not previously seen in twentieth-century Britain, characterized by a new ugliness and a new species of modern conveniences, affecting the urban landscape and rural environment, the working day, domestic chores and the pursuit of leisure, the rôle of women, and the nature of education. Hitherto individual technologies had impinged separately on society, now the concept of one unified technology, based on what its apostles termed 'the systems approach', was beginning to influence every aspect of social organization. New production techniques brought down the price of consumer goods while making it possible to pay higher wages.

Despite recurrent economic crises, the reality for the vast majority of British people was that at last the country seemed to have entered into the kind of high-spending consumer society long familiar from American films. Most of these developments owed little to the deliberate actions of politicians, though the general drift is quite well encapsulated in certain political utterances. The keynote had been sounded in June 1954 by the then Conservative Chancellor of the Exchequer, R. A. Butler, when he asked, rhetorically, 'Why should we not aim to double our standard of living in the next twenty-five years, and still have our money as valuable then as now?' A remark made by the Conservative Prime Minister, Harold Macmillan in 1957, taken out of context, entered popular lore in a vulgar joke which tore round the country during the 1959 election campaign. a woman complains to the police that she has been raped by one of the candidates, who, she insists, was the Conservative, she knows this, 'because she's never had it so good'. In the 1964 election campaign, Harold Wilson, as leader of the Labour Party, moved two steps forward by speaking of 'the white heat of technological revolution'.

White heat was perhaps not quite the right image; much of the new technology was concerned with suds, shine, and phoney flavours. Still there could be no doubt about the benefits brought by technology: disinfectants and detergents enormously improved health and hygiene; food was generally purer and fresher than before the war. The British end of the giant multi-national conglomerate, Unilever, had set up its first research establishments in the aftermath of the Second World War. By 1963 there were three, when a fourth was established at Welwyn, the team investigating problems of texture and flavour in oils and fats and problems relating to ice-cream moving there from Port Sunlight; the capacity released at Port Sunlight was used for expanded research on detergents. The research was needed, for detergents were already choking up the country's sewers with foam; however, by 1965 a method was found of breaking down detergents biologically. Canning was a traditional method of preserving food (the upper classes in the thirties believed that the feckless working class lived off tinned food); now came freezing and drying as efficient methods of producing convenience foods. The electrical industry directed itself towards producing smaller and more efficient refrigerators, as well as washing machines, spin-driers, dishwashing machines, and bigger and better television sets. Certainly there appeared to be, as disciples of American capitalism had always maintained, a cunning inter-relationship between technology, the market, and the forces of communication. Advertising on commercial television did much to build up and sustain the demand for the new appliances. The chemicals industry produced new plastics. To put the appropriate sheen on the new laminated surfaces new polishes were produced. All of these developments fitted into a social scene where a greater proportion of women than at any time since the war were going out to work and where domestic labour was in short supply They were also crucial in the movement in the British economy away from the traditional heavy industrial base to the new technological industries.

The systems approach, appropriately dressed up in its own awful jargon, seemed vindicated. Computers were essential to the process known at Unilever as 'Programme Evaluation and Review Technique', translated by Professor Charles Wilson (in his history of the company) as 'the planning not only of research projects but of research, development and marketing projects so that operations were carried out in the most logical and economical fashion'. The 'scientists' were entering upon their heritage, and in the sixties for the first time they began to appear in numbers on the boards of directors of the major companies dealing in consumer products. (I C I, the larger of the two British chemicals' giants, had been the pioneers of placing scientists in important executive positions.) At the receiving end, as it were, of the sophisticated new trading mechanism, supermarkets and self-service stores began to appear. As wages rose, working-class people bought less fish and more meat. Mac Fisheries began to turn their chain of fish shops into small supermarkets selling vegetables and groceries as well as fish. Greater and greater emphasis came to be placed on packaging and advertising. Advertising in itself became a major new growth industry. In 1965 the Chairman of Unilever explained to the shareholders why advertising and packaging had become so important: 'If your goods are to be sold by self-service your package is fighting for you against every other package directly or indirectly competing. You cannot expect it to get much help – at least in self-service stores and supermarkets – from the people running the shop.'

The full version of C. P. Snow's 'The Two Cultures' was delivered as the Rede Lecture at the University of Cambridge in 1959, and published the same year. It quickly aroused a great deal of attention. The incoming Wilson Labour Government of 1964 established a Ministry of Technology with the powerful trade-union leader, Frank Cousins, at its head, and with Snow as Parliamentary Under-Secretary; at the same time Dr B. V. Bowden, Principal of the University of Manchester Institute of Science and Technology, was appointed Minister of State in the Department of Education and Science, being, like Snow, given a peerage. Once again the changes were more paper than reality; within two years Cousins, Snow, and Bowden had all resigned their posts.

On the world's stage momentous events took place at a medical conference held in Tokyo in 1955. The intra-uterine device for contraceptive purposes had been experimented with in the 1920s and 1930s, but had produced such disastrous side-effects that it had been abandoned. At Tokyo, the Japanese reported the successful re-introduction of the intra-uterine contraceptive device. At the same conference the American biologist Gregory Pincus reported his successes with hormonal oral contraceptives. The process by which ovulation is initiated, controlled, and regulated had been understood for fifty years. In the mid-1930s synthetic oestrogens were developed which could prevent the release of pituitary gonadotrophins, so that ovulation would be inhibited and conception controlled. Still lacking, however, was a cheap source of synthetic progesterone-like steroids. Then in the 1940s another American biologist, C. L. Markert, demonstrated that certain plants, particularly the Mexican yam, were rich sources of steroids from which orally effective gestagens could be synthesized cheaply. It was during the year prior to the Tokyo conference that Pincus and his colleagues successfully tried out the combined oestrogen-gestagen product in Puerto Rico. 'The era of the Pill,' a leading medical historian (Dr N. E. Himes) has written, 'had begun.' Always, though, there is a time-lag between scientific discovery and general usage. We shall be discussing later the social consequences of new contraceptive methods, but it may be noted here that the pill only began to be at all widely used in Britain in the late 1960s. And even then, as a 1970 survey reported, only 19 per cent of married couples under forty-five were using the pill, while 29 per cent were using the condom and 37 per cent were using no contraceptive method at all.

New appliances flowing down from the commanding heights of technology formed one of the streams entering the millpond of 1960s Britain; rising income levels formed the other. Even if the phrase had not been invented by Professor J. K. Galbraith for his classic denunciation of American society of the fifties for allowing public squalor to exist side-by-side with private wealth, a distinctive condition, well described as 'the affluent society', undoubtedly existed in the Britain of the 1960s. Back in 1951 the average weekly earnings of men over twenty-one had stood at £8·30 per week. A decade later the figure had almost doubled to £15·35; in 1966 it was £20·30, in 1968 £23·00, in 1969 £24·80, in 1970 £28·05, and in 1971 £30·93. Of course, there was a touch of inflation around as well. Between 1955 and 1960 retail prices rose by 15 per cent; by 1969 they were 63 per cent higher than in 1955. But against that, weekly wage *rates* rose 25 per cent between 1955 and 1960, and had risen by 88 per cent in 1969. When overtime is taken into account, we find that average weekly *earnings* rose 34 per cent between 1955 and 1960, and 130 per cent between 1955 and 1969. This last figure was almost exactly matched by the average earnings of middle-class salaried employees, which rose 127 per cent between 1955 and 1969. While prices of food and other necessities were steadily rising, the prices of small cars, in relation to earning power, were falling, and the many products of new technology, such as television sets and washing machines, were, despite inflation, actually costing less.

New appliances altered the home more than they altered the work place. Most of the new technological wonders of the consumer age were in fact put together by routine, repetitive work on the assembly line. Where systems approaches prevailed, where research and development really was important, there was employment for the growing breed of 'white-coated workers' who required special training and skills and whose working environment was of a salubrious nature unknown on the assembly line or in the old heavy industries. Many technocrats did indeed come from working-class backgrounds and were well on the way to establishing themselves securely within the middle class. But it was not so much that old work places changed; rather that new work places were created for the fortunate and the upwardly mobile.

Work was much studied by academic researchers towards the end of the sixties. Investigations by Fraser, Warr, Wall, and many others brought out its fundamental dualistic character. On the one hand it is the curse by which almost all human beings are afflicted; on the other it is the activity through which most people establish their identity, feel pride, and, perhaps, find fruition: or, at least, it is the activity which fills the largest slice of any person's time between birth and death. On the whole upper-class (top professional and business) and middle-class (other business and professional) occupations offered most scope for personal satisfaction; lower-middle-class and working-class occupations least Yet, obviously, the crucial significance of work at all levels cannot be ignored A factory apprentice spoke to Fraser of 'the unforgettable claustrophobic comradeship' of the factory:

It is a friendship generated of common experience, common income and common worktasks. Out of this shared pattern of experience grows a common culture of the workplace And like other cultures it can never be fully understood by the outsider On that first morning at work I began to learn all the expected patterns of response, all-the rewards and sanctions, just as an infant learns its native tongue. I quickly learned the harsh language of aggressive friendship; the need to identify myself with the workgroup in opposition to all forms of authority from the chargehand up. Nothing must be allowed to threaten the cohesion of the workers, for only through this 'sticking together' could we solve the problems facing us.

But another of Fraser's interviews, also recorded in his *Work: Twenty Personal Accounts* (1968), this time with a machine-minder in a knitwear factory, well caught the agony of repetitive, yet highly stressful, work:

Watching the cones, checking the fabric, attending the machines which constantly break down, you're on the go all the time If a machine stops, it must be started, and when it is going the cones are running out and have to be replaced. Hour after hour without break, from one machine to another and back, putting up ends, changing cones, starting the machines and trying to watch the fabric. The machines aren't designed for the operator You bend low to see the fabric, and climb up on the machine to reach the arms holding the thread. To see all the cones you have to walk twenty-five feet round Usually an operative has three machines with a total of 150 cones – many of which you can't see immediately because they're on the other side of the machines; you have to memorize which cones are going to run out. With bad yarn the machines snag constantly; it's gruelling keeping everything running ...

Hey, the machine's stopped. A top red light? Find a stick, disentangle the thread – break off the balled-up yarn, put the end up, check the thread is not caught, press the button, throw the handle Peer at the fabric – needles? lines from tight yarn? Feel the yarn as it runs, alter the tension; we're not supposed to, it's the supervisor's job but he's too busy. Change a tight cone. A red light above droppers – cone run out? press-off? A yellow light – the stop motion has come up, maybe something is out of position on the needles, a build-up of thread or a broken needle. Clear the build-up, change the needle, start the machine again. And the other machines, are they all right? One of them stops every other minute on average. Can't spend more than thirty seconds looking at one, leave it for the two others, make sure they're all right, come back to the first. May take five or ten minutes to clear. By the time the trouble's clear, another one's stopped. Break off the bad yarn, disentangle the cone, restart the machine – a few seconds later do the same again.

Working on his thesis 'The perceived determinants of job satisfaction and job dissatisfaction in a chemical firm', Toby Wall received this account from an employee:

If I thought there was no hope of ever having more variety than continuously running out batches and cleaning jobs, but to stand under a blender in one position, day after day, just opening and shutting the valve, it's not my idea of satisfactory. Though, as they say, somebody has to do it, but I don't see why it should be me.

Many schemes were mooted in the middle fifties for improving productivity, in particular incentive production bonus schemes and the increased use of automation. The Secretary of the National Motor Joint Shop Stewards' Committee, in June 1956, produced a neat reaction to automation proposals at the British Motor Corporation.

Don't let anyone kid you, Brothers, that we don't welcome automation – we do, but the workers must be in a position to have a say in how automation should be used and to have a fair share of the profits. I don't grumble when I get home from work because my wife has been able to sit down in the afternoons because I have bought her a washing machine, a vacuum cleaner and an electric sewing machine. That is the beginning of automation – making the workers' lives easier. Has it made your life easier? I doubt it. We don't welcome mass introduction of machinery just to help the Government get half-a-million on the dole.

Perhaps the very visible growth in the acquisition of durable consumer goods was necessary to help workers forget the conditions of the work place. In 1956 only about 8 per cent of households had had refrigerators; this rose to 33 per cent in 1962 and 69 per cent by 1971. Television sets had been a rarity in the early 1950s; but by 1961 75 per cent of families had one, and by 1971 91 per cent. By 1971, also, 64 per cent of families had a washing machine. Although technological developments elsewhere were matched in the realm of telecommunications, there was not quite the same expansion in households having a telephone. Subscriber trunk dialling was introduced in Bristol in 1958, in London in 1961, and thereafter was slowly extended to other parts of the United Kingdom. In 1951 1·5 million households had had a private telephone; by 1966 this figure had risen to 4·2 million; nevertheless at the end of the decade more than a half of all households, as yet, had no telephone.

The British in general have not been distinguished for their interest in the culinary skills nor for the quality and variety of the food they eat. Affluence brought important changes, though not always absolutely for the better. After meat rationing ended in 1956, average consumption of all meat, meat products, and poultry ran at something above 2 lb. per week. By 1967 consumption had risen only slightly, but fish was re-assuming a more important rôle in the diet, mainly, however, in the form of pre-packed frozen 'steaks' or 'fingers'. (Fish and chips from that traditional institution, the fish-and-chip shop, of course, retained a constant popularity.) All in all, convenience foods accounted for about a fifth of expenditure on food in 1960; by 1970 this had risen to a quarter.

As world oil supplies dry up and pollution takes its toll of the environment, it is easy to mock the concept of the private automobile as an instrument of personal freedom and power. Yet, if it is not unapt to speak of 'roads to freedom', it is not, perhaps, inept to stress the importance of the cars which ran along them. The expansion in car ownership began in the fifties, but accelerated rapidly in the early sixties: 2,307,000 cars and vans in 1950; 3,609,000 in 1955; 5,650,000 in 1960; 9,131,000 in 1965; 11,802,000 in 1970. In November 1959 the first modest stretch of the M1 motorway was opened. A new era of cultural spoliation and environmental vandalism, but also of undreamt-of mobility, was opening. If the expansion of private transport

threatened chaos on the roads and the possibility of bankruptcy
for the nationalized railways, who better fitted to assess the
problem than one of the new scientist-industrialists? In 1961
Dr Richard Beeching was appointed Chairman of the British
Transport Commission. A couple of years later, the Beeching
Report on the railways recommended the axing of all branch
lines, reducing the railway network from 13,000 to 8,000 miles
with a concentration on freight and inter-city services. In the
upshot, the system was stabilized at 11,000 miles, but many
small towns lost their railway connections none the less.
Mobility, perhaps, was fine for those with cars; for many without, in the country areas, there was almost a return to pre-
industrial conditions. At the other end of the scale, domestic
air travel doubled between 1961 and 1971 from 1,000 million to
2,000 million passenger kilometres.

Thus there were great changes in industrial organization,
social geography, and, in lesser degree, in conditions of work.
Technology showed itself in one of its most pernicious forms in
the beer industry. Here, small breweries were closed down, and
large ones built to produce chemicalized beer. While some of
the traditional industrial concentrations remained, as, for
instance, in sections of the much shrunk coal-mining industry,
on the whole the 1960s was the decade in which the new industry superseded the old. Conditions in light engineering
works and motor factories were often as tedious as heavy industrial work had always been; but they were generally less dirty
and less arduous.

Hopes were not yet gone that the growth of the fifties and
sixties, channelled and shaped by the planning ideals of the
forties, could yet create a genuinely better environment, though
perceptive commentators noted that such great environmental
planners of the war years as Barlow and Abercrombie had
scarcely bargained for the new technological civilization of the
sixties. As one geographer wrote, neatly encapsulating the complacent optimism and pleasantly fearful exuberance of the time:

The achievements of the post-war years have been great and
London's expansion has been braked, if not halted; new development
has taken place in a controlled, not in a haphazard, fashion; redevelopment has created and is creating inner areas of which Londoners

need no longer be ashamed; the new towns are built. Yet the circumstances of 1960 are very different from those envisaged by Sir Montague Barlow or Sir Patrick Abercrombie, and new forces have risen to promote further growth.

In 1963 the Buchanan Report recommended urban motorways as the remedy for traffic congestion in towns. Planners and developers came together in a clouded vision of brave new architectural concepts, a wish to set up concrete symbols of progress, a need to accommodate to the motor car, and a desire to make affluence yield a decent profit. So the guts were torn out of such cities as Newcastle, Glasgow, and Birmingham and replaced with an ugly jungle of urban motorways and high-rise buildings.

8. Critiques, Boutiques, and Pop

Never is there an era in which no writers or artists are expressing criticism of the society in which they live. It would be wrong to overstate the case for the late fifties and the sixties as a time of special social criticism; indeed, much that was newest and most characteristic rather formed a self-regarding part of the new culture than a forceful criticism set apart from it. Still, a number of influences, often inter-related, often quite different in strength or in kind, can be detected which together produced that transformation in British ideas and modes of behaviour which can, without quite slipping into bathos, be described as forming a 'cultural revolution'.

First, after the parochial post-war years, there was a new openness to ideas and attitudes from both the Continent and the United States. At the most rarefied level philosophers seemed at last to be peering out from the tunnel of linguistic philosophy, and three works of 1959 can be taken as marking a re-kindling of interest in the wider metaphysical issues which had continued to preoccupy the continentals: *Individuals* by Peter Strawson, *Thought and Action* by Stuart Hampshire, and *Words and Things* by the expatriate Parisian Jew Ernest Gellner. The most powerful (and influential – the book went through six impressions by 1970) demonstration of a new mood in philosophy and of the gathering strength of the social sciences was Peter Winch's *The Idea of a Social Science and Its Relation to Philosophy* (1958): 'Any worthwhile study of society,' he declared, 'must be philosophical in character and any worthwhile philosophy must be concerned with the nature of human society.' Historical writing, too, seemed to be shaking off the dead-hand of relativism which had lain across it for so long, and historians began to take an interest both in the non-European world and in the methodology of social science. Above all, structuralism – put simply, the attempt to find the underlying structures in apparently the most impressionistic and diverse of human activities – in part through the diffusion of the ideas of the French anthropologist Claude Lévi-Strauss, greatly influenced the humanities and the social sciences, most strikingly, perhaps, in the realm of English literature, so long the softest of all the arts subjects. Structural linguistics, and pursuit of the universals in all human language, were advanced by the disciples of the American Noam Chomsky, particularly at Edinburgh University under the influence of the leading Chomskyite, Professor John Lyons.

Certain other American influences were of such a specific character that they must be separated out into a second category of their own. The point was that America had for years had the style of advanced economic and technological society into which Britain was now edging. Earlier American responses now struck a chord in Britain. Herbert Marcuse's *One-Dimensional Man* (1964) and Marshall McLuhan's *Global Village* (1968) became clichés, along with Galbraith's *Affluent Society*. There was no one political trend: broadly the critiques were of the soullessness and standardization involved in mass technological society; yet from Daniel Bell's *The End of Ideology* (1960) came the view that the old political divisions were redundant.

A more positively political trend, thirdly, was the revivification of the intellectual left. A greater opening to continental influences, and an emphasis, above all, on the lesser-known early writings of Karl Marx, helped to create the more humane 'New Left' which turned away from economic determinism towards the concept of the alienation inherent in contemporary industrial society. The *Universities' and Left Review*, founded in 1957, merged in 1960 into the *New Left Review*.

But, fourthly, there was another purely indigenous school of commentators concerned with the twin problems of Britain's rather poor economic showing (despite affluence) compared with her, by now, flourishing competitors, and her decline in world influence. On the former there was general agreement among those who were to the right of the Labour Party or the left of the Conservative Party that in some way or another Britain had gone 'soft', on the latter there was disagreement between those who accused Britain of maintaining delusions of world grandeur, and those who attacked her for, in the brilliant phrase of John Mander (*Great Britain or Little England?*, 1963), taking a 'holiday from history'. Among those Mander had in mind were members of the Campaign for Nuclear Disarmament (CND) founded in 1958. Like Richard Hoggart's *The Uses of Literacy* (see below, page 128), CND very much marked a period of transition in British society. Its leaders were largely upper class and upper-middle class; it was very much in the tradition of British radical dissent. Yet it pointed the way towards the participatory sixties: it involved housewives (though usually middle-class ones), and, as opinion polls showed, it had the support of between one quarter and one third of the British public. The campaign reached a peak in 1960 when the annual Labour Party Conference adopted a resolution in favour of Britain's unilateral nuclear disarmament. Thereafter, however, the campaign seemed to lose impetus; a similar resolution was rejected by the following year's Conference, in itself a rather arbitrary matter, given Labour's block-vote system of 'democracy', but, more significantly, the polls suggested a decline in public support.

Typical studies of the economy were Michael Shanks's *The Stagnant Society* (1961), Eric Wigham's *What's Wrong with the Unions?* (1961), and Rex Malik's *What's Wrong with British Industry?* (1964) – all published in paperback by Penguin Books. A wider front was covered by Anthony Sampson's *Anatomy of Britain* (1962), Brian Magee's *The New Radicalism* (1962), and the collection of essays edited by Arthur Koestler, *Suicide of a Nation* (1963). In February 1963 Koestler wrote in the *Observer*:

> In no other country has the national output been crippled on such frivolous and irresponsible grounds. In this oldest of all democracies class relations have become more bitter, trade union politics more undemocratic than in De Gaulle's France and Adenauer's Germany. The motivation behind it is neither communism, socialism, nor enlightened self-interest, but a mood of disenchantment and cussedness.

Much of the economic and political analysis was rather shallow. Far more profound was the shift, in the world of intellect and imagination, away from the literalism and representationalism which had dogged British literature and drama, and to some extent also the visual arts, since the war. At last technology was allowed to influence artistic form. At last intellectuals began to overcome their contempt for the film as a form of expression. New aesthetic concepts influenced art and architecture. There is so much in all this that detailed exemplification must await the closing sections of this chapter. For the moment my concern is to pin down the whole gamut of influences and changes.

Fifthly, then, there were the reactions of those within the little world of art, entertainment, thought, and religion towards the new consumer society in which hitherto underprivileged and silent groups now had, if not a voice, certainly purchasing power. These reactions involved both a general populism, and a special veneer of appealing to and being influenced by youth. Perhaps the best single example is the attempt of the Anglican John Robinson to popularize the more libertarian *avant garde* theology in his book with the catchpenny title *Honest to God* (1963). At its most appealing the reaction within the world of entertainment burst out in the 'satire boom' of the early sixties, which was itself very much grounded in exuberant undergraduate irreverence for authority. Its two major products were the weekly magazine *Private Eye* and the television show *That Was the Week That Was* broadcast, wonder of wonders, by the BBC.

A sixth force is that of youth. At root this was an economic phenomenon related to the new spending power created by the new technological high-wage society. Youth, of course, can mean many different things depending upon the standpoint. The 'angry young men' were certainly not youths. But their writings, and the publicity which surrounded them, helped none the less to create the notion of a culture led by individuals of a rather younger age than had hitherto been usual: there was a kind of 'shunting' effect – intellectuals were now fifteen or twenty years younger than they used to be, so the age of popular entertainers and fashion-setters, too, was shunted back by fifteen or twenty years. Technological developments, allied with the particular turn taken by popular music, were, as we shall see, to give youth a particular hegemony over that aspect of popular culture.

When we speak of youth we begin to move away from influences mediated through the upper and middle classes, or rather through minorities belonging to these classes. And so we make a quantum leap to consider something rather different and of great significance in its own right: the emergence of a new conception of the nature of the working class and its rôle in society. It became fashionable to speak of the cultural ambience of the sixties as 'classless': a number of individuals from working-class backgrounds did indeed achieve personal eminence, and this is a fact of some considerable significance. But the crucial development was the beginnings of a perception of the working class not as stereotype, not as banner-bearer of the future, but as itself, on its own terms. The seminal work was written by a product of the Leeds working class, a graduate of Leeds University who occupied a faintly low-status appointment on the fringes of academic life at a not very celebrated provincial university: Richard Hoggart was Senior Staff Tutor in Literature at the Department of Adult Education, Hull University, when his *The Uses of Literacy* was published in hardcover in 1957: it was reprinted as a Penguin thirteen times between then and 1977.

Hoggart cautioned against two romantic idealizations of the working class: as the earnest Jude the Obscure seeking after knowledge, or as the class-conscious political activist. Of the seekers after knowledge Hoggart commented: 'They are exceptional, in their nature untypical of working-class people; their very presence at summer schools, at meetings of learned societies and courses of lectures, is the result of a moving-away from the landscape which the majority of their fellows inhabit without much apparent strain.' Those who idealized the political activists, he said, 'overrate the place of political activity in working-class life' and 'do not always have an adequate sense of the grass-roots of that life'. He then went on:

A middle-class Marxist's view of the working classes often includes something of each of the foregoing errors. He pities the betrayed and debased worker, whose faults he sees as almost entirely the result of the grinding system which controls him. He admires the remnants of the noble savage, and has a nostalgia for those 'best of all' kinds of art, rural folk art or genuinely popular urban art, and a special enthusiasm for such scraps of them as he thinks he can detect today. He pities and admires the Jude-the-Obscure aspect of working people. Usually, he succeeds in part pitying and part patronizing working-class people beyond any semblance of reality.

I have spoken of openings towards populism, towards youth, towards the working class. But that certainly did not mean a new culture, more inclusive, more unified than ever before. The very pace of technological change, the very multiplicity of new inputs, meant the opening of a gulf between the proponents of the new culture and the older generation. It was perhaps this, above all, that led the new culture to present itself in an over-emphatic, and sometimes even shrill, manner. Always, of course, there has been an *avant garde* cut off from the mass of res-pectable society. But the new culture was much more widely diffused than any *avant garde* culture had ever been; and it was not necessarily, anyway, in any sense 'progressive'. But the ten-sion between old and new was undoubtedly there, and I would rank that tension eighth of the forces we are now discussing.

Ninth is the point that out of all the flux and upheaval new groups were formed protesting against established society on behalf of various minorities. In general there was a current of opinion in favour of what came to be termed 'permissiveness'. This actually had two distinct origins. There were those who argued vociferously for freedom as a part of a human need for self-expression and went to lengths which to others seemed to transgress the frontiers of civilized behaviour. The other source lay with the highly civilized, who saw themselves at the head of a long tradition favouring toleration, dating back to John Stuart Mill and earlier. But there was no one-way trend. In 1964 Mrs Mary Whitehouse set up her 'Clean-up TV' campaign. A running battle between the advocates of permissiveness and tolerance and those of purity and censorship was joined: that battle in itself served to publicize the fact that change indeed was taking place.

Many of these forces came together in what was a kind of overarching characteristic: an attack upon the cosiness, the clichés, the stereotyped assumptions, and the parochialism of British society. But this attack itself became a trend, itself almost became a part of the cosiness of British society. However, that is to debunk too much. In the end, for all the tinsel and for all the posturing, there was an almost un-British vibrance in popular culture, in verbal expression, and in the arts and entertainment, which adds up, as far as anything ever can, to a cultural revolution. Some of the detail will be studied later in the chapter.

Two non-fiction works, published in 1957, both illustrate many of the forces just described and helped to accelerate them. In introducing the collection of essays entitled *Declaration*, which he had edited, Tom Maschler explained that 'a number of young and widely opposed writers have burst upon the scene and are striving to change many of the values which have held good in recent years'. These writers, who had recently achieved fame as 'the angry young men', were, Maschler reminded his readers, 'in their twenties and thirties'. Notably missing from the line-up was Kingsley Amis, whose reply on being invited to contribute had been: 'I hate all this pharisaical twittering about the "state of our civilization" and I suspect anyone who wants to buttonhole me about my "rôle in society". This book is likely to prove a valuable addition to the cult of the Solemn Young Men; I predict a great success for it.'

First among those who did contribute was the socialist novelist Doris Lessing, then in her late thirties. 'British life,' she wrote, 'is at the moment petty and frustrating. The people of these islands are kindly, pleasant, tolerant; apparently content to sink into ever-greater depths of genteel poverty' – the poverty, in her view, was caused by the heavy expenditure on armaments. 'The working people,' she continued, 'get their view of life through a screen of high-pressure advertising; sex-sodden newspapers and debased films and television; the middle classes, from a press which from *The Times* to the *New Statesman* is debilitated by a habit of languid conformity which is attacking Britain like dry rot.'

Colin Wilson, twenty-six at the time *Declaration* was published, stuck to a personal exploration of his own philosophical position, essentially a pseudo-Nietzschean glorification of certain 'outsider' figures, including Nietzsche, T. E. Lawrence, and himself. John Osborne (twenty-eight), while also self-centred, was very pungent. The phrase 'There aren't any good, brave

causes left' to which critics of *Look Back in Anger* had attributed
a central explanatory rôle, he explained as merely an expression
of 'ordinary despair'. 'At every performance of any of my plays,
there are always some of these deluded pedants, sitting there im-
patiently, waiting for the plugs to come singing in during
natural breaks in the action ... There they sit, these fashionable
turnips, the death's heads of imagination and feeling, longing
for the interval and its over-projected drones of ignorance. Like
the BBC critics, they either have no ear at all, or they can
never listen to themselves.'

The fullest and most subtle historical analysis was provided by
John Wain (thirty-two). He suggested that great social changes
had been initiated at the beginning of the century but had then
never been consummated. In the forties writers and intellectuals
could still impress by simply being portentous and solemn, but
in the fifties a more critical appraisal of society had become
imperative: 'How *can* anyone say that he accepts, or rejects, the
twentieth century *en bloc*? It is too full of unresolved muddles
for that.' Kenneth Tynan and Bill Hopkins, the drama critic
and the novelist, both just thirty, confined themselves to the
brief of talking about their own special fields. Lindsay Anderson (thirty-four, and second in age only to Doris Lessing) also
wrote on his special concern as a film director but managed to
make a number of points of considerable general significance. His
essay began:

Let's face it; coming back to Britain is always something of an
ordeal. It ought not to be, but it is. And you don't have to be a snob
to feel it. It isn't just the food, the sauce bottles on the café tables, and
the chips with everything. It isn't just saying goodbye to wine, goodbye to sunshine. After all, there are things that matter even more than
these; and returning from the Continent, today in 1957, we feel these
strongly too. A certain, civilised (as opposed to cultured) quality in
everyday life: a certain humour: an atmosphere of tolerance, decency
and relaxation. A solidity, even a warmth. We have come home. But
the price we pay is high.

For coming back to Britain is also, in many respects, like going
back to the nursery. The outside world, the dangerous world, is shut
away: its sounds are muffled ... Nanny lights the fire, and sits herself
down with a nice cup of tea and yesterday's *Daily Express*; but she
keeps half an eye on us too ...

After the shock of encountering nanny, one might reflect that at that time not too many British people did go to the Continent, though no doubt many of those who did belonged to that class which employed nannies. In the familiar way, Anderson actually describes himself as 'upper-middle-class', his father having been an army officer, his mother the daughter of a wool merchant; he had been educated at a preparatory and at a public school. However, the open attempt to place himself socially was significant. He then went on to point out that the British cinema had produced practically no proper working-class films. Indeed, he found working in the cinema a great cause for despondency: the British simply did not take film as a serious and creative medium in the way in which foreigners did.

Finally, there was a statement both more personal and more sweeping than any of the others, by Stuart Holroyd, at twenty-four the youngest of the contributors, who, on leaving school, had worked as an author and critic before going to university and becoming a professional philosopher. His declaration was that 'A sense of crisis is one of the first things needful in the writer today. He must see the crisis of our time as a threat to human freedom, and must seek to restore freedom in the only way possible: by deepening inwardness and, by means of his psychological vision, extending the limits of consciousness.'

Against *Declaration* I want to place Hoggart's *The Uses of Literacy*. I have already stressed Hoggart's perception of the working class as it really was, rather than as a figment of upper-class intellectual imagination. Perhaps more graphically than it had ever been done before, Hoggart brought home the physical reality, the geography, of class. Working-class houses, he said,

are fitted into the dark and lowering canyons between the giant factories and the services which attend them; 'the barracks of an industry' the Hammonds called them. The goods-lines pass on embankments in and around, level with many of the bedroom windows, carrying the products of the men's work to South Africa, Nigeria, Australia. The viaducts interweave with the railway lines and with the canals below; the gas-works fit into a space somewhere between them all, and the pubs and graceless Methodist chapels stick up at intervals throughout. The green stuff of the region forces its way where it can – and that is almost everywhere – in stunted patches. Rough sooty grass pushes through the cobbles; dock and nettle insist on a defiant life in the rough and trampled earth-heaps at the corners of the waste-pieces, undeterred by 'dog-muck', cigarette packets, old ashes; rank elder, dirty privet, and rosebay willow-herb take hold in some of the 'backs' or in the walled-off space behind the Corporation Baths. All day and all night the noises and smells of the district – factory hooters, trains shunting, the stink of the gas-works – remind you life is a matter of shifts and clockings-in-and-out. The children look improperly fed, inappropriately clothed, and as though they could do with more sunlight and green fields.

That Hoggart was writing very much at a time of transition in British social history is brought out by the stress he places on the geographical immobility of the working man:

The car has not reduced distance for him; the trains are no faster than they were three-quarters of a century ago. True, he will usually travel by bus if he has to travel, but the point is that he normally has to undertake very little travel except within a mile or two. The local quality of the day-to-day life of a working-class man is well-illustrated by the way he will still trudge half-way across town with a handcart or old pram, transporting a sixth-hand kitchen table he has picked up cheap from someone who knew someone. It will take the better part of an evening, but seems normal procedure. One is reminded of Tess of the d'Urbervilles moving from one valley to another and seeming, to herself, to move from one country to another. The contrast is not so acute, but the working-man in this instance is nearer Tess than he is to the city solicitor who runs out seven miles for a round of golf. For plenty of working-class people a bus journey to relatives half-way across the county is still a matter for considerable thought and upheaval.

While stressing the cultural homogeneity of the working class, Hoggart also put a special emphasis on what was to appear as one of the characteristic figures of the time, the working-class scholarship child 'emotionally uprooted from their class, often under the stimulus of a stronger critical intelligence or imagination' and who can never escape from 'an underlying sense of some unease'.

However, the dynamic concern of Hoggart's book was with the way in which, while material conditions improved, many of the accompanying cultural changes, particularly the debased popular reading matter referred to also by Doris Lessing, were destroying some of the best things in the working-class heritage.

... it would be a mistake to regard the cultural struggle now going on as a straight fight between, say, what *The Times* and the picture-dailies respectively represent. To wish that a majority of the population will ever read *The Times* is to wish that human beings were constitutionally different, and is to fall into an intellectual snobbery. The ability to read the decent weeklies is not a *sine qua non* of the good life. It seems unlikely at any time, and is certainly not likely in any period which those of us now alive are likely to know that a majority in any class will have strongly intellectual pursuits. There are other ways of being in the truth. The strongest objection to the more trivial popular entertainments is not that they prevent their readers from becoming highbrow, but that they make it harder for people without an intellectual bent to become wise in their own way.

... The new-style popular publications fail not because they are poor substitutes for *The Times* but because they are only bloodless imitations of what they purport to be, because they are pallid but slicked-up extensions even of nineteenth-century sensationalism, and a considerable decline from the sinewy sensationalism of Elizabethan vernacular writers.

Hoggart was no Jeremiah. He noted as encouraging the fact that although the working class might be exploited through the pushing of trivialized entertainment, at least they had now 'to be approached for their consent'. He could see that some of the worst developments that he feared might be a temporary facet of a particular development in technological society. The challenge was to maintain the freedom of an 'open' society while the process of centralization and technological development continued.

The upper-class end of the new social critique of the late fifties was kept up by the publication in 1959 of *The Establishment*, edited by a young diplomat who was to turn historian, Hugh Thomas. As Thomas later explained it, this collection of essays was 'dedicated to the theme that the most sensitive institutions in England were dominated by the same anachronistic master class'; the phrase 'the establishment', meaning this 'master class', had gained a certain currency earlier in the fifties. Nine years later, Thomas published another collection, *Crisis in the Civil Service*, which serves as quite a good measure of the progress of this particular social debate over the 1960s. The assumption in 1959 'was that once class was swept away, proud old England would reassert herself as a society both humane and industrially efficient and capable of exercising by her example a moral force for good in the world'. But by 1968 British weaknesses were rather seen as due to 'well-established and broad national attitudes rather than those of an élite'.

Throughout this book I have stressed the importance of class; I have also stressed the significance of the geographical variety of British society. If we are to talk of new critiques and new social trends we have to try to distinguish between what had a relatively limited impact within London itself, and what spread across the outlying provinces. Boutiques figure in the title of this chapter because they symbolize so many of the points laid out in my opening paragraphs. They represented a reaction against the mass presentation of department stores and big advertising. They had absorbed a *soupçon* of continental dash. Their appeal was to the youthful. They became a self-regarding and self-serving trend. It was actually in 1955 that Mary Quant and Alexander Plunkett-Greene opened their first Bazaar in the King's Road, Chelsea; within a year or two John Stephen had arrived from Glasgow and was opening his first shop in Carnaby Street, near Oxford Circus in London. It took a dozen years or more before boutiques were to be found in every provincial urban centre.

Accompanying the rise of the boutiquier went the rise of the photographer. Cameras were to art and advertising what washing machines were to domestic life: they fitted well into the international (the Germans were the great innovators) and, fairly, classless world of gadgetry. Where an upper-class figure, Anthony Armstrong-Jones, led the way, he was quickly followed by two upwardly mobile products of the London working class, David Bailey and Terence Donovan.

But the central feature, undoubtedly, of the cultural revolution was the transformation of the popular music scene. The pop revolution had all the ambivalence of the other developments characteristic of the sixties. It sprang out of the separate culture of youth, yet it depended upon the spending power of the affluent teenager. It expressed protest against established society and the organized music industry, yet it became a massive commercial enterprise. It was genuinely innovative musically, yet it spawned a mass of repetitive trivia. It had a true do-it-yourself participatory element, yet it became closely bound-up with the wonders of electronics.

American rock and roll music first hit Britain in the middle fifties. The film *Rock Around the Clock* crossed the Atlantic in 1956; Bill Haley went on his epochal tour in 1957. The local, do-it-yourself, response came in the form of skiffle groups. In 1956 two working-class lads, John Lennon and Paul McCartney, were playing in the Liverpool group, The Quarrymen. By 1960 the beat group the Silver Beatles had been formed to play in the Liverpool clubs, such as the Cavern and the Jacaranda. Visits to Hamburg equipped the group with new hairstyles and a new cosmopolitan image and exuberance. Decca, Pye, Columbia, HMV, and EMI all refused to record them but in May 1962 they were taken on by George Martin of Parlophone. With a new drummer, Ringo Starr, especially brought in, they recorded and released their first record, 'Love Me Do': it reached the top twenty. Thereafter a series of number-one hits followed. The phenomenon was in origins a local and Liverpool one, though a number of other groups also enjoyed a wider national success through the sale of their records, Gerry and the Pacemakers being the best-known.

The Beatles' publicity success reached its peak, and was sustained for several years thereafter, with their American tour of 1964. At the same time, they received the attention of serious music critics. Richard Middleton (in *Pop Music and the Blues*, 1972) has summed up the principal characteristics of their work as including:

first, rhythms, concepts of structure and function and of theme and texture derived, *via* Rock 'n' Roll, from blues, second, a melodic combination of pentatonic and tonal elements, the latter being mostly simply diatonic and folk-like but sometimes having a touch of chromaticism; third, a complex use of harmony, which combines and juxtaposes in different ways tonal progressions of varying complexity, modal progressions, parallel triads and harmonic ostinato, relationship of tonal and non-tonal elements often resulting in an ambivalence of scale and 'key'; fourth, a blues-like but typically 'innocent' vocal style; fifth, a use of vocal response and backing [of a special type]; and sixth, the frequent use, alongside blues-like structures, of verse-and-refrain form, probably derived from folk song and previous popular music traditions. It is the perpetual tempering of one element by another in such a cultural mixture as this (as well as what is retained of the traditional blues techniques of objectification) which is responsible for the sense of irony and control characteristic of the music.

For national and international fame the only possible rivals to the Beatles were the London-based rhythm and blues group the Rolling Stones, who had a stronger pro-youth, anti-establishment, and altogether wilder image than the Beatles. They also came from a social class above the Beatles: when the group was founded, Mick Jagger, lead singer, was a student at the London School of Economics and two other members were at the Sidcup Art School.

Despite the commercial success and hullabaloo attending upon the famous names, this music very definitely had its roots in the hundreds of groups performing in pubs and clubs up and down the country: any collection of young people with a modicum of musical talent could put together the equipment necessary to set themselves up as a pop group. The commercial companies did not initiate the trends; they followed shakily behind. The old song-writer practically disappeared as groups developed their own music and songs. The printed music sheet was passing away, too. A proper record of any number, with all its electronic effects, had to be just that, a *record*. In the fifties, the hit-parade had been judged on sales of sheet music: now it was compiled from the sales of individual records.

It could scarcely be said that the newspapers moulded opinion. More and more, they were themselves a part of mass consumer society. Tighter consolidation of ownership and sharper polarization between quality press on the one side, and popular press on the other, took place. After 1960 a further five national newspapers disappeared; and in 1964 the attempt to run a Labour daily newspaper with some serious political content was finally given up when the *Daily Herald* was transformed into the *Sun*. Between 1959 and 1961 the former Daily Mirror Newspapers Ltd emerged as the massive combine, the International Press Corporation. Roy Thomson took over Kemsley Newspapers, including the *Sunday Times*, in 1959; and in 1966 he bought *The Times* from the Astors. Unlike the Lord

Beaverbrook of an earlier era, the great press magnates were not interested in pressing their own personal opinions through their columns: they let the market decide the character of their papers. The deeply entrenched unions in the newspaper industry made sure that however much new technologies might dominate other aspects of British society, they would be kept at bay in the world of newspapers. Yet, in many respects, as money appeared still to be splashing around, such quality papers as the *Sunday Times*, the *Observer*, and *The Times* rose to a level of journalism probably above that seen before in the twentieth century.

Newspapers now had the full competition of television, and the BBC had the full competition of commercial television, which by 1961 was reaching into the homes of 95 per cent of the population. For technical standards, competition proved beneficial; overall the standard of current affairs programmes was high. However, social comedies and dramas showed a ham-handedness which revealed that television was not yet ready to grasp the serious realities of British social structure; broadcasters, and some investigative programmes touching on questions of class, both betrayed the dated upper-class style. The greatest breakthrough was achieved by commercial television when, in late 1960, it presented the first edition of 'Coronation Street', whose characters really did breathe the essence of working-class existence.

But after pop, the most potent evidence of intellectual and artistic renewal in Britain was to be found in the cinema. Three tendencies, relating to what was said at the beginning of this chapter, can be detected: a perceptive social criticism and social satire; an authentic presentation of working-class life-styles; and genuine innovation both in technique and in breaking away from the purely naturalistic film. The classic satire was the Boulting Brothers' film of 1959, *I'm All Right Jack*, which with ruthless gusto exposed the unwitting collusion between the pigheaded, work-shy working class, and the snobbish, arrogant, and corrupt upper class. (Yet within the year, the same production team, without any comment whatsoever, had used a public school setting as the natural background for a vacuous comedy entitled *The French Mistress*.) Clive Donner's *Nothing*

But the Best (1966) was a brilliant satire of the enduring upper class: Denholm Elliott, as the black sheep of an upper-class family, coaches Alan Bates, a lower-middle-class clerical worker in a large financial institution, into becoming an accepted member of the upper class: he does not actually have to be able to do anything, but he has to have the right accent and manners, and the proper arrogance. The lower-middle-class ambience, contrasted with the upper-middle-class one, lay at the heart of *Room at the Top* (1959), whose social criticism had a sharper cutting-edge than that provided by John Braine's original novel.

The classic portrayal of the working-class environment seen from within was Karel Reisz's interpretation of Alan Sillitoe's *Saturday Night and Sunday Morning* (1960). The disaffection (it is too diffused to be called anger) of the young factory worker is directed against organized society and its bureaucrats, and against the more docile members of the working class, rather than against any identifiable class enemy. Lindsay Anderson had his commercial opportunity with *This Sporting Life* (1963), which, with great subtlety, brought David Storey's inarticulate rugby league footballer to the screen. After the initial failure of his play *The Birthday Party* (1960), Harold Pinter, with his menace-laden plots concentrating on the sudden shifts of dominance in human relationships, emerged as the major play-wright of the decade (*The Caretaker*, 1960; *The Homecoming*, 1965); when he teamed up with American-born film director Joseph Losey, British cinema at last abandoned its slavish adherence to the naturalistic conventions (*The Servant*, 1963; *Accident*, 1967). Towards the end of the decade, Lindsay Anderson was responsible for *If* (1968) which after a realistic public school beginning explodes into a futuristic rebellion against this microcosm of British imperial and class rule.

Along the way I have mentioned some of the novels which illustrate the main trends of the times, or were converted into films. As a social commentator, Kingsley Amis became a literary institution: between *Take a Girl Like You* (1960) and *I Want It Now* (1968) a whole sexual revolution had indeed been con-summated. John Burgess Wilson, having in 1958 produced *English Literature: A Survey for Students*, emerged briefly in 1963 as Joseph Kell, author of *Inside Mr Enderby*, but was already on the permanent way to literary esteem when, as Anthony Burgess, he published (1962) *A Clockwork Orange* (a futuristic study of excessive mindless violence perpetrated by youth). An imaginative range going outside the traditional novel of social custom was also shown by John Fowles in *The Collector* (1963), *The Magus* (1966), and *The French Lieutenant's Woman* (1969) (which, for example, broke with the naturalistic tradition in offering the reader a choice of conclusions to the story). At middle-brow level – sign indeed of these scientific times – science-fiction was building up a following greater than that ever commanded by thrillers or detective fiction.

Changes were taking place in the means whereby books reached their public. Both the great London commercial circulating libraries and the local twopenny libraries withdrew from business in the early sixties. Two institutions filled the gap. First of all, the public libraries, which up till the Second World War had seen their duties as being basically concerned with the lending of non-fiction works, by the 1964 Libraries and Museums Act had their position confirmed as the officially recognized centre for making books available; libraries were now, as a number of commentators have remarked, the national health service for books. Secondly, the small shops switched over to selling paperbacks. It has been argued that neither development fostered creativity and originality in the production of fiction.

The British were the greatest library users in the world, with about one third of the population registered with a public library; but as buyers of books the British ranked well below the Americans and most West Europeans. The absolute number of books produced shot up in the sixties as publishers endeavoured to cash in on affluence by publishing works of history, popular sociology, and so on; the number of novels dropped slightly as compared with the fifties. In 1963 2,375 new novels were published which does not compare very impressively with the 2,153 published in 1937. Sales, in general, were poorer than they had been in the thirties. To break even, a first novel had to sell about a thousand copies. An average sale of 1,200–1,400 might be expected, but of this 90 per cent went to libraries. British novels, at 60,000 words, tended to be short compared with American. This, according to John Sutherland, author of *Fiction and the Fiction Industry* (1978), was so that dedicated readers could read six novels a fortnight in the half an hour allocated each evening in bed. Despite innovations elsewhere in Britain, and despite the major experiments taking place on the Continent, the British novel remained fundamentally naturalistic. It now brought in new areas of experience, particularly that of the working class and of women, but in form it was not much changed. Margaret Drabble, successful author of a number of novels, including *A Summer Bird-Cage* (1963), *The Millstone* (1965), and *The Waterfall* (1969), essentially related to the rôle of women in contemporary society, declared in 1967: 'I'd rather be at the end of a dying tradition, which I admire, than at the beginning of a tradition which I deplore.'

For literary innovation, it was necessary to go to the theatre. A whole clutch of new playwrights, John Mortimer (*What Shall We Tell Caroline?*, 1958), Peter Shaffer (*Five-Finger Exercise*, 1958), Arnold Wesker (*Roots*, 1959), Shelagh Delaney (*A Taste of Honey*, 1959), as well as Harold Pinter, appeared at the end of the fifties. Mortimer declared himself to be particularly concerned with the decline of the upper-middle class; Wesker, unusually for a British playwright, had a very overt, idealist-socialist 'message'. In 1965 Edward Bond exploded violently on to the scene with *Saved*, which explored the condition of society's rejects and their predisposition to senseless violence. The mighty, imaginative, new school of directors went from strength to strength: Peter Hall took over at Stratford in 1960, Peter Brook put on his incredible *Marat/Sade* in 1964. Perhaps partly inspired by transatlantic example, a number of new, often experimental, smaller theatres were opened. In 1959 the Mermaid Theatre opened in the City of London; in 1962 came the Chichester Festival Theatre; in 1963 the Traverse Theatre in Edinburgh; and in 1964 Charles Marowitz began his Theatre of Cruelty (he, like the founder of the Traverse, Jim Haines, was an American). London, in the 1960s, really could claim to be the drama centre of the world; and the provinces were not doing badly either.

The international artistic style most in vogue in the post-war years had been abstract expressionism. Also from America, there now emanated pop art – the realistic presentation of subjects drawn from advertising, comics, popular idols, and the banal apparatus of everyday life – and optical art. Three British artists, in particular, demonstrated the special vitality of British painting in the 1960s, and were in themselves symbols of their times. Two were women, one, when he achieved overnight success, a mere youth. In many ways Elizabeth Frink was the most original and most appealing: toughly and uncompromisingly female (rather than feminine) in her powerfully realized, though far from exactly representational, male nudes and portraits of horses. Bridget Riley became one of the international leaders of the op-art movement; the critic David Thompson has spoken of 'a kind of optical situation which constantly recurs in her later work – that of a dominant formal pattern under pressure of disintegration'. David Hockney, a lower-middle-class boy from Bradford, vegetarian and conscientious objector, took to etching at college because he could not afford the materials for painting, visited New York on £100 he had managed to save, and produced the series of etchings, The Rake's Progress, which made him £5,000 while still a student. He showed an eclecticism and inventiveness worthy, at times, of Picasso; he drew upon pop art, and showed a healthy disrespect for the canons of wisdom handed down in the colleges: 'I have stopped bothering about modern art, in that at one time you would be frightened of doing things in painting because you would consider them almost reactionary. I have stopped believing that it's possible for art to progress only in a stylistic way.'

Architectural developments, which so closely mirrored the rise and fall of hopes in respect of social policy and social planning, I leave to the last chapter of 'Roads to Freedom'. The achievements of domestic and industrial design, however, were considerable and fit in well with the more optimistic trends discussed in this chapter. First of all, the careful, rational work of the Council of Industrial Design went steadily ahead, its endeavours enjoying added prestige when the former Anthony Armstrong-Jones, now (as Lord Snowdon) Princess Margaret's husband, joined the Council in 1961. Secondly, design shared in the new populism, the new reaction against supermarket and mass-produced shoddy. As with so much in this era, there was a certain ambivalence about the key event, the establishment by Terence Conran of his shop Habitat in South Kensington in 1964. Instead of individuals (middle-class, of course, rather than working-class) having to search around for their own individual items of style and charm, Habitat and its imitators would do the work for them. As Conran said: 'We hope we have taken the foot-slogging out of shopping by assembling a wide selection of unusual and top quality goods under our roof. It has taken us a year to complete this pre-digested shopping pro-gramme and we are confident that many women will take to this new style of buying with enthusiasm.' Still, many of the shops put on sale items made at home by amateur designers. Nowhere was the reaction against supermarket mass produc-tion stronger than in the field of children's toys: Galts, Play and Learn, and several others brought a new standard to British toys.

A third influence was that of pop, introducing the jokey and self-indulgent, the use of new plastics and of psychedelic colours. It might seem that the sober-sides of the Council of Industrial Design were being left behind. In the Society of Industrial Arts journal, Michael Wolff stated:

Basically it is true that the sort of designers in Britain who have really given people a bang in the last two years are Ken Adams, Art Director of the James Bond films; Frederick Starke, with his clothes for Cathy Gale [a popular TV character]; and Ray Cusick, with his daleks [the robots in the children's TV series *Doctor Who*]. People like Mary Quant and John Stephen have had the same sort of impact on a more limited age range. It is their zing, and their zest, and their vigorous understanding of what design is all about which should be one of the main contributions of industrial designers to modern society. It'll be a great day when cutlery and furniture designs (to name but two) swing like the Supremes.

True, there was a tension between pop culture and established culture. But the best of serious design, and pop design, were not necessarily totally antithetical. Paul Reilly of the Council of Industrial Design suggested that:

We are shifting, perhaps, from attachment to permanent universal values to acceptance that a design may be valid at a given time for a given purpose to a given group of people in a given set of circumstances, but that outside those limits it may not be valid at all; and conversely there may be contemporaneous but quite dissimilar solutions that can still be equally defensible for different groups – miniskirt for the teenager, something less divulging for the matron; painted paper furniture for the young, teak or rosewood for the ageing – and all equally of their times and all equally susceptible to evaluation by a selection committee. All this means is that a product must be good of its kind for the set of circumstances for which it has been designed.

Above all, the Council of Industrial Design was at its most successful in its efforts to persuade British industrialists of the importance of contemporary design. 'It had,' wrote Fiona MacCarthy, 'won a famous victory, with questions in the House, over the design of the new Cunard liner, demolishing forever the tendency in industry to leave design decisions to the Chairman's wife.' Council of Industrial Design policies for industry overlapped with a fourth influence discussed in Chapter 7: that of the systems approach dependent on computerization.

The ideas, the images, the literature, the life-styles all showed much of the old cosiness simply transformed into trendiness. But there was a liveliness and a spirit of innovation not seen in British society for generations and which, as never before, had penetrated through so many layers of this still stratified society. In very truth, things would never be quite the same again.

9. The End of Victorianism

The changes in what, in the nineteenth century, the great lawyer-historian A. V. Dicey had called 'law and opinion' – that which was acceptable both in duly constituted courts of law and to prevailing social convention – had little to do with the tenets of socialism or of capitalism. Nor, however, did they just happen. There were pressures from the market place, pressures from youth and popular culture, but also reasoned arguments in favour of a civilized and tolerant society put forward by politicians. The leftist and liberal proponents of a civilized society no doubt had no desire to create a gamblers' paradise; many of those who argued for the individual's rights to waste his money as he willed wanted neither free abortions nor tolerance of homosexuals: but whatever the little local disagreements, all of the 'reforms' of the late fifties and sixties marked a retreat from the social controls imposed in the Victorian era by evangelicalism and non-conformity.

The introduction of commercial television has already been mentioned several times. Next came the introduction in 1956 of the first public lottery since the eighteenth century, the Premium Savings Bonds scheme. Up till 1960 the very strict and somewhat arbitrary legislation governing betting and gaming, itself largely a product of Victorian evangelicalism and snobbery, had resulted in widespread evasion of the law, especially in the form of the passing of betting slips on street corners and in pubs. The main purpose of the 1960 Betting and Gaming Act was the sound conservative one of restoring respect and credibility to the law by openly legalizing certain forms of gambling: street betting shops, gambling clubs, and bingo followed. As the racketeers moved in on the new clubs, it became clear that perhaps there was something to be said for Victorian controls after all.

In the mid nineteenth century drugs had been widely accessible, and controls were established only in the late Victorian
period. In the 1950s, drug control was administered in accord-
ance with the best and most liberal paternalistic principles. Drug
users, very largely the middle-aged and elderly, were registered,
and could receive their particular poison on the National
Health Service. British officialdom prided itself on this open
system, which seemed to have preserved the country from the
horrors of the illicit drug trade which went on in the United
States. As the wonders of science marched forward, hand in
hand with the wonders of the National Health Service, more
and more people, mostly older women, became dependent on
the new psychotropic drugs, that is to say, sleeping pills, appetite
suppressants, tranquillizers, and anti-depressants. By the early
sixties it was clear that the official complacency over the work-
ings of British drug control was quite unjustified: doctors were
consistently, though innocently and ignorantly, over-prescrib-
ing, and the surplus was finding its way into a new black market.

The new element on the scene was that prosperous and
aggressive youth which has been referred to already on several
occasions (though it was still far from true that young people
were the main drug addicts). In understanding the growth and
influence of drug consumption in the 1960s it is important to
distinguish between four major areas. First of all, the amphetamines and other pills and capsules operating upon the central
nervous system; second, heroin and the other 'needle drugs':
together these had been the main sources of narcotic indulgence
by adults in the fifties; third, cannabis, a source throughout
the ages for a minority, but in the sixties the characteristic drug
of youth and the older figures who identified with youth
culture; finally, the new invention, LSD, and the other psychedelic drugs.

In 1951 the major pharmaceutical company Smith, Klein,
and French came up with the new amphetamine Drinamyl:
served up as a blue triangular-shaped pill, it was eventually
to become notorious as the 'purple heart'. By the early 1960s
it was clear that there was a racket in purveying purple hearts
and other amphetamines to certain adolescents, many from
a working-class background. The spread of amphetamines

coincided with the rise of the particular conservatively dressed youth groups known as the 'mods'. Officialdom was stirred out of complacency and, in what may well seem a contradiction of the general trend against social controls described here, the 1964 Drugs (Prevention of Misuse) Act was passed, making the possession of amphetamines without a prescription an offence.

The central development of the sixties was the spectacular growth in the availability and use of cannabis. *Cannabis sativa* is the name of the hemp plant which grows throughout the world: the flowering leaves and tops provide marijuana, popularly known as pot, and the form most usually taken in the United States; cannabis resin provides hashish, the form usually found in Britain, though here too it is sometimes referred to as pot. Cannabis did become very much the basic drug of a widespread youth culture; and by the later sixties it was also being taken by many of those, no longer young, who were in occupations related to the burgeoning popular culture, or who were in the universities, or who were even in the more traditional professions. The Wootton Committee, reporting in 1968, reckoned that there might be anything from 30,000 to 300,000 cannabis users; other estimates suggested that in 1970 there might have been anything from one million to two million.

LSD (lysergic acid diethylamide) is a synthetic drug which was discovered in 1938 by the Swiss scientist Hofmann; it is derived from ergot, a substance produced, rather easily, by fermenting rye. LSD was used therapeutically, though perhaps dubiously, in Britain from 1954 onwards. Above all, in the middle sixties, it was the drug of the San Francisco underground culture. Its spread to Britain was probably on a very limited scale. However, hashish and LSD were, together, thought of as 'mind-expanding' drugs: they were associated with the San Francisco scene, with resistance to the Vietnam War, with support for peace in general, with transcendentalism, and with 'flower power'. In the summer of 1967 the American hit, Scott MacKenzie's 'San Francisco', also reached the top of the hit-parade in Britain. The influence of the psychedelic drug culture on British popular music after 1967 could be seen, for instance, in such titles as the Beatles' 'Lucy in the Sky with Diamonds' (the initials, of course, spelling out LSD) and Procul Harum's 'A Whiter Shade of Pale'.

The flower-power, psychedelic, dream quickly went sour in America. The wide use of cannabis undoubtedly continued in Britain, but there was also a new, tragic swing in the use of amphetamines: from 1967 onwards certain groups of adolescents were taking amphetamines intravenously in the style of American 'speed freaks'.

For the most part, though, it must be stressed, the use of cannabis proceeded unobtrusively and harmlessly. Illicit drug taking was only a small part of a new sense that, suddenly, the forces of law and order, so painstakingly established in Victorian times, were now suddenly breaking down.

The acceleration in the crime rate was apparent from the mid-fifties onwards. From the mid-thirties to the mid-fifties offences of violence against the person had risen by about 6 per cent a year. From then onwards they went up by about 11 per cent a year. The total figures for crimes of violence went like this: 5,869 in 1955, 11,592 in 1960, 15,976 in 1964, and 21,046 in 1968. The increase in criminality was a feature of the population as a whole, but it was most significant in the seventeen to twenty-one, the fourteen to seventeen, and even the eight to fourteen age groups. The seriousness of the general situation seemed to be highlighted by such spectacular events as the great train robbery of 1963, with its brutal attack on the engine driver, the Moors murders of 1965, which involved particularly sadistic and grisly murders of children, the Shepherds Bush police murders of 1966, and the arrest and trial of the notorious East End criminals, the Kray brothers, in 1969 which brought out just what a vicious, and again sadistic, pair they were. The 1966 general election campaign was the first one in which 'law and order' featured as a major campaign issue.

Some careful researches by Michael Zander have suggested that even a massive increase in the police forces would have very little effect on the actual number of crimes committed; similarly, increasing the severity of penalties seems to have little effect. The roots of the rise in crime must be sought in the economic and cultural changes which we have been discussing.

The Committee on Children and Young Persons, reporting
in October 1960, offered some wise words on the rise in
juvenile crime:

During the past fifty years there has been a tremendous material.
social and moral revolution in addition to the upheaval of two wars.
While life has in many ways become easier and more secure, the whole
future of mankind may seem frighteningly uncertain. Everyday life
may be less of a struggle, boredom and lack of challenge more of
a danger, but the fundamental insecurity remains with little that the
individual can do about it. The material revolution is plain to see.
At one and the same time it has provided more desirable objects,
greater opportunity for acquiring them illegally, and considerable
chances of immunity from the undesirable consequences of so doing.
It is not always so clearly recognized what a complete change there
has been in social and personal relationships (between classes, between
the sexes and between individuals) and also in the basic assumptions
which regulate behaviour. These major changes in the cultural background may well have replaced the disturbances of war as factors which
contribute in themselves to instability within the family.

With regard to youthful offenders, one might stress the new
aggressiveness and hostility to authority of youth in general;
one might stress the temptations of the affluent society, going
often with frustrations for those who found that in fact nothing
opened before them but dead-end jobs. For the crime rate in
general, one might stress the acquisitive aspect of the ethos of
'having it good' and the destabilizing influence of a situation
in which, although living standards were generally rising, often
the contrasts between those who were prospering and those
who weren't were becoming sharper; but that would perhaps
seem to make too many excuses – much of the villainy of the
time was cold and calculated, and carried through with the
ruthlessness of a business operation. Perhaps the standards of
civic loyalty and respect for law and order had never been as
high as conservative romantics affected to believe. There is no
easy way of rooting out deviants in society; but certainly the
special conditions of the late fifties onwards gave deviants full
rein.

Perhaps the increase in crime should be seen more as a return
to Victorianism rather than a move away from it, but there

can be no doubts about the most significant of all the pieces of civilizing legislation, the abolition of capital punishment. In October 1965 an Act got through Parliament abolishing hanging as a five-year experiment. But before the five years were up, late in 1969, James Callaghan, the Home Secretary, decided to make abolition permanent. The first three years of the experiment had demonstrated convincingly, as was well known in any case to all authorities on the subject, and had been demonstrated from foreign experience, that there was no clear connection between the number of murders committed and the existence of the death penalty.

The solid, respectful, friendly British 'bobby', in so far as he ever fully existed in reality, was the product of the police reorganization of the late Victorian period (and makes some of his most solid appearances in the Sherlock Holmes stories). In the post-war years, the image (strongly presented in the original Dixon of Dock Green film *The Blue Lamp*) was remarkably unchanged, though the TV series *Z Cars* brought a more realistic image in the sixties. Two particular features distinguished the British police from their continental counterparts. First was the manner in which the separate forces (157 of them in the early sixties) were administered locally not nationally; only the Metropolitan Police was directly under the authority, through the Metropolitan Police Commissioner, of the Home Secretary. Second was the fact that, save, very occasionally, for a very few officers under very special circumstances, the British police were not armed. The Police Act of 1964 did strengthen the supervisory powers of the Home Secretary over all police forces, and at the same time a movement began towards amalgamating the smaller police forces. The spectacularly violent crimes of the sixties produced a situation in which the police themselves were having greater resort to firearms than the traditional image warranted. In 1965 the Special Patrol Group (SPG) of the Metropolitan Police was established on the analogy of the various riot control groups to be found on the Continent. In general the appearance was of a tougher, more professional, police force. In 1964 there were about 80,000 (policewomen as well as policemen) in the various forces; by 1973 there were over 111,000, though this was still below the paper 'establishment'. The legal system and the administration of justice remained little affected by social change in the sixties. Only in the early seventies did standing committees and commissions begin to wrestle with the Herculean task of dragging the law and its procedures out of the nineteenth century.

One of the first public signs of a significant relaxation in the Victorian moral code was the result of the trial for obscenity in 1960 of the publishers of *Lady Chatterley's Lover*. Since its completion by D. H. Lawrence in the 1920s, *Lady Chatterley's Lover* had not been available in this country: Penguin Books took a calculated decision to republish it. With many expert literary witnesses speaking for the defence, and with the prosecution counsel making an ass of himself in a peculiarly significant way by asking the jury whether the book was one they would wish their servants to read, Penguin Books were acquitted, and it was clear that books containing the same sort of explicit sexual material as Lady Chatterley would now be widely available.

The year 1967 was something of an *annus mirabilis* as far as liberal legislation in the sphere of sexual mores was concerned. First, the Abortion Act, put forward by the Liberal MP, David Steel, but supported by the Government, and also by several Conservatives. It had been possible in recent years for the well-off to secure abortions through private clinics, where doctors and psychiatrists were able to steer through the uncertainties of the existing law dating back to the Victorian era. However, penalties for well-intentioned medical men could still be extremely severe. More critically, for the less well-off woman suffering from an unwanted pregnancy the choices were two: to go through with the birth, or to seek a back-street abortion, with all its attendant horror and danger. That classic film of the affluent working-class swinger, *Alfie* (1966), brought the situation out well enough. Under the new Abortion Act, it was merely necessary that two doctors should be satisfied that an abortion was necessary on medical or psychological grounds: the number of private nursing homes providing this service now greatly expanded, but at least their fees were greatly reduced; it was now possible, though often with the prospect of having to go on a waiting-list, to get an abortion on the National Health Service. The National Health Service (Family Planning) Act of the same year made it possible, for the first time, for local authorities to provide contraceptives and contraceptive advice.

Secondly, thanks to the efforts of a private Labour MP, Leo Abse, the Sexual Offences Act ended (in England and Wales) the long and barbaric tradition whereby homosexuals had been subject to persecution and blackmail: a homosexual act between two consenting adults in private would no longer be a criminal offence. The effects of these three Acts were cumulative: gradually, 'gays' (as homosexuals now started calling themselves: ordinary citizens had tended to talk of 'queers' or 'poofs') began to 'come out'; advertisements began to appear in public places providing information on contraception and abortion. Matters which the Victorians had buried under shame and evasion by the barrel load were now entering fully into the public domain.

For any but the very rich, divorce was practically unobtainable in the Victorian era; and even then it was much easier for a husband to divorce his wife than for the wife to divorce the husband. Right on into the sixties the pejorative concept of 'matrimonial offence' remained; without such an offence being committed by one or other party no divorce could be obtained. Representing a special feminist aspect of the Victorian tradition, Dr Shirley Summerskill claimed that the Divorce Reform Act of 1969 was a 'Casanova's charter'. To most people, feminist and non-feminist, it offered freedom to both sexes from an irksome and unjust social control. Clause One of the Act tore apart the shrouds of centuries: 'After the commencement of this Act the sole ground on which a petition for divorce may be presented to the court by either party to a marriage shall be that the marriage has broken down irretrievably.' Henceforth, if a couple had lived apart for two years, and both consented, they had a right to divorce. If separation had lasted five years then either partner was entitled to a divorce, even if the other partner did not agree. Broadly, the trend in this and other legislation was towards recognizing women as independent individuals. The Matrimonial Property Act of

1970 established that a wife's work, whether as a housewife within the home or as a money-earner outside it, should be considered as an equal contribution towards creating the family home, if, as a result of a divorce, that had to be divided. In the same year was passed the Equal Pay Act. There were exceptions and loopholes, and the Act was not to come fully into law for another five years; but at least the principle of equal pay for equal work had been adumbrated even if not universally established.

Theatrical censorship was abolished in 1968. Theatre-going (like divorce) is a minority activity. But if the crudity and the nudity, the frankness and the four-letter words were to be met at their meatiest in the experimental theatre, openness and explicitness spread more widely both in respectable newspapers and in what could be accepted as polite conversation. The censorship system remained for the cinema but there was a noticeable relaxation here too in what was regarded as acceptable.

In part, the new legislation was due to the exertions of active feminists, though it owed more to deeper social and economic forces favourable to a general liberalization of statutes and attitudes. In the middle and later sixties, the feminist movement in Britain was still only in its springtime; the full summer was yet to come. Springtime is an apt metaphor as liberation, in a very non-political sense, showed itself in the fashion, first, for mini-skirts, and then for hotpants. This sort of liberation, as many steelier feminists grumbled, might well mainly mean a picnic for men. Quite simply, as, of course, the Victorians had always known, a girl scantily dressed was a good deal easier to seduce than one more voluminously clad. Under certain circumstances a girl might feel it better to strengthen her defences by opting to wear a pair of jeans. The attitudes and behaviour quickly summed up at the time as 'permissiveness' resulted from a conjunction of circumstances which helped to remove old restraints and fears and positively encouraged the active sexual life as 'normal'. The pill was not the sole factor – many of the sexually active never touched it – but its advent contributed to a general sense of security for women and girls and to a situation in which contraception (something no respectable girl would have dreamt of mentioning ten years before) could be spoken of openly. Much is sometimes made of the influence of the mass media; it is often forgotten that the most potent means of communication is by word of mouth – that is how girls learned what to do to avoid trouble, and what to do when they found themselves in trouble.

Much in arrears of America and many continental countries, women's liberation in its full political sense was scarcely in evidence in Britain at the end of the 1960s. Perhaps this was another facet of that 'secular Anglicanism' which I have mentioned once or twice: there was still something of a tolerance and genuine courtesy as between men and women which softened the potential antagonisms which in America were already producing such violent and hysterical manifestations as SCUM (Society for Cutting Up Men). The critical event, in so far as there was one, in the development of the contemporary feminist movement in Britain was the publication in 1970 of Germaine Greer's *The Female Eunuch*. This work was to influence the seventies rather as *The Uses of Literacy* had influenced the sixties; it will be discussed in the final part of this book.

On the broader question of citizen's rights, and local participation in decision-making, the British were not just far behind the Americans, they were scarcely in the race at all. But in the sixties middle-class groups did begin to stir into action, offering resistance to urban spoliation in the interests of the easy penetration of the motor car. The turning point came in 1965 when a local group in the newly fashionable Barnsbury enclave in Islington in North London successfully resisted a general LCC development order; there were similar movements in Bath, Oxford, and elsewhere.

A crucial aspect of the liberalization of the 1960s was the major development in the realm of higher education. Many colleges, particularly in the spheres of art and design, were up-graded, as were teacher training colleges; quasi-university status was given to leading colleges of technology – rechristened poly-technics, their degrees were awarded by one *national* body (a sharp break with tradition, this), the Council for National Academic Awards (CNAA), founded in 1964; certain colleges of higher technology became full universities, and totally new universities were created: at the top of the prestige scale was Sussex, followed by York and Kent; with Warwick, Lancaster, and East Anglia in the middle; while Essex and Stirling came lowest in the scale. The student movement of 1968 was relatively mild, and in many ways imitative, compared with the French example – secular Anglicanism at work again perhaps. It took its sharpest forms in the austere environment of Essex, or the cramped urban quarters of the London School of Economics. Youth was certainly not made an enemy of by established society; and a section of it, at least, was incorporated in the political nation, by the lowering of the voting age in 1971 to eighteen.

There were profound changes in other sectors of education as well. By 1964 the arguments against the eleven-plus by sociologists, psychologists, and committed social egalitarians were becoming almost deafening. The new Labour Government in July 1965 issued Circular 10/65 calling upon all local authorities to submit proposals for establishing comprehensive schools. Great impetus was certainly given to the replacement of education divided between secondary modern and grammar schools by comprehensive schooling but within a context of great confusion and inconsistency. Government intentions in regard to direct grant schools were far from clear; local authorities anyway had plenty of licence to go their own ways. Confusion was confounded, inconsistency compounded when the new Conservative Government, in June 1970, issued Circular 10/70 which stressed that the reorganization of secondary education was entirely a matter for the local authorities. Thus there was no unified comprehensive system; but at least deep inroads had been made into a system which, with more than a whiff of Victorianism about it, had essentially selected those from deprived backgrounds to go to secondary modern schools, and those from relatively privileged backgrounds to go to grammar schools.

Where innovation most in accord with the other changes that have been discussed took place was in the primary schools. For long enough children had been reared under the shadow of the Victorian faith in the three Rs. One of the first major initiatives towards bringing imaginative new approaches to curriculum design came from a private source, the Nuffield Foundation. In 1964 the Schools Council for the Curriculum and Examinations was set up, with finance coming from the local education authorities. From the Schools Council came many initiatives towards making the primary school curriculum more flexible, more imaginative, and more enjoyable. Of course, just as many respectable and far from wrong-headed citizens deplored what was happening in the universities, old and new, and argued that the spread of comprehensive education was destroying the high academic standards once the pride of the grammar schools, so there were many who thought that primary school children were being given far too much latitude while failing to learn the necessary basic skills.

In so many ways, then, British society seemed to have broken out of the straitjacket of dullness and conformity which had pinioned it since Victorian times. It would be wrong to exaggerate changes in everyday life. The growth in wine drinking, the proliferation of foreign restaurants: these things still affected only a minority. But it would be fair to say that there was a new hedonism abroad in the land; that life was lived with greater gusto than ever it had been since the evangelicals set their stamp upon the mores of the middle class. A symbolic case study was provided by Association Football. The abolition in 1962 of the maximum wage, an achievement of the Professional Footballers' Association under the leadership of Jimmy Hill, enabled the best players to escape into a world of high earnings which, though most players remained working-class in background and manner, had something of that veneer of classlessness to be found in other branches of the entertainments industry. Football became fashionable. As well, participatory sports which had once been the preserve of the prosperous or the eccentric became available to people in most sections of the community: new provision was made for sailing and mountaineering, and new leisure and sports centres were built.

One must be careful over the placing in time of the different changes. The absurd Lady Chatterley trial and the sad fuss over the Profumo episode of 1963 show how persistent were the old morality and the old hypocrisy at the beginning of the decade. (John Profumo, Conservative War Secretary, had consorted with Christine Keeler, member of an expensive call-girl circle with which Captain Ivanov, formerly of the Russian Embassy, and Stephen Ward, a society osteopath, were also associated; charged with living on immoral earnings, Ward confirmed the allegations which Profumo had at first publicly denied. During his own trial Ward committed suicide.) Many of the changes, such as the new feminist movement and the citizen's rights movement, just apparent at the end of the decade, only really moved on to their full strengths in the 1970s.

10. *Social Structure and Social Strains*

When the cultural innovations of the sixties were spoken of as being 'classless', the word was being used in a very limited and rather inaccurate way: certain leading cultural phenomena had sprung out of genuinely working-class antecedents; some working-class individuals had achieved great success; regional accents (middle-class as well as working-class) were no longer smoothed into a sort of standard southern English pronunciation but were boldly projected, red in tooth and claw.

Certainly, the British people were under no illusion as to the disappearance of class boundaries. Regularly throughout the sixties interviews and opinion polls showed that well over 90 per cent of the population recognized the existence of social classes. When, on one typical occasion, a representative sample were asked, without prompting, to allocate themselves to a social class, 67 per cent said they were 'working-class' and 29 per cent said they were 'middle-class'. Of the remainder, 1 per cent said 'upper-working-class', 1 per cent said 'lower-middle-class', and 1 per cent said 'upper-class'; this left only 1 per cent unable to allocate themselves to any of the traditional classes, including 'one twenty-five stone eccentric' who said he belonged to the 'sporting class'. When pressed to allocate themselves to the 'upper' or 'lower' parts of their class, most were reluctant to do so: only 3 per cent of the middle class moved themselves up into the 'upper-middle class', with 4 per cent moving themselves down into the 'lower-middle class'; 10 per cent of the working class moved themselves up into the 'upper-working class', with only 4 per cent allocating themselves to the 'lower-working class'. This suggests a very strong awareness of the broad divisions between the traditional social classes rather than a sensitivity to the subtle distinctions between different occupations, so often insisted upon by social scientists.

A second survey of Banbury conducted between 1966 and 1968, though not published till 1975, it is true, was unable to confirm the clear-cut class distinctions discovered in the first survey; but as the authors say in their introduction 'much had changed in sociology between the two studies'; perhaps that was more important than what had actually changed in Banbury. Reserving the word 'class' to a somewhat pernickety usage, the authors were still prepared to admit the existence in Banbury of 'three social levels', and to hint that something of an upper class was still to be found in the surrounding areas. Actually, there were still plenty of examples of the upper class's image of itself to be found. A leading local lady, interviewed by Ronald Blythe for his study of *Akenfield* (1969), said: 'I suppose we would be called upper class – in fact, we could hardly be called anything else.' Simon Raven, who ought to have known since his father had had independent means and he was himself brought up in 'Surrey stockbrokers' country', educated at an expensive prep school, at Charterhouse, and at King's College, Cambridge, defined the upper class as controlling or consuming 'the cream of the country's resources, its cash, its offices, its perquisites, its youth – and only have to open their mouths in a yawn to be assured of an attentive and nationwide hearing'. In a little piece of heart-searching, Richard Crossman stumbled on a marvellous phrase about the 'facility of freedom and an amplitude of life' which can well be taken as an upper-class hallmark of the 1960s:

I am sitting here in comfort and am therefore bound to wonder whether that fierce old Tory, my brother Geoffrey, is reasonable when he says that I can't be a socialist and have a farm which makes good profits. I tell him the two are compatible provided that as a member of the government I'm ready to vote for socialist policy to take those profits away and even, in the last resort, to confiscate the property. Nevertheless that isn't a complete answer. Having Prescote deeply affects my life. It's not merely that I am more detached than my colleagues, able to judge things more dispassionately and to look forward to retirement, it's also more crudely that I am comfortably off now and have no worries about money. I can eat, drink and buy what I like as well as adding seventy acres to Prescote Manor Farm. Ann and I have a facility of freedom and an amplitude of life here which cuts us off from the vast mass of people ...

In his study *Middle Class Families* (1968), based on Swansea, Colin Bell neatly summarized a distinction between those who had made it into the upper class, and those who remained in the middle class: Swansea, he wrote, 'may appear in the first chapters of the autobiographies of the famous; it rarely appears in the last'. Awareness of the distinction between middle class and working class are also brought out in two contrasting career autobiographies presented by Colin Bell. A thirty-eight-year-old chemist remarked that there had been a time 'when I used to think that I was a cliché – the working-class boy who made good, a member of the new middle class, the meritocratic technocrat'. The 'whole question of identity' had been 'very difficult for me and my kind'. But this was no longer a problem 'because I now think I know where I am going'. If, he concluded, 'I can get another couple of notches up I will be able to send the boys to a boarding school ...'. The family of a thirty-nine-year-old wholesaler, on the other hand, had 'always been comfortably off'. As he was the eldest, it had always been assumed that he, at least, 'would go into Dad's business'. Describing those now working for him in his warehouses, he remarked that 'about twenty-two men' were 'what you would call working class'.

Older working-class communities, of the type described by Hoggart, continued to exist in the sixties. In writing of Huddersfield, Brian Jackson stressed the continuing importance of the working men's clubs, noting that there were very few businessmen or small tradesmen in the clubs and that those few preferred to keep a very low profile. The view in Huddersfield was:

They've got their own clubs and political clubs. It's all working men here. Unlike even the pub, the club has the atmosphere of the working man's home: 'I never go into a pub at all now. Clubs are much more sociable like. Look at this. I couldn't rest my legs across a chair in t'pub. Here it is like being at home. As long I don't put me feet on t'seat, I'm all right.'

There was a clear boundary to the community of mill workers; floor managers, clerical workers, and minor officials were excluded. While they collected a general dislike and mistrust, there was, Dennis Marsden found, 'a grudging respect' for the mill owners. You could, said Jackson, 'trace a line through Huddersfield marking the point where the gap showed between middle-class and working-class life'.

The famous Goldthorpe, Lockwood, Bechofer, and Platt survey of 'the affluent worker' in Luton, covering assembly line workers at Vauxhall Motors, machine operators, and craftsmen servicing machines at the Skefco's Ball Bearing Company, and process workers and craftsmen engaged on process maintenance at Laporte Chemicals, did suggest some fragmentation of traditional working-class images and some blurring of class lines. Fourteen per cent claimed for themselves definite 'middle-class' status, while 8 per cent took the view that they could be described equally well as 'working'-class or 'middle'-class. Yet, 67 per cent had no difficulty in allocating themselves to the 'working class'.

Actually, these 'affluent' workers were still a million miles away from middle-class job satisfactions or from middle-class aspiration after social mobility. The Luton workers stressed the unpleasantness of their work, giving the high pay as its only advantage (70 per cent of white-collar workers, by contrast, did not mention pay, and two-fifths – the highest single group – gave the nature of their work as their greatest source of satisfaction). The Luton workers expressed no very strong feelings against separate canteens: 'I don't like the idea of the boss breathing down my neck at meal times,' said one; 'We wouldn't want *them* listening into my conversation,' said another. All three of the Luton firms encouraged promotion from the shop floor to supervisory, technical, and managerial grades. But in fact, the mass of the labour force did not 'think of themselves as one day likely to become something more than merely wage workers'. In brief, Goldthorpe, Lockwood, Bechofer, and Platt concluded, 'for the large majority of men in our sample the possibility of promotion was of no real significance'.

To be working-class in the sixties, then, despite the occasional instance of rapid upward mobility, meant a 'life sentence' of hard manual work where, by an implicit irony, the attainment of middle-class living standards was only possible through expending, on overtime, even more excessive amounts of energy in a traditionally working-class way. At the top, to belong to the upper class still offered disproportionate access to positions of power. More than one third of the Labour Cabinet of 1964 were traditional upper-class figures ('patricians' Dr Timothy May calls them), and six Cabinet members were products of the most exclusive public schools, the 'Clarendon Schools'. Only two Ministers had graduated from universities other than Oxford. It is in that context that one has to see the emergence as Prime Minister of the lower-middle-class, but Oxford-educated, meritocrat, Harold Wilson.

The fruits of social mobility over several generations, and the upper-class socialization process, are well brought out in the career of Edward Heath. His great-grandfather had been a merchant seaman, his paternal grandfather, after running a small dairy business which failed, became a porter at Broadstairs Station on the Southern Railway. His son, Will, Heath's father, became a carpenter. His maternal grandmother was the wife of an illiterate farmworker. On leaving school at fourteen, her very good-looking daughter had gone into domestic service with a middle-class family from Hampstead who spent their summers in Broadstairs. Her mother was proud of this position, with its opportunity for learning middle-class ways, but she was not at all pleased with her daughter's association with Will Heath. She lamented that 'with her looks she could do a lot better'.

The First World War, that great engine of social mobility, provided Will Heath with the opportunity to take a job building air frames at the Vickers Aircraft factory in Crayford in North Kent. After the war, he was employed at a good wage by a local builder, while at home his wife worked hard to introduce the middle-class standards she had learned in service. Around 1930 Will Heath took over a small firm which became 'W. G. Heath Builder and Decorator' and the family, as Andrew Roth puts it, 'crossed the line' between the skilled working class and the lower-middle class.

At the age of ten Edward Heath won a scholarship to a grammar school in Ramsgate, which not only set high academic standards but imitated the forms of the public schools. He failed his open scholarship to Balliol but his parents, assisted by a loan, were prepared to fund him; then, after a year, he won the Balliol

Organ Scholarship. Heath was well on the way; and the Second World War, in which he ended up a lieutenant colonel in the prestigious Honourable Artillery Company, consolidated his position. He entered the House of Commons in 1950: 'That intake in the Commons,' writes Andrew Roth, 'was exceptional in the large proportion of its new Tory entrants who were ex-officers – and who were professionally competent and had made their way without benefit of family wealth and connections.'

Significantly, however, Heath himself remarked that 'for the new member who has been a member of the Oxford or Cambridge Union, coming to those benches is like coming home'. And Heath quickly showed a knack for associating with the traditional upper-class members of the Conservative Party, though curiously, particularly for a man of his musical talents, he never managed to get the accent right. David Wood of *The Times* noted perceptively that for all his image of 'Wilsonian classlessness', Heath was well in with the Tory 'magic circle', and that 'his is the kind of classlessness that takes on the protective colouring of the company he keeps'. Heath became the first-ever elected leader of the Conservative Party in 1965.

Class showed itself in inequalities in the distribution of power and wealth, and in life-styles and life-chances; above all, it showed itself in the gathering cold war which affected British industrial relations, with a snobbish, and often uninformed, management entrenched on one side, with an immobile, unambitious, workforce, deeply attached to its long traditions, on the other. Class, too, was the biggest single determinant of voting preferences. Yet there was no open evidence in Britain of class conflict: though class distinctions were undoubtedly affecting economic performance, they could still well be held, socially, to be an integrating factor.

The special strength and the special homogeneity of the British working class are represented in two distinctive institutions, the British Labour Party and British trade unions. To be employed as a manual worker in any major British industry was almost certainly to be a member of a trade union. In 1951 male trade-union membership was 7,745,000, 56 per cent of all male employees; in 1961, 1966, and 1971 respectively, the figures were 7,911,000 (53 per cent), 8,003,000 (53 per cent), and 8,382,000 (58 per cent). Trade-union membership figures for women were: 1951, 1,790,000 (25 per cent of female employees); 1961, 2,005,000 (24 per cent); 1966, 2,256,000 (23 per cent); and 1971, 2,753,000 (32 per cent). Since the term 'employees' covers most of those in middle-class as well as working-class occupations it can be seen that union membership among working-class males must have been a good 80 per cent throughout the period since the war.

From the period before the First World War trade unions had enjoyed a special position under the law: even if through strike action unions inflicted considerable financial damage on employers they could not be sued, an entirely reasonable provision in that the strike was the basic weapon wielded by unions in protection of their members' standards of living. Despite their special legal status, unions had not been particularly noteworthy in the inter-war years for asserting economic power. What really was crucial in gauging the relative strengths of unions, employers, and government was the actual state of the economy. In a time of general economic growth and relatively high demand for labour, as was the period after the Second World War, trade-union power was greatly enhanced.

As union membership seemed to bring results, so there was more and more pressure on all employees to join a union, while the truly active membership, those doing the work and making the decisions, tended (in keeping with the non-participatory tradition of British political culture) to be quite a small minority. As we have seen, gross membership figures rose steadily in the fifties and sixties, though at the end of the fifties and in the first half of the sixties trade-union membership actually fell behind the overall growth in employment. In the later sixties trade unions began to grow again, so that in 1971 58 per cent of all male employees and 32 per cent of all female employees belonged to a union. Some of the expansion was due to the way in which white-collar, lower-middle-class unions were beginning to expand (an expansion which really exploded in the 1970s).

In the period with which we are concerned here (that is, essentially, the late fifties and the sixties) the number of strikes, the number of strikers, and the number of days lost due to strikes remained remarkably constant and only a little above those for the period of 'consensus'; only at the very end of the sixties was there a sharp upward turn. For the period 1945–54 the annual averages were, for strikes, 1,791, for workers involved, 545,000, and for days lost, 2,073,000. For the period 1955–64 the annual averages, respectively, were 2,521, 1,116,000, and 3,889,000; and for the period 1965–9 they were 2,380, 1,208,000, and 3,951,000. However, in 1970 the number of strikes had gone up to 3,906, and the number of days lost was up by two and a half times to 10,980,000. The actual number of strikes fell to 2,228 in 1971, but days lost were up again to 13,551,000.

Up till the end of the sixties strikes fitted well into the description I gave above of 'industrial cold war'. Most were not officially sanctioned by the appropriate union, but arose spontaneously from the tensions of the work place. As H. A. Turner put it in 1969, most stoppages 'are over before the unions which might have members involved have even heard of them'. When the Royal Commission on 'Trade Unions and Employers' Associations', chaired by Lord Donovan, reported in 1968 its main criticism of the unions was the failure of union leaders to exercise control over their members; neither the Commission, nor any other informed commentators, held that union leaders were heedlessly or villainously forcing their men into unwanted strikes.

After 1968 circumstances altered: not only was there an increase in strike activity, but an increasing proportion of strikes were now 'official' and led by large unions. The origins of this change of emphasis lay in growing resistance to Government policies aimed at wage restraint and, after 1970, in a wider hostility to the political philosophy of the Heath Conservative Government. It did give some credence to arguments that leaders of major unions could now too readily wield power seriously damaging to the economy. Yet careful study of the actions of union leaders shows them continuing to act with great responsibility and restraint. The surface evidence, as we move on into the early seventies, is of increasing conflict (in so far as strikes represent conflict) between employers and employees,

and even between Government and employees; and while
Britain's strike record compared with other countries had
hitherto been rather good, it now became slightly worse, as
Table 1 shows.

Table 1: International trends since Donovan

| | Stoppages per 100,000 employees | | Striker-days per 1,000 employees | |
	1965–9	1970–74	1965–9	1970–74
United Kingdom	9·5	12·0	156	585
Australia	31·4	45·2	217	581
Belgium	1·9	5·1	73	242
Canada	7·6	8·8	659	773
Denmark	1·2	4·1	30	360
Finland	4·2	44·7*	84	600*
France	9·6†	17·7	126†	166
German Fed. Rep.	(not available)		6	49
Ireland	10·2	15·4	543	434
Italy	16·3	25·6	817	1,070
Japan	3·0	6·2	68	115
Netherlands	0·6	0·7	5	48
New Zealand	12·8	30·4	103	187
Norway	0·4	0·8	8	52
Sweden	0·5	1·9	25	56
United States	6·4	6·7	492	531

* Official criteria for recording strikes changed during this period
† 1968 excluded from average
Source: International Labour Office, *Yearbook of Labour Statistics*

The basic point to be stressed is that if up till the late sixties,
at any rate, trade-union activity undoubtedly demonstrated the
deep sense of cultural identity and class *awareness* of the British
working class, it did not provide evidence of the existence of
sharp class conflict in British society. At the same time, if we
are following up the 'What Went Wrong?' theme it can be seen
that industrial relations in Britain were worsening and that there
was a case to be made out that in certain spheres trade
unions could exercise powers menacing to the community as a
whole.

A new source of open social conflict was race. In this book
I have already suggested a number of different landmarks in-

dicating the point of change between the post-war age of consensus and the new age of cultural change. Another such land-
mark occurred in August 1958 when violent race rioting broke
out between the heavy concentration of West Indian immigrants in Notting Hill, in West London, and local whites. West
Indians had started coming in soon after the war, and the matter
had first attracted attention in the early fifties.

One may perhaps detect something of a class division in the
way in which the British reacted towards the question of
immigration. Those in governing circles were still very much
influenced by the notion of Britain's great imperial heritage
which, as a concrete legacy, had left a situation in which West
Indians, Indians, Pakistanis, and Africans were all full British
subjects and entitled, without let or hindrance, to settle in
Britain itself. Those in governing circles were also aware of the
shortage of labour in post-war and early fifties Britain. Those
in the working class and lower-middle class, living in the poorer
areas in which, perforce, the new immigrants congregated, were
more aware of the disruptions and strains brought to their own
everyday lives. Almost a third of all immigrants were concentrated in certain parts of London; there were also heavy concentrations in the West Midlands, in Bradford, and in other
impoverished urban areas. Among working-class activists, as
well as liberal-minded middle-class and upper-class politicians,
there was also a genuine sense of outrage at any discrimination
based on race, creed, or colour. While upper-class politicians
might become increasingly aware of the mythical quality of
Britain's imperial or Commonwealth rôle, they were also aware
of the growing need to maintain tactful relationships with India,
Pakistan, and the West Indies. Politicians, of course, were not
totally unaware of the potential problems of overcrowding and
racial friction. While on the one hand there was some talk in
Conservative circles in 1955 and 1957 of bringing in controls on
immigration, on the other hand the Institute of Race Relations
was set up in 1958.

The cause-and-effect relationship between actual legislation,
or the announced intention to legislate, and the increase in
immigration has been much argued over. It seems that there
was something of an upturn in 1960, then came the Govern-

ment's announcement of its intention to legislate, followed in
turn by a much greater influx than ever before: in the first ten
months of 1961, 113,000 immigrants arrived from India,
Pakistan, and the West Indies. The Immigration Bill proposed
a quota system for ordinary immigrants, with vouchers for
those who actually had jobs or who were possessed of special
skills; it was hotly attacked by the Labour opposition, but
eventually became law on 27 February 1962. An opinion poll
at the end of the previous year had indicated that 90 per cent
of the population at large supported the new legislation. However, it undoubtedly gave a further stimulus to immigration
and perhaps encouraged permanent settlement by those who
would otherwise have simply sought temporary employment.

Many Labour members actually abstained in the February
vote, and steadily, as complaints arose from working-class areas,
Labour moved towards a belief in the need for controls. Once
immigrants were in, a complete *laissez-faire* policy was observed: no education, no special training, no attempt at geographical dispersion. Again polls indicated that at least 80 per
cent of the population felt that there were too many immigrants
in the country already. The immigrants were, indeed, making a
valuable contribution to the British economy, usually in the
lowest-paid, most unskilled jobs, though a significant contribution to the National Health Service was also being made by
Commonwealth doctors. But there were also special social
strains, in the schools, and in the community generally; many
immigrants had little or no English. The British, at the best of
times, are a xenophobic people. For their part, the immigrants
had long-standing and deeply felt cultural and religious traditions of their own.

To hope for integration, let alone assimilation, was perhaps
to hope for too much. Roy Jenkins, Labour Home Secretary
and protagonist of the civilized society of the sixties, offered
a definition of integration 'not as a flattening process of assimilation but as equal opportunity, accompanied by cultural
diversity, in an atmosphere of mutual tolerance'. But Jenkins
also recognized that there was a 'social factor' putting limits
upon the numbers that could be absorbed. Already, in February
1965, the Wilson Government had introduced stricter restric-

tions on the number of unskilled workers entering the country. But it also set out positively to legislate against discrimination. Britain's first-ever Race Relations Act set up, in 1966, a Race Relations Board aiming at conciliation in cases of proven discrimination on grounds of race or colour. The two-pronged policy was continued in 1968 when a rather more substantial Bill against discrimination was coupled with new legislation to control entry, the latter being in part a reaction to events in Kenya which seemed likely to provoke a large-scale immigration of Kenya Asians holding British passports. The new Act endeavoured to combat discrimination in employment and housing.

British sentiments, quite simply, were confused. There had been a marked absence of a constructive lead from policy-makers. Deep grass-roots hostility to immigrants, and, above all, to further immigration went along with popular support for some kind of legislation against racial discrimination. Respectable parliamentarians, Labour, Conservative, and Liberal, were agreed in trying to prevent race from becoming a national political issue, agreed on a policy of both maintaining and strengthening controls while at the same time endeavouring to outlaw discrimination against those already settled in the country. Yet race as a political issue led to the establishment, through a fusion of existing groups, of the National Front, as a minority right-wing party, in 1966. Then on 20 April 1968, while Parliament was discussing the new stronger Race Relations Bill, the Conservative front-bench spokesman for Defence, Enoch Powell, delivered a speech in Birmingham in which he envisaged a staggering growth of the non-white population: 'like the Romans, I seem to see "the River Tiber flowing with much blood"'. Apart from a Gallup poll showing 75 per cent of the population broadly sympathetic to the sentiments expressed by Enoch Powell, there were also a number of working-class demonstrations in his support. But Powell was instantly dismissed by Edward Heath from his position in the Conservative Shadow Cabinet.

There were also some home-born stresses upon national cohesion. A new active phase of Scottish Nationalist revival began around 1962. In one of its statements the Scottish Nationalist

Party hit off exactly the radical technocratic image of the hour: 'The Scottish Nationalist Party stands for an independent and up-to-date Scotland, and believes this country cannot become up-to-date until it is independent.' The symbol of the 1962 revival was the West Lothian by-election in which the SNP candidate, William Wolfe, a chartered accountant, came a creditable second to Labour, and the Conservative lost his deposit. Thereafter progress was by no means consistent, but the party felt sufficiently confident to put up fifteen candidates in 1964, compared with five in 1959. There were no further significant developments until post-1966 disillusionment with Labour rule began to take effect. In the spring of 1967 the SNP vote in the Pollok (Glasgow) by-election was sufficient to ensure a Conservative victory, and in October Mrs Ewing carried through the greatest Nationalist triumph thus far by winning the by-election at Hamilton. This victory did not necessarily mean that henceforth Nationalist candidates could count on success in similar seats throughout Scotland, but it did provide a tremendous stimulus to party recruitment, with membership reaching 80,000 at the beginning of 1968.

The collapse, in the late seventies, of the movement for a separate Scottish assembly inevitably casts a long shadow backwards over the question of how truly significant the nationalist revival of the sixties really was. Much of it must be seen purely as a protest movement, protest on behalf of Scotland's declining industry, protest against neglect by Westminster, and also against geriatric local Labour politicians and complacent (to put it at its most innocuous) local Labour councils, all mixed up with the cultural upheavals of the time. But there was also a core of very genuine nationalism, a deep and real fear that Scotland as a separate nation, with a distinct and valuable cultural tradition, was doomed to extinction through emigration and the invasion of alien values, unless she resumed complete control of her own affairs. No doubt this sentiment was consistently held only by a small minority, though, as other concerns pressed in, it was capable, from time to time, of firing the enthusiasm of others.

The successes of Plaid Cymru, the Welsh Nationalist Party, were not quite so striking, though their President, Gwynfor

Evans, won the Carmarthen seat in July 1966. But Welsh nationalism was perhaps even more closely intertwined than Scottish with the cultural movements of the sixties, and the revived interest in roots and origins. Probably the most significant single event was the Act of 1967 which placed the Welsh language on a par with English in Wales. For some, this was a powerful triumph; for others, it was an unmitigated nuisance as proceedings on committees, at universities, and elsewhere now took twice as long as they were conducted first in one language then in the other.

To many Labour MPs of the more solid sort, those who had never comprehended the romantic appeal of nationalism, the issue was one of regionalism rather than of nationalism. As it became clear in the sixties that the relocation of industry policies of the post-war years were not necessarily solving the problems of the old depressed areas, and as expanding affluence sharpened the distinctions between those who were doing pretty well and those who were doing only moderately well, a certain geographical sectionalism began to appear. Strong competition developed in the late 1960s for allocation of the regional funds made available by the Labour Government in order to try to stimulate flagging industrial areas. While class remained the classic division in British society and while it would be wrong to speak of a 'revolt of the provinces', none the less, taking into account the growth of race, of nationalism, and of regionalism, it could be argued that in this period of change Britain was beginning to be touched by some of the characteristics formerly more closely associated with the United States (though now, perhaps, to be considered common features of all Western industrialized, or post-industrial, countries).

But what of that essential glue of the social fabric, the family? For once in a while the statistics speak volumes (Table 2). No evidence, certainly, of any decline in the popularity of marriage; the proportion of married to single people in the total population remains remarkably constant as between 1951, 1961, and 1971. One specially sad burden borne by women, caused by the greater vulnerability of the male of the species (apart from other factors, the Second World War was still showing its savage effects), can be seen in the tragically high figures for

Table 2: Marriage in the United Kingdom 1951–71 (figures in thousands)

	Males			Females		
	1951	1961	1971	1951	1961	1971
All ages:						
Single	10,811	11,340	12,014	10,846	10,829	11,055
Married	12,358	13,279	13,976	12,488	13,355	14,050
Widowed	} 944	760	762	} 2,769	2,860	3,139
Divorced		102	200		185	318
Age groups:						
0–14:						
Single	5,781	6,321	6,873	5,544	6,015	6,515
15–19:						
Single	1,556	1,850	1,921	1,542	1,709	1,713
Married	8	20	40	68	116	159
Widowed	—	—	—	—	—	—
Divorced	—	—	—	—	—	—
20–24:						
Single	1,267	1,139	1,350	929	719	848
Married	379	501	779	811	941	1,244
Widowed	} 1	—	—	} 4	2	2
Divorced		1	3		2	10

Source: CSO *Annual Abstract of Statistics* (1980), table 2·8

widowed women compared with widowed men. The greatly
increased number of divorcees as between 1961 and 1971 is also
clearly brought out. If we seek the true seed-pods of social
change we must scrutinize the figures for the fifteen to nineteen
year olds and the twenty to twenty-four year olds. Here we can
see how marriage at an early age became more and more
fashionable for both males and females (though at all times,
many more young women were getting married than young
men) into the late fifties and all through the sixties. Certainly the
divorce rate goes up sharply at the end of the sixties (though
this was only the dawning of the real age of ready divorce of
the seventies): the numbers of divorces were – 1968, 45,794 (3·7
per thousand of the married population); 1969, 51,310 (4·1 per

thousand): 1970, 58,239 (4·7 per thousand); 1971, 74,437 (6·0 per thousand).

Generalizing about family size, or indeed about long-term birth-rates, is not as easy as might be thought (indeed much Government planning went badly awry on the latter score). The huge families of the late nineteenth century had certainly gone for good; but whereas in the inter-war years there had been almost universal pressure to limit family size to, say two children, many couples in the sixties were showing a happy predisposition to ignore such old-fashioned prudence. The actual rate of births per thousand of the total population, standing at 16·0 at the beginning of the fifties, rose to 17·9 in 1961, 18·3 in 1962, 18·5 in 1963, 18·8 in 1964 – the peak year, since in 1965 the rate was 18·4, in 1966 it was 18.0, in 1967, 17·6, in 1968, 17·2, in 1969, 16·7, in 1970, 16·3, and in 1971 back to its fifties level of 16·2.

Much of the more engaging detail, which the official statistics leave out, was revealed in the survey which Geoffrey Gorer carried out in April and May 1969, published in 1971 as *Sex and Marriage in England Today*. The results of this survey can be compared with the earlier one of the 1950s, presented in *Exploring English Character*. On courtship, the broad situation had not changed much. Twenty-four per cent of married couples had first met at a dance, 15 per cent at work, 12 per cent at social gatherings, parties (a particularly middle-class phenomenon, this), and outings; 12 per cent had also first met through mutual friends, and again this was a particularly middle-class phenomenon. Eighty-six per cent of women and 74 per cent of men considered that they had really been in love at the time of marriage; 23 per cent of men and 11 per cent of women said that they had not. Twenty-six per cent of men and 63 per cent of women were virgins at the time of marriage; a further 20 per cent of men and 26 per cent of women had married the person with whom they had first had sexual relations.

A clear sign of the emancipation of women achieved in the sixties was to be found in the much higher proportion now declaring sexual love to be very important in marriage: 67 per cent of women made this point, as against 65 per cent of men.

Averages and medians almost certainly mean very little in this sphere, but, for what it is worth, Gorer found that the median rate of sexual intercourse per married couple was twice a week. Twenty-four per cent of married couples had what he called 'a high rate of intercourse', three times a week or more; 36 per cent had a medium rate, one to three times a week, and 37 per cent had a low rate, once a week or less.

Despite the developments of the sixties two fifths of all couples were not using any form of birth control: of the 19 per cent of married women on the pill, there was a marked concentration in the younger and also in the wealthier groups. Gorer quoted the views on the pill of a twenty-four-year-old wife of a school teacher, a pious non-conformist: 'Good. I was very biased against it medically when I first heard about it – but nothing based on real scientific knowledge. In all other respects it makes the love side of marriage so much freer, it can only be a good thing.' Gorer's findings did not suggest that the pill was leading to infidelity among the married. To the question, 'Now that the pill provides absolute safety, do you think faithfulness is or is not as important as ever in marriage?', 92 per cent replied in the affirmative.

Of the unmarried interviewed by Gorer, 44 per cent said that they had a special girlfriend or boyfriend. Gorer's general findings supported the view that sexual permissiveness was very far from rampant in the late sixties. What he really found was nothing too surprising: the immense variousness of human behaviour. However, the signs clearly are of a definite trend away from older social controls. Half of those with a regular boyfriend or girlfriend spoke of being on terms of 'real physical intimacy', but for a quarter of these, apparently, this did not include full sexual intercourse. On the one hand there was the twenty-one-year-old daughter of a railway worker who said: 'I have been brought up to believe that you should wait until you are married; and I think if you love someone enough you can be prepared to wait until marriage.' On the other hand was the nineteen-year-old lorry driver, who had been sexually active from the age of fifteen and who remarked: 'If it comes along you don't turn it down'; and the eighteen-year-old daughter of a skilled worker, hoping to go to university, who had been sexually active at sixteen and replied: 'Twice a week if I like the boy. It depends on exams!'

Gorer's findings can be amplified by the more detailed study of 1,873 young people aged fifteen to nineteen carried out by Schofield. Of these, only 12 per cent of the girls had had sexual intercourse, but of the engaged ones, 37 per cent were sleeping with their boyfriends. Another study, this time of third-year university students at Durham carried out in 1970, revealed that 93 per cent of the girls had been virgins when they came to university, but that by the third year only 49 per cent were still virgins.

Use of contraceptives, or perhaps one should say effective use of them, had not kept pace with sixties changes in moral attitudes. Gorer found that the majority of the sexually active unmarried were not regularly using any form of birth control. To turn back to hard official statistics, the number of illegitimate births had been 5 per cent of the total at the beginning of the fifties, was 5·8 per cent at the beginning of the sixties, and had risen to 8·2 per cent at the beginning of the seventies; this was an indication, of course, not merely of promiscuity but of the way in which illegitimacy was losing its Victorian stigma.

The family is usually, and very properly, seen as a force holding society together. However, the family had always also been a source of potential violence: most murders took place within a family context, and by the late sixties attention was coming to be given to the plight of battered wives. As women demanded equal rights, and attempts, though rather faltering ones, were made to try to enforce these, some commentators began to ask whether, just as white was being set against black, and Welsh nationalist against English chauvinist, a new social stress was not also opening between men and women. Again one must not anticipate developments which only reached significance in the seventies but one pregnant statistic, not usually sufficiently stressed, deserves mention. In 1971, in the total population of the United Kingdom, there were still many more women than men: 28,562,000 as against 26,952,000. But already the balance, which for centuries had favoured surviving males, had altered: if we look at the crucial fifteen to twenty-nine age group, we find that in 1951 there were 5,255,000 women and girls to only 5,073,000 men and boys; but already in 1961 there were 5,159,000 men and boys as against 5,100,000 women and girls, and the balance had tipped further in 1971 to 5,915,000 men and boys to only 5,764,000 women and girls. For many men, the advent of permissiveness in the sixties was to prove to be a last golden age; never again would they have it so easy.

What of the stresses and strains between youth and age? In the middle sixties much critical attention was directed at the violent and destructive encounters taking place on Bank Holidays at popular holiday resorts between rival teenage groups of 'mods' and 'rockers'. Yet perhaps one of the most revealing indicators of the condition of British society in the 1960s was the muted and derivative character of the student protests of 1968 and 1969. The older universities were stuffy and authoritarian in their style and government; some of the new universities were bleak and short of cultural amenities. There were good pragmatic reasons for revolt. But much of the student movement was frankly imitative of the much more impressive events taking place in California, Paris, and elsewhere on the Continent. There was no link-up between the students, mostly upwardly mobile members of the middle class, and other dissenting groups. All passed off remarkably uneventfully, with universities making timely concessions in regard to student representation and quietly dropping the more irritating conventions and regulations. As there was not that stridency in male–female relations already to be found in contemporary America, so there was a mildness about the student protest movements. Yet all was not bland in British society. A new activism was afoot among middle-class residents' groups which broke through the standard apathy of British political culture. Motorway schemes, urban and rural, the siting of new airports, the invasion of suburban streets by heavy goods vehicles, all of these brought militant, and often highly successful, protest groups of (relatively) ordinary citizens into being, giving some real substance to the word 'participation' which now, with 'permissiveness', began to be bandied around as part of the signature tune of the late sixties.

Belatedly, for better and for worse, Britain was showing the variety of characteristics familiar for a decade or more in the United States. But still social cohesion held up remarkably well; still, there was that comfortable blanket of secular Anglicanism.

11. *False Optimism*

Generalizing about 'the mood of the country' is the stock-in-trade of journalists; historians should know better. Of criticism and dissent there was plenty in the Britain of the sixties. Although income levels in fact kept ahead of inflation, there was much frustration among those who were more conscious of rising prices than of periodic wage increases; some sections of the community, anyway, got left far behind. Yet when all the qualifications and exceptions have been totted up, it is not unfair to speak of there being an optimism abroad in British society during the sixties. The austere and slightly prissy good intentions, and the shrill *Daily Express* conservatism which was its reverse, of the forties and early fifties had largely gone; the joyful irreverence that never really stretched social cohesion added to, rather than subtracted from, complacency and good feeling. One of the many choice remarks which one could quote occurs in the autobiography (published in 1967) of Walter Greenwood, author of the great working-class novel of the 1930s, *Love on the Dole*. He speaks of the former slum area in Lancashire where he was brought up:

Bulldozers are at their work of destruction here ... Over three decades have passed since I stood on the threshold of what proved to be for me a wonderful year, decades that have witnessed another world war, the voluntary liquidation of the Empire and the establishment of a social revolution of which this demolition is but a local aspect.

Bulldozers we shall return to shortly. As for the 'social revolution', even if that phrase must seem exaggerated and inapposite, there actually were very significant developments in the principles and practice of the Welfare State in this decade Although radical Conservatives were declaring that the notion of a permanent Welfare State was 'not ennobling but degrading', the Welfare State, despite the usual windy posturing of politicians, was scarcely now a matter of political debate. Medical advances, innovations in social theory, greater professionalization and professionalism: these were the forces behind the developing Welfare State of the sixties.

By the late fifties it was clear that while flat-rate contributions to National Insurance were quite burdensome for the lowest-paid, the flat-rate benefits themselves were falling far behind the sort of income expected within an affluent society. Thus, in 1959 there came a new scheme whereby better-off employees paid an additional graduated contribution which in return qualified for an additional earnings-related pension Employers, provided they paid a higher flat-rate contribution, were permitted to contract out of the scheme if they offered their own employees an adequate pension scheme, protected on change of employment. The new principle was actually extended by the Labour Government in 1966 when it introduced earnings-related contributions and benefits to cover the first six months of loss of earnings from other causes than retirement. The major positive contribution to income security was the Redundancy Payments Act of 1965, which laid down that lump-sum payments, financed partly by the employer and partly by compulsory contributions from all insured employees, must be paid to employees with over two years' service dismissed simply because of a change in the employer's requirements or circumstances.

The most important piece of welfare legislation of 1966 was the Ministry of Social Security Act which, among other things, sought to remove some of the stigmas still attaching to National Assistance by replacing it with Supplementary Benefits. The growing view in official Labour, as well as Conservative, circles was that the universalist principle of 1945 was in reality wasteful of resources in that it spread inadequate benefits too thinly across the entire nation, giving a little to those who had no need, and too little to those who were in deep need. Thus Supplementary Benefits both depended upon a means test, and were administered in a flexible way, with much depending upon the discretion of local officials. Payable to those not in full-time employment, Supplementary Benefits were intended to bring income up to a scale calculated according to the number and age of dependent children together with a rent allowance. Humane and sensitive in many respects (great efforts were made to bring to the attention of the deprived the benefits to which they were entitled), the scheme as it worked in practice had two particularly obnoxious features. First there was the bureaucratic device of the 'wage-stop' designed to ensure that Supplementary Benefits did not act as an encouragement to the work-shy. Those who, when in employment, earned less than the income normally provided by Supplementary Benefits were deliberately, when out of work, paid a level of benefits slightly below their potential earnings when in work. Thus such people were placed in a poverty trap from which, short of a miraculous change in their employment prospects, there was no prospect of escape. Second, there was the 'cohabitation rule': single, separated, or divorced women claiming benefits, often for the support of their children, could have their benefits stopped if the snoopers of the Department of Health and Social Security discovered that they were in fact cohabiting with a man who could then be held to be providing them with financial support.

But the main story is of the deliberate seeking-out of sources of deprivation ignored in the grand strategy of 1945–8: the Rating Act of 1966 allowed for rate rebates for those in need and the National Insurance (Old Persons and Widows Pensions and Attendance Allowance) Act of 1970 directed new benefits towards the disabled and the very old.

The experience of the National Health Service suggested that some commercialism and freedom from the universalist control of the State could co-exist with the maintenance of the ideal of a high-level national service. Medical insurance schemes, offering both care in private nursing homes and access to pay beds in National Health Service hospitals, greatly expanded: they had about a million members at the beginning of the seventies, compared with only fifty thousand at the end of the forties. Supporters of such schemes argued that they actually brought more resources within the national system; opponents argued, probably with greater cogency, that they enabled the wealthy to jump the queue for treatment of non-acute conditions.

A major problem of the Health Service in its first dozen years was the desperate shortage of hospitals. To this, because of

Government miscalculation, was added by the late fifties a shortage of doctors. In the sixties genuine attempts were made to deal with both problems. A ten-year hospital building programme was announced by the Conservatives in 1962; the shortage of general practitioners reached a peak in the middle sixties when many doctors actually had more than the maximum permitted number of 3,500 patients on their lists. But after 1966 special additional allowances were earmarked for practice in certain designated areas and by 1971 the average number of patients per doctor was down to 2,421. Attempts to expand private practice, it may be noted, were not greatly successful at this time. A new private scheme launched by the British Medical Association in 1965 came to an unlamented demise within three years. Doctors within the National Health Service had meantime gained a more generous system of remuneration which, in particular, now tended to reward the better and more progressive doctors.

One sphere in which British society had always shown itself to be particularly uncaring was that of mental health. The epoch-making Mental Health Act of 1959, which brought a new flexibility and informality to the treatment of mental disorder, could not of itself carry through a revolution. In the sixties there were disclosures of ill-treatment of mental patients in some of the large, badly managed, and under-staffed institutions. These were followed by the setting-up of the Hospital Advisory Service and a general move towards attending more closely to the plight of mental patients.

On the whole the sixties saw a massive retreat from the original principle of a free health service. Having resisted the imposition of charges in the early fifties, the Labour Party, in office in 1968, reintroduced medical prescription charges and dental charges amounting to half the cost of the treatment. It became a commonplace that Britain was putting less into its health service than other more prosperous Western nations (4·9 per cent of the gross national product was being spent on the National Health Service in 1972 compared with 3·8 per cent in 1962) and there were plenty of commentators to point out that, whatever the achievements of the sixties, crisis was never far away. Still, the majority of the population would probably have echoed Sir George Godber, Chief Medical Officer of the Department of Health and Social Security, when in his Annual Report for 1972 he remarked that 'in time of need for myself or my family I would now rather take my chance at random in the British National Health Service than in any other service I know'.

The arena of most conspicuous boom was that of education, and higher education in particular. If we are to seek 'mood' documents for this period, among the best examples are the Robbins Report on Higher Education and the Newsome Report on Secondary Education (both 1963, and both postulating expansion and envisaging greater social mobility and a society appreciative of the values of education), but also the Plowden Report (1967, directing attention to the needs of primary education, particularly among the socially deprived) and the James Report (1972, calling for a more systematic training of the country's teachers, with the aspiration, eventually, of an all-graduate profession). Universities were built, colleges of education expanded, there were new jobs at all levels. The publishing trade moved in; academics really had never had it so good; more and worse 'academic' books were published than ever before. Still, it is too easy to let eighties sourness cloud the vision of the sixties. Some of the new developments brought British universities up to the standard of the best American ones and at the end of the sixties the university system, judged as a whole, was in most respects better than any to be found abroad, though in engineering and technology there was still nothing to compare with MIT and Cal. Tech. in the USA. Already at the end of the decade, too, the most ambitious plan of all had come to fruition in that it was in 1969 that the first academics were appointed to the new distance-learning institution for mature students, the Open University.

If educational developments speak volumes for the optimism of the sixties, and some of the false assumptions which underlay it, it is in architecture and redevelopment that we see false promises made concrete. Some magnificent buildings were erected. On the one side was the monumental terraced style of Sir Denys Lasdun, as seen in the University of East Anglia and the National Theatre, as also in Patrick Hodgkinson's Brunswick Centre in Bloomsbury. On the other hand was the gentler more flexible style of, say, Sir Basil Spence with his Sussex University, strongly influenced by Le Corbusier's Jaoul houses in Paris and discreetly blending echoes of a Roman colosseum into a magnificent landscape, or of Sir Robert Matthew in his Edinburgh Airport, with its appropriate Scandinavian styling. It was a very laudable part of the orthodoxy of the time that client and architect should work very closely together. Unfortunately, when the client was a public authority and the actual users ordinary people with no say at all, things began to go sadly wrong.

Yet in the early sixties the spoliation carried out in central Newcastle by T. Dan Smith and his colleagues received the praises of the left-wing intellectual journal the *New Statesman*. When the Kirby housing estate near Liverpool – later to become a paradigm of dereliction and vandalism – was opened, Barbara Castle, left-wing member of the Labour Government, told the local Labour Party: 'This is your chance to build a new Jerusalem.' Those bulldozers lauded by Walter Greenwood appeared to be on a destructive foray against close-knit older communities for the poor trade-off of disruptive urban motorways and ugly, unloved high-rise housing.

In 1968 a gas explosion brought the collapse of Ronan Point, a system-built tower block in East London. Much else collapsed as well; and architects and planners must be given credit for the fact that by the time the seventies had begun they were obviously aware that they had an architecture and planning crisis on their hands. Involved in this was the whole principle of planning ('the architect knows best') and revelations about the commercial exploitation of systems building, and inadequate and often fraudulent support services and amenities. A new emphasis on conservation and a halt to the building of high-rise public housing were announced, though low-cost housing estates of dubious popularity would go on being built, and thousands of people would continue for many years to be marooned in flats hundreds of feet above the ground. (The well-off, however, liked being marooned in such prestige high-rise developments as the Barbican in the City of London.)

The overwhelming majority of people in any country at any time have very little understanding of economics, and do not talk much about such issues as the balance of payments, devaluation, and the money supply. They thus differ from economists and politicians, who talk a lot about the balance of payments, devaluation, and the money supply, and, no doubt, are complete masters of the particular economic theory to which they adhere. In 1964, when the Conservatives left office, there was an enormous balance-of-payments deficit. Left-wing Labour politicians argued for a siege economy, with barriers against imports; right-wing Labour MPs argued for a speedy devaluation; Conservatives, and others, called for curbs on the unions. All thought that if their remedy were adopted, the essential soundness of the nation would reassert itself. The Wilson Government, in the event, did what its Treasury advisers told it to do. It was unable, in face of the opposition of its own supporters, to carry through any changes in trade-union law. There was a great sterling crisis in 1966, a devaluation in November 1967, and further rumblings of crisis in 1968. For those who cared about such things, the country, it seemed, was in a mess. Yet after measures of wage freeze and austerity, which did not, in practice, halt the general upward movement in real living standards, the balance of payments was again in respectable surplus by 1970. Many of the authors of the earlier critiques had focused on the inadequacies of central administration and of local government, as well as on poor industrial relations. The sixties, in fact, was a time of considerable reorganization in central Government; old ministries bit the dust, new departments rose in their place. By the turn of the decade, plans were well advanced for local government reform. As they were, too, for the decimalization of the currency, finally carried through in 1971.

Winning the election of 1970, the Conservatives went hard for a policy of expansion. Edward Heath spoke enthusiastically on television of how export companies had full order books. The year 1972 was one of apparent buoyancy: a good year certainly for finance companies and property speculators. Certainly, trade-union activism, as we saw, was getting more threatening. Even so, Britain's record for days lost because of strikes still wasn't noticeably worse than that of her competitors.

To return, then, to 'moods'. Critics might argue that the British had lost their appetite for work, were no longer interested in the creation of wealth, that the key problems were low productivity and low investment. Yet life was good and all seemed far from lost. Still there was joy in the present, and hope for the future.

Part Three

The Time of Troubles
1973–80

12. Gloom on the Man-Made Island

If, in broad outline, the period of 'consensus' with which this book began could be seen as containing the story of the determination to escape for ever from the Depression conditions of the 1930s, the story of the middle and late seventies might well be seen as one of a return to the gloom of that 'devil's decade'. Apart from a general sense of a worsening economy and declining living standards, the special doom-laden features which contemporary commentators singled out were the outbursts of militancy, violence, and terrorism, the revelations of corruption in high places, and the break-up of the optimistic consensus which had, according to one point of view, successfully carried Britain through the difficult post-war years into the affluence of the sixties, or, according to another, had mischievously concealed the desperate realities of Britain's true predicament.

There is no sharp line of divide. The 'roads to freedom' ran on through the seventies, often wider and smoother. Small 'wild-cat' strikes, the characteristic phenomenon of the industrial scene since the early days of the war, ceased to be so around 1968, when observers began to be much more worried by the rise of the large, official strike. The Conservatives, it is true, ousted Labour in 1970; yet a political historian might well prefer to treat 1964–79 as one 'period' of, in general, Labour hegemony. Heath and his Chancellor of the Exchequer Anthony Barber at first propagated a philosophy of expansionism. It was only at the end of 1973 that the spurious boom in share-dealing and property collapsed. The most bitter year since the war of confrontation between Government and unions was certainly 1972: it was the year of the IRA bomb outrage at Aldershot in which five civilians died; and it was also the first year since before the First World War in which a union picket lost his life (albeit in an unfortunate accident). Yet the full-blooded IRA campaign of violence on the British mainland did not materialize till 1974, which was also the year in which Kevin Gately lost his life in the anti-National Front demonstration at Red Lion Square, London. Overall economic trends, no doubt, were downward – as perhaps they had been for a long time; but there were fluctuations. Only in 1976 was it absolutely clear that unemployment was on the up and up. The percentage unemployed out of the total number of employees stood at 2·6 per cent in 1970, rising to 3·5 per cent and 3·8 per cent in 1971 and 1972 respectively, with a fall back to 2·7 per cent in 1973 and 2·6 per cent in 1974; in 1975 it rose to 4·1 per cent, in 1976 to 5·7 per cent, in 1977 to 6·2 per cent, with a slight remission in 1978 to 6·1 per cent, then up again in 1979 and on into 1980.

In 1978, the total population of the United Kingdom was 55,835,000 (that is, including the 1,539,000 who lived in Northern Ireland), divided between 27,170,000 males and 28,666,000 females. There had been something under a 10 per cent increase in the total population since 1951 when for the United Kingdom it had been 50,290,000 (1,373,000 in Northern Ireland), divided between 24,152,000 males and 26,138,000 females. It is within these overall totals that we can best assess the significance of regional and local fluctuations in population. The striking national fact which gave pause to the thoughtful and provoked pessimism in the excitable was that in 1975, 1976, and 1977, for the first years since population records began, the population fell slightly. The cause was a sharp fall in the birthrate. Births in 1977 just outnumbered deaths, but were not sufficient to make up for a net migration out of the country. Figures at the end of the decade suggested a slight rallying, so that statisticians were predicting that on through the rest of the century there would be a steady but very slow increase in population; no bad thing for a crowded island, perhaps. However, it was also noted that a steadily increasing proportion of the population fell into the dependent category, either old people, or the young, together supported by a declining proportion of actual earners. While all that was being digested, it turned out that personal incomes, which had enjoyed an average annual rise of 4·4 per cent from 1950 onwards, actually fell by 0·2 per cent in 1976, and by a further 1 per cent in 1977.

The over-riding economic fact was the shrinkage in Britain's industrial base; there was also, as had been the case in America for many years, a growing mis-match between the characteristics of those seeking work and the kinds of jobs which were available. The total numbers in manufacturing employment declined by 2·2 per cent between 1971 and 1974, and by a further 6·1 per cent between 1974 and 1977. After 1974 the number of males in employment fell, whereas between 1971 and 1976 a further one million married women moved into employment.

Whatever different policies Governments followed, they did little to alter the fundamental facts. In January 1974 the Conservative Government of Edward Heath found itself in confrontation with the miners and involved in an international energy crisis, so that major industries were closed for two days out of five in every week. In the 1940s, Government intervention in industry had been directed towards building, on the basis of the war experience, a post-war Britain in which the mass unemployment of the inter-war years would be abolished. The interventionist policies of the incoming Labour Government after 1974 had more the character of a desperate attempt to shore up failing industries. Certainly considerable sums of money were dispensed, and Britain's only indigenous car firm, British Leyland was taken into state ownership. Between 1970–71 and 1975–6, Government expenditure on 'trade, industry, and employment' increased (at constant, 1975, prices) from £1,800,400,000 to £2,586,600,000, an increase of 44 per cent. Government, it might be said, was doing its best to preserve or create jobs. Yet, with very minor fluctuations, unemployment figures steadily rose. For Great Britain, they went over the million mark for the first time since the Second World War in August 1975. In 1978 (under Labour) and considerably more drastically in 1979 (under the Conservatives) there were massive expenditure cut-backs, and unemployment continued to soar up towards two million.

Before we go again on our British journey, something old and something new. The something old is that, although Britain remained one of the world's most densely populated countries

(593 persons per square mile in Britain, 920 per square mile in England, and 11,432 per square mile in London), considerable parts of the country are quite sparsely populated and the nation was still far from being one continuous urban sprawl; in fact, almost 80 per cent of the land surface was still taken up for agricultural uses, 7 per cent being covered by forest, and only 8 per cent being taken up by towns and cities. The new point is that in the early seventies a complete re-drawing of the local government map had taken place. Obviously the essentials of social geography do not change – the new political lines were intended to recognize such of the social realities as had changed – but on our tour we will find that some historic names had disappeared, and some strange ones had appeared. The new Local Government Acts were passed into law in 1972 (Scotland, 1973), with the new boundaries taking effect in the spring of 1974 (Scotland, 1975). In England and Wales smaller counties were grouped together and the conurbations were formally recognized as metropolitan counties: Tyne and Wear, South Yorkshire, West Yorkshire, West Midlands, Greater Manchester, Merseyside, and Humberside and Cleveland. Scotland was divided into regions (with the bulk of the population going into Strathclyde), and the major cities, for example the City and Royal Burgh of Edinburgh, were now given the undignified title of 'local government district'.

If we start our tour once again in Scotland, we find that whatever optimism there had been in the late 1940s had by now almost completely evaporated, but that a new harbinger of possible wealth was over the horizon. The two most significant features of Scotland's economy were, from the late fifties right through, a deepening depression in the old heavy industries, and from the early seventies onwards the advent of North Sea oil and all its accoutrements. Unemployment ran well above the national average in Scotland: 4·5 per cent in 1973, 4 per cent in 1974, 5·2 per cent in 1975; it rose to 6·9 per cent in 1976, 8·1 per cent in 1977, and 8·2 per cent in 1978. Yet by 1976 around sixty thousand people were in employment directly or indirectly related to oil.

The growth area was the North-East (the new Grampian

region). In the post-war years Aberdeen had led a life to match
the texture and colouring of its granite buildings. Now it became the capital of the Scottish oil industry. In the process it
lost its gentility without gaining many of the attributes of prosperity. Pubs, under new Scottish licensing regulations which in
the last years of the decade permitted all-day opening (leaving
England far astern), took on a slight transatlantic character.
Where once the city's finest restaurant had stood a massive bar
brought together oilmen, citizens of various avocations, and
ladies of the town. Some historical documents have a special
evanescence. The list of drinks on offer in this bar at Easter
1980, rough-hewn into poetic abbreviation, forms a statement
of social custom which ought to be recorded:

Whisky	45p	Export	50p
Rum		Lager	50p
Vodka		Pt Bot	
Gin		Cider	48p
De Lux	48p	Bots	
Bacardi		Export	33p
Brandy	58p	Lager	33p
Liqueurs	58p	Carls	35p
S'Comfort	58p	Carls Spec	47p
Port	44p	Guins	35p
Sherry		Stout	33p
Aperitifs		Macks	
Juices	25p	St Ale	35p
Coke	25p	Brown Ale	
Babies	20p	Whits	50p
Cham	35p	Pils	47p
S'Ball		Cordial	4p
Lemonade	24p	Crabbies	7p
		Dashes	4p

The scribblings on the shops at Pompeii are scarcely more
evocative.

The black fingers spread further afield than the Grampian
coastal towns of Aberdeen and Peterhead. Docking facilities for
tankers and construction yards for oil platforms were in demand. Of course, the Highlands had long had hydro-electric
schemes, aluminium works, a missile base, a missile testing
range, and an atomic energy station. Now they were well on

the way to becoming a type of region specially associated with late twentieth-century civilization: wild, remote, beautiful, neglected, with dotted here and there the advanced industrial-technological complexes which the inhabitants of more developed, more populated, areas preferred not to have sited in their midst. However, one man's environmental poison is another man's daily bread.

But, also, one man's fish is another man's environmental disaster. International agreements on the conservation of fish stocks badly hit Scottish fishermen (who formed nearly half of all fishermen in Great Britain). The tragic story of the Scottish fishing industry highlights the point that the Highlands were still basically in decline, despite the new technological marvels. However, a further point is as relevant to consumer society in general as it is to social life in this particular part of Scotland. As well as new sources of energy, society, or rather a few more affluent members of it, demanded certain luxuries: thus there was modest prosperity to be found in the Harris tweed industry and in the malt whisky distilleries dotted round the perimeter, from Islay in the south-west, through Talisker in Skye, to Highland Park and Scapa in the Orkneys, and right round to the classic Speyside area in Grampian.

Here and there in the towns and cities of the Lowlands (the new regions of Strathclyde, Central, and Lothian) industry, as heavy engineering declined and electronics expanded rapidly, had moved into the age of automation and the white-coated worker. But for the majority it was a case of working in the old way, or, more and more, of not working at all. One industry (located throughout the Lowlands and Southern Uplands and in Grampian and the North-East) that was doing well was agriculture. There was some prosperity, too, for the quality tweed and knitwear industries in the small towns of the Southern Uplands. And, of course, there were the nuclear power stations, at Hunterston and at Chapelcross.

In many respects the new local government map of England still failed to meet the realities of economic geography as perceived by the central Government. For the purposes of central planning, there was one 'standard region' of the North, which included the historic counties of the North-East, Northumberland and Durham, the new county of Cleveland, the new metropolitan county of Tyne and Wear (old Newcastle-upon-Tyne writ large), and the old North-West, now corresponding with most of, but not the whole of, the new county of Cumbria. This North region was the most depressed of all in Great Britain, for it remained most dependent on traditional industries and most constrained by the worthy but inadequately thought-out policies of the late forties. In 1972 the unemployment rate in the North was, at 6·3 per cent, marginally better than that in Scotland. Although 1973 and 1974 were better years for the country as a whole, it was during them that the North slipped firmly behind Scotland. In the bad year of 1976 the unemployment rate in the North was up to 7·4 per cent, and in 1977 and 1978 it reached 8·3 per cent and 8·8 per cent respectively. The derelict coal-mining villages of Northumberland and Durham set a new bench-mark for dilapidation and deprivation in contemporary Britain. Gloom was least in the farming areas, still vitally important in both Cumbria and Northumberland, and among the new technological complexes on the Teesside area of the metropolitan county of Cleveland.

In preparing their standard textbook *Geography of the British Isles* N. J. Graves and J. T. White visited the Northumbrian market town of Hexham, one of those towns with a population of around ten thousand which so often get neglected in studies of contemporary Britain. Livestock sales took place there at the auction market four days a week, with cattle being brought from as far away as Ireland, coming via Liverpool docks. In the late seventies as many as 2,000 head of cattle would be auctioned daily. 'In one day,' one of the authors reported, 'I saw lorries from Wooler in the North, Carlisle and Penrith in the West, Northallerton and Knaresborough in Yorkshire.' Many specialized firms had grown up close by the markets, supplying farm machinery, fertilizers, seeds, feed stuffs, and advice and services to farmers. As in so many similar market towns the pubs had special licensing hours to cater for those attending the market. The biggest change during the seventies was the building of a vast car park. Bus services were not good; though the authors might have mentioned, but did not, the frequent train service to Newcastle.

Teesside had the largest concentration of chemical plant in the whole British Isles. It had modern port facilities, and a massive modern steel complex, which was, however, already having its production cut back as the eighties began. The people of Teesside were relatively prosperous, but at the expense of living in an atmosphere often made foul by the chemical works in their midst.

Lancashire still survived as a county and the standard region based on it was recognizably the same distinctive region it had been in the late forties. The North-West, comprising the metropolitan counties of Greater Manchester and Merseyside and the counties of Lancashire and Cheshire, had not seemed to be doing too desperately badly at the beginning of the seventies. However, by the end of the decade unemployment rates here, too, were up above 7·5 per cent. Cotton was no longer king, and the old textile towns of Bolton, Stockport, Oldham, Blackburn, Preston, Rochdale, Burnley, and Bury had, with considerable success, diversified into both man-made fibres and carpets and engineering. Manchester no longer drew prosperity from textiles, but remained Britain's second most important commercial and financial centre and was still, by grace of the Manchester ship canal, an important port. It was a centre, now, of electrical and heavy engineering, electronics, petrochemicals, clothing, dye stuffs, and pharmaceuticals. Among the old chemical towns, Warrington achieved a new fame for its production of vodka. Leyland, home of the original Leyland motor company, now maintained the only really successful division of British Leyland, the one manufacturing commercial vehicles. Blackpool, not quite the holiday centre it once had been as holiday patterns changed, had reasonably successful chemical and other light industries, as had Lancaster itself, never a heavily industrialized town in the nineteenth century, but now, among other things, home of one of the new universities. The farm land of Lancashire is very fertile, and on the whole the agricultural industry did well. There was a nuclear power station at Heysham.

Manchester's great rival, Liverpool, now enveloped in the new metropolitan county of Merseyside, could still boast of being, after London, the largest centre for processing and converting imported foodstuffs and raw materials, such as grain, oils, fats, tobacco, sugar, and rubber. But Liverpool provided the classic case of the city whose heart – in this case the old dockland areas – was dying, and whose prosperity, such as it was, was to be found around the periphery. The geographer Peter Hall had cities like Liverpool in mind when he described the dilemma of the inner city and the predicament of its inhabitants: 'A significant minority of these residents are poorly educated, are unskilled, have incomes too low to travel far, and perceptions too limited to know the possibilities. They could perform the heavy, simple jobs needing much strength but little skill, that were once plentiful. But in the new age of the automated machine and the computer, there is no place for their modest talents.'

Yorkshire we spoke of, when making our earlier tour, as 'an industrial museum'. Compared with other old industrial areas Yorkshire was in fact doing slightly less badly in the later seventies. Standing at 2·8 per cent in 1973, unemployment had risen to 6 per cent in 1978. The 'standard region' is termed Yorkshire and Humberside, and in the new functional (more or less) local government scheme the romance of the Ridings, as divisions of Yorkshire, have gone; instead there are the metropolitan counties of West Yorkshire (Leeds, Bradford, and their surroundings) and South Yorkshire (Sheffield and its surroundings). Again it is just worth remembering that though this area is in parts very heavily industrialized, more than four fifths of Yorkshire and Humberside is open country. The development of new man-made fibres had given the Yorkshire textile trade a slight lift; there had also, as we noted in regard to Harris and the Scottish borders, been a revival in the demand for good woollen products. At the end of the seventies about 70 per cent of Britain's worsted and woollen industry was located in West Yorkshire, with Bradford still having a little of the *cachet* of being the commercial centre of the wool trade. Doncaster and Barnsley continued to be basically coalfield towns, but were profiting from some diversification. York had always stood apart from industrial Yorkshire: it was not doing too badly on two very contemporary trades, tourism and chocolate. Hull and Grimsby, on Humberside, were surviving reasonably well at the beginning of the seventies, their dependence upon fishing balanced out by the establishment of port facilities for European trade together with food processing and cold storage plants. But they were hit hard by the general slump in fishing, and in 1980 the entire Hull trawler trade went bankrupt. Mighty symbol of Humberside's fluctuating fortunes, and Britain's industrial problems in general, was the Humber Bridge, still, after massive expenditure, and one serious accident, uncompleted in 1980, by which time it was being argued that most of the commercial need for it had already vanished.

It was in the Yorkshire coalfield, and in its continuation into the East Midlands, that automation had gone furthest. The geographer (David M. Smith) who wrote that 'the miner in the white coat is the symbol of the 1970s' was exaggerating, but without any doubt automation, based on the inexhaustible possibilities for computerization presented by the silicon chip, for better or for worse, was now beginning to bite deeply into conditions of and opportunities for work. There were huge new power stations around Castleford. Coal made up about one fifth of the industrial output of the East Midlands; major industries were hosiery, knitwear and footwear, trades which, short of a total general depression, tended to do reasonably well as vital parts of contemporary consumer society. Unemployment did not reach 5 per cent in the East Midlands till 1977 and it remained steady at that figure in 1978.

The West Midlands had been the great success area of the war and post-war years. Under the local government reorganization this whole region formed one metropolitan county, with many historic towns now being defined as mere 'districts': Birmingham, Coventry, Dudley, Solihull, Walsall, and Wolverhampton. The area, however, was very dependent upon the vicissitudes of the motor industry, and after having very low unemployment rates in the early seventies, the West Midlands had a 7·5 per cent unemployment rate by 1978. Yet, for seeing what was going on in Britain in this time of troubles, the region was a good one to visit. The Midlands' cities, Newcastle-under-Lyme, as well as Birmingham and Coventry, had early gone into the business of tearing down their town centres in order to make a land fit for motor cars to live in. In the later seventies, unsteadily because of lack of funds, the attempt was made to restore the conservationist balance. The area's aspiration towards a North American future was best represented in the building and opening of the National Exhibition Centre on the outskirts of Birmingham which sought to destroy the monopoly which London had so long held on national and international congresses. The region had two quite successful new towns, both based on the metal industries, Telford and Redditch.

On the outermost fringes of the 'Home Counties' (the counties clustered round London), where they begin to merge into the South Midlands, the most famous of all new towns, the new city of Milton Keynes, began to shake itself into some sort of life in the later seventies, and to become as famous a topic for popular journalism as the Loch Ness Monster. Built very much like a large piece of American suburbia, Milton Keynes was much criticized for its 'rabbit-hutch' housing, and for the obvious segregation of its different classes of housing estates. Still, when, according to *New Society*, the community television station, as an April Fool's joke for 1979, broadcast a message saying that the entire city (100,000 inhabitants, half the planned total, at the end of the decade) was to be ploughed back into the ground, a viewer declared that he was not going to go back to London: 'Milton Keynes had given him a garden, something he'd never had before, and he was damned if he was going to give it up now.'

In *Wales: A New Study* (1977), edited by David Thomas, there is, in the chapter by Graham Humphrys, a map of industrial South Wales, showing the collieries still open as black dots, and the collieries closed since 1950 as white dots; the white quite overwhelms the black. The fundamental fact about Wales since the early 1950s has been the concentration of coal production in the deeper central parts of the coal basin, with a drying-up of production around the edges. Small mines closed down leaving only large collieries employing at least five hundred workers. The old life of the village perched on top of the pit was breaking up; the new collieries were often quite some distance from the old villages. If the men did not all work in white coats, though Humphrys speaks of 'a new breed of mining technocrats' replacing 'the men skilled in the arts of manual labour', they were certainly at one with 'post-industrial' twentieth-century civilization in that they had considerable distances to travel to work. For most of the seventies closures did not mean a high level of redundancy; instead there was simply a steady population drift away from South Wales. Hardest hit of all was the anthracite region to the west.

Hopes were still high in the early seventies over the potential of the South Wales steel industry: they had all come crashing down by the end of the decade. First there had been the closure of the small inland works, and a concentration on the vast coastal complexes; but even those were under threat in 1980. Attempts were made to continue and extend the policies of the forties. Substantial growth took place in the electrical goods industry, but the jobs created mainly went to female labour. Historic Merthyr Tydfil was now best known for its Hoover washing machine factory, whose demand for labour fluctuated with the consumer economy as a whole. Various motor component plants established in the sixties suffered with the problems of the British motor trade in the seventies. In 1971 Wilkinson Sword had established a garden tool manufacturing plant at Waterton Industrial Estate. L'Oreal opened a cosmetics factory at Llantrisant in 1972. There were oil refineries at Milford Haven and Llandarcy and a giant petrochemicals complex at Bagland Bay. There was one nuclear power station at Wilfa on Anglesey and, as a final earnest of the determination of the man-made world to dominate the world of nature, there was another at Trawsfynydd in the middle of the wild and beautiful national park of Snowdonia.

In the West Country (the standard region of the South-West), where, save for the creation of the county of Avon as an expanded version of the former county borough of Bristol, the historic counties had been left intact, the main change since the early fifties was the growth of light engineering and of the various branches of the electronics industry. In addition the West Country had three nuclear power stations, at Berkeley, Aldbury, and Hinkley Point. The South-West had been troubled by unemployment at the end of the sixties (2·8 per cent in 1970), and in 1977 unemployment was running at 6·8 per cent, with a slight drop to 6·5 per cent in 1978.

In the later sixties London and the whole South-East region had been the most prosperous in Britain, with unemployment standing at 1·6 per cent in 1970. This region continued to suffer less than any other, and in 1977 and 1978 was the only region to have unemployment below 5 per cent (4·5 per cent and 4·2 per cent respectively). Yet London itself was steadily losing both employment and population. There was a developing outer ring of light industry, but many of the most characteristic technological developments of the age were being located somewhat outside of Greater London itself: for example the computer industry had important bases at Hemel Hempstead and Letchworth, and the electronics industry was developing at Chelmsford. A special factor in the decline of London's East End was the opening of new deep-sea port facilities down the Thames at Tilbury. There were major oil refineries on both the Thames and the Medway. Finally, another characteristic of the contemporary age, the major London airports at Heathrow and Gatwick were in themselves now major employers. Outside of London the South-East continued to enjoy a modest prosperity, probably on a rather higher level than was to be found anywhere else in the country. There were nuclear power stations on the south coast at Dungeness. The population of the South-East began to decline after 1972 (when it was 17,600,000); in 1978 it was down to 16,832,000.

In simple cash terms London, though by no means London alone, benefited greatly from the manner in which Britain was becoming a major tourist country, with a record 11·5 million visitors in 1977, spending £2,179 million. But there were those who complained that parts of London, particularly the West End, where tourists took the form of shoppers rather than sightseers, and such towns as Stratford-on-Avon and Edinburgh, were, in high season, unbearably overcrowded. Many were the new hazards of life in contemporary Britain.

One of the few regions (though, in regard to population, a very tiny one) to show steady growth was East Anglia, which grew from 1,683,000 inhabitants in 1971 to 1,843,000 in 1978. Many East Anglian towns were still steadily absorbing 'overspill' from London, and the old port towns of Great Yarmouth and Lowestoft had expanded their trade with the Continent as well as becoming North Sea oil bases. The most significant development was the building of the massive continental container port at Felixstowe. There was a nuclear power station at Size-well.

Yet, again, we must not forget rural England. While the 'revolution in farming' did bring some prosperity to rural areas, the exodus from tiny villages to the towns where the electronics and other technological industries were located, and the drastic changes in British transport policy were leaving less happy consequences. When the petrol crisis of late 1973 first struck, and rationing seemed imminent, the strongest arguments for special consideration came from car owners in East Anglia and other country areas. But for the older and less affluent there were other limitations upon mobility than those threatened by restrictions in the private petrol supply. This and other points were developed in a fine piece of journalism by Philip Norman in the *Sunday Times* of 29 January 1978, when he described a visit to the East Anglian village of Sudbourne in Suffolk.

There was a different village here. It exists now only in clues ... School Road, Hospital Road, lead one blandly, each to a cul-de-sac of distance and forest edge. The school has become a private house, its gothic classroom windows shortened, its teachers' quarters severed and lately sold to a barrister from London. Hospital Road divulges only four fir trees in a clump, the scene of fire. There was once a shop, they say, at the Red House. Its vanished window haunts it still in a shape of paler bricks. Inside the telephone kiosk a plaque informs the user he is speaking from 'Sudbourne Post Office and Stores'. Looking out, he sees a white house front, a new double garage, a pale blue, exclusive-looking door.

The Post Office shut down three years ago ...

The bus time-table, fixed to a wall outside the Chequers, is like a gauge of isolation. It tries to be cheerful, with its promise of money-saving excursions, yet wherever the name Sudbourne occurs on its columns, one might deduce an almost malign wish to keep the village out of step with everywhere. The time-table ordains Woodbridge, eleven miles away, as the nearest town; Saxmundham, Leiston and Aldeburgh, all nearer, are inaccessible from Sudbourne by bus. The morning Ipswich service, calling at Sudbourne just before eight, reaches Woodbridge too late to catch a train. If you take the early evening

bus, there is no getting back the same night. The full journey of an hour-
and-three-quarters ... costs £1 each way ...

For all practical purposes Sudbourne depends on local authority
transport, that modern form of charity. School buses take its children
to Orford, Butley or Woodbridge. A mobile library calls on alternate
Fridays, staying half-an-hour. Once a fortnight, a county council mini-
bus takes the elderly to Orford, to collect their pensions and enjoy a
half hour's shopping in the metropolitan atmosphere of a post office,
a sweet shop and Elliott's General Store.

The invasion of the rich into the rural territory of the poor,
taking over their homes, and everywhere pushing up rates and
house prices, was in many places mightily resented. That resent-
ment, allied with nationalism, resulted, early in 1980, in an arson
campaign in Wales against the owners of second homes. Still,
contemporary discontents should not obscure long-term gains.
In Sudbourne, as in villages in Wales and elsewhere, the universal installation of electricity and sewerage was very much an
achievement of the period since 1945.

Increasingly, observers were declaring that the crucial divide
in British society was one of social geography: between a prospering innovative South (the Midlands, and everything to the
south, but excluding Wales), and a backward, depressed North
(everything beyond the Midlands). In the general election of
1979, the South, thus defined, overwhelmingly voted Conservative; it was in the North that Labour kept its hopes alive.
Throughout the North wages were lower while more was collected in social security benefits. Scotland had fewest cars per
head, but the highest rate of prosecutions for drunken driving.
The Times summed up Central Statistical Office tables for 1979,
in the headline: 'Dirtier, less healthy North; a wealthier South'.

Yet, beneath the geographical and regional variations, there
was developing a grimmer social and demographic pattern. All
over the country it was becoming difficult for school leavers to
find jobs, and older men, unable to acquire newer skills, formed
a high proportion of those unemployed. While much unemployment was still relatively short-term, over the country
the proportions of those unemployed for over six months and
unemployed for over twelve months were remarkably consistent. These dismal points are brought out graphically in Table 3,

prepared from Department of Unemployment figures by Kevin Hawkins for his study *Unemployment* (1979).

Table 3: Regional analysis of male unemployment by duration and age, January 1978

Region	Male unemploy-ment rate %	Long-term male unemployed as a proportion of all male unemployed		Proportion of all male unemployed	
		Over 6 months	Over 12 months	Under 20	Over 40
South-East	5·8	39·2	21·1	11·2	40·3
East Midlands	6·3	41·6	25·1	11·6	44·1
West Midlands	6·5	47·3	29·0	13·4	40·3
East Anglia	6·6	39·2	24·0	11·5	44·7
Yorks/Humberside	7·3	42·2	25·7	12·4	41·2
South-West	8·9	42·2	24·8	13·4	40·3
North-West	9·2	49·2	29·9	14·7	35·6
Wales	9·9	44·2	26·6	13·6	36·3
North	10·4	46·0	28·5	13·3	39·2
Scotland	10·6	42·1	24·6	11·5	34·6
Great Britain	8·1	43·3	25·4	13·2	39·3

Work had not lost its double-edged quality; but by the beginning of the eighties a job was becoming again, as it had been in the 1930s, something that you began to thank your lucky stars you had. The paradox of the late seventies was that although a crucial aspect of industrial relations was dominated by the Employment Protection legislation enacted in 1974 which seemed to affirm the responsibility of society to provide everyone with a job, the economy was so depressed, the provision of new industrial skills so lacking, and the workforce itself so immobile, that, while redundancy payments could be claimed, redundancies themselves were a threat as they never had been since the Second World War. A tentative move towards establishing work as a social right had foundered on adverse economic circumstances and perhaps, indeed, was incompatible with favourable ones. The industrial worker was still at the greatest risk, though his 'rights' had been strengthened; the privileged security of the middle class lay under threat.

In 1955 the first motorways were only promises on the planner's pen. In 1980 there was a widely held predisposition against the building of any new ones. At one level communications, apart from the occasional bottleneck, such as that on the old two-lane stretch of the M1 just north of London, were probably better than they had ever been in the country's history. Much of the rail network was electrified and the Inter-city 125 services on major routes offered journey times as good as any in the world; Cardiff, for instance, was brought within two hours of London and against the tale of South Wales decline can be placed the siting of Companies' House there. It was at the more local level, and in the remoter areas, as we have noted, that transport facilities were declining, though probably almost all individuals, through the irrepressible institution of the extended family, had, in time of need, access to transport by private car. A totally new communications phenomenon was to be found in the pipe lines established to transport gases, natural and otherwise, and petroleum.

It would be wrong to see the environment at the beginning of the 1980s as dominated totally by money-making technologies and their accompanying spoliation and pollution, by the demands of commuter and industrial transport, and by rural decline and the whims of the owners of second homes; and still more wrong to forget that industrial pollution was as old as industry itself. On the side of the angels were three major government bodies: the Standing Royal Commission on Environmental Pollution, the Clean Air Council, and the Advisory Council on Noise; and a whole host of voluntary societies: the National Society for Clean Air, the Noise Abatement Society, the Keep Britain Tidy Group, the Friends of the Earth, and the Council for Nature.

13. *Class, Race, and Nationalism*

The previous chapter indicated various possible divisions in British society, suggesting, on one plane, the emergence of a division between a deprived North and a relatively prosperous South, and, on another plane, a nationwide divide between young people unable to secure jobs and the rest of society. Clearly both local deprivation and such major structural changes as were brought about by North Sea oil could be expected to have considerable relevance to the progress of nationalism. Already Britain was a society marked by race discrimination and racial tension; often, in the economic gloom, it was the members of racial minorities, particularly the young ones, who could not get jobs. New economic circumstances, then, could be expected also to intensify race divisions.

But for all that, class was very far from losing its traditional significance in British society. In that judgement sociologists, journalists, and commentators of all descriptions seemed to concur, for the seventies ended in an unprecedented flurry of studies of class. From the middle seventies onwards discussions of the all-absorbing topic rumbled through the letter and feature columns of various newspapers. Storm-centres were created by: a Labour Party television broadcast late in 1976 which boldly portrayed a selfish and ineffectual upper class; an acrimonious controversy over the relationship between education and class centring particularly on the relative merits of comprehensive and grammar schools and on the Labour Party's announced intention, at last, to attack the entrenched position of the public schools; and the case, presented most bluntly in the sections of a Milton Friedman American television broadcast shown in this country, that Britain was handicapped compared with her foreign competitors by her rigid class system.

In December 1976, the novelist Lynne Reid Banks in a letter

to the *Observer* summed up a widely expressed opinion: 'Class is so deeply embedded in our national sub-conscious it is poisoning every aspect of our lives. Not just industrial relations and politics, but our choice of districts to live in, jobs, schools, friends – even which bar to drink in at our local. It's a kind of civil war we are perpetually fighting, wearing out our energy and emotions, wasting our time and money. It holds back progress, destroys prosperity, impedes social and working relations on every side.' Three years and two months later (late January 1980) the same writer, this time in a feature article, had moved from a general critique of British society to a more embattled class position: 'Why should I feel ashamed of the indisputable fact that we, the middle classes, fill the better schools with our children and the theatres with ourselves?' Middle-class idealists, she continued, had given up on the comprehensive educational system: 'What drives them to it is the awful realization that the working people of this country, on the whole, are not interested in educational or cultural self-improvement. They have no ambition for their children apart from material ambition.'

Earlier, a left-wing Labour MP (Robin Kilroy-Silk, writing in *The Times*, December 1976) had welcomed the return to 'a fearless and radical examination and critique of class in Britain today'; the Labour Party, he said, did not seek to divide society, it was divided already. Nowhere was this more clear 'than in the factories where manual workers enter by one gate, eat in segregated canteens and work longer hours in worse conditions than their "betters"'. Also in *The Times*, a right-of-centre Labour MP (John P. MacKintosh) wrote on 'Them and Us: What we can do to heal our divided land': many managements, he noted, would not dream of sitting down to lunch with their shop stewards. The Conservative reply was that 'some form of class structure is inevitable'. The thesis of *Class on the Brain: The Cost of a British Obsession*, written for the right-wing Centre for Policy Studies by Professor Peter Bauer, was that, if class-conscious and variegated, British society was also open and mobile, with the very evident badges of class enhancing mobility by providing additional incentives to hard work and enterprise. This, significantly, is a defence, not a denial, of class distinctions; what characterized all the debates was an open recognition of the existence of classes. The old decade ended with the publication of the lighthearted, but shrewd, study of class by the highly successful journalist Jilly Cooper; and the new one opened with the heavy-footed, but sound, studies of class and social mobility, and class and education, written, respectively, by John Goldthorpe and A. H. Halsey.

There was still no consensus among those who commented so profusely, and indeed promiscuously, over what constituted the upper class, if indeed there was one, or over where the divide came between such an upper class and the upper-middle class. There is no consistency of popular usage, and therefore no rule, over who are included in the upper class and over where the divide comes between the upper class and the upper-middle class. Back in the sixties, in introducing his book *The English Gentleman*, Simon Raven had, as we have seen, revealed that his father had independent means, and that he himself was brought up in 'Surrey stockbrokers' country', educated at an expensive preparatory school, and at Charterhouse and King's College, Cambridge; yet he denied being himself a member of the upper class. In 1979, Jilly Cooper presented a somewhat similar disclaimer:

My paternal grandfather was a wool-merchant, but my paternal grandmother's family were a bit grander. They owned newspapers, and were distinguished Whig MPs for Leeds during the nineteenth century My mother's side were mostly in the church, her father being Canon of Heaton, near Bradford. Her mother was a beauty. Both sides had lived in the West Riding of Yorkshire for generations. They were very, very strait-laced. To this day there has never been a divorce in the family.

My father went to Rugby, then to Cambridge, where he got a first in two years, and then into the army. After getting married, he found he wasn't making enough money and joined Fords, and he and my mother moved, somewhat reluctantly, to Hornchurch, where I was born. At the beginning of the Second World War he was called up and became one of the army's youngest brigadiers. After the war we moved back to Yorkshire, living first in a large Victorian house. I was eight and, I think for the first time, became aware of class distinction. Our next-door neighbour was a newly rich and very ostentatious wool-merchant, of whose sybaritic existence my parents disapproved ...

Soon after that we moved into the Hall at Ilkley, a splendid Georgian house with a long drive, seven acres of fields for my ponies, a swimming pool, and tennis and squash courts. From then on we lived an élitist existence: tennis parties with cucumber sandwiches, large dances, and fêtes in the garden.

Jilly Cooper, in effect, defines herself as 'upper-middle class', though she admits that to upwardly mobile, hardworking middle-class professional people, she might well seem 'upper class'.

For myself, I have to say that I would regard both Simon Raven and Jilly Cooper as falling within that 2 per cent or so of the population that I would describe as 'upper class'. By that definition, just to clarify things, an ordinary professor such as myself, well-paid, but without influence and totally dependent upon my own earnings, belongs to the upper-middle class. Another usage, just as reputable, though, I think, less exact, would agree with the valuations given by Simon Raven and Jilly Cooper and put them in an upper-middle class which, by all practical indicators, has much the same power, influence, and wealth as the small upper class, restricted in this case to the 'true' aristocracy and gentry, while putting me and my like solidly in the middle class.

In what follows I shall continue to speak of an 'upper class', but readers who do not accept my analysis must then take this category of 'upper class' as including both the upper class and what they would refer to as the 'upper-middle class'. That such a social grouping, whether taken as one integrated entity, or split into two parts, continues to exist is not within the realm of dispute.

Again I must refer to two metaphors employed earlier. First, there is still the upper-class 'box' of ethos, attitudes, and education which perpetuates the tradition and absorbs those not born to the manner. Secondly, this upper class is a 'reservoir'. Not all members of it wield power through being on the boards of multi-national companies or finance corporations; not all members of it stand in the limelight through being Cabinet Ministers or influential backbenchers; not all members of it manipulate the substance of power through the civil service or diplomatic corps. Many other jobs, now, are taken on by sprigs of the upper class, particularly in publishing, journalism, and television. But the point is that all jobs, if wanted, are more accessible to this privileged 2 per cent or so of the population (750,000 individuals; man, woman, and child, or, perhaps, 150,000 family units).

Arguments about the disappearance of a unified upper class are based, we have noted, on the thesis of the 'managerial revolution', on the thesis that influential owners of capital have been displaced by professional managers. Much good work published in the seventies has effectively challenged this gauche thesis. One unique and specially valuable publication, itself a product of one of the more positive and hopeful developments of the 1970s, was the pamphlet *The Making of a Ruling Class* published in 1979 by the Benwell Community Project of Newcastle-upon-Tyne. The careful, detailed, research on which this publication was based brought out very clearly how the descendants of Newcastle's old coal-owning, industrial, and banking families of the eighteenth and nineteenth centuries were now powerful components of a nationwide upper class. Inter-marriage had created great dynasties, such as those of the Joicey, Barnett, and Dickinson families, of the Buddle, Browne, and Brackenbury families, and of the Priestman, Pumphrey, Peile, Bosanquet, and Hodgkin families, as well as families able to go it alone, such as Noble, Pease, and Stephenson. As matters stood in 1980, biographical studies revealed recurrent characteristics: members of these dynasties tended to sit on local authorities (such as the Northumberland County Council), on local planning bodies, on the boards of finance corporations and multi-national companies (where they were also substantial shareholders), had usually been educated at Eton, Harrow, Winchester, or Rugby, held substantial family seats in rural Northumberland, belonged to the Northern Counties Club in Newcastle's Hood Street, and (in the case of eighteen families) to the following exclusive London clubs, Brooks's, the Turf, Pratt's, and the Carlton. 'It is not uncommon,' the authors remark:

to hear the argument that the boards of directors of the banks and in-surance companies are purely window dressing; that they are full of titled members of no particular importance, and that effective power lies with the cadre of highly skilled and trained professionals who have worked their way up to the top through the ranks. Thus Anthony

Sampson quotes the cartoon in an old Insurance Guild journal showing a decrepit old man staggering through the office: '*No, that's not an accident claim, Clogg,*' said one clerk to another, '*that's a director.*' While this view seriously underestimates the importance and significance of the interlocking directorships between the finance capital and industrial capital sectors, it is also fundamentally misleading about the class background of the key executives in banking and insurance. The men from the west Newcastle dynasties who have held or now hold some of these key positions are 'professionals' in that they are career accountants, bankers or insurance managers, but there is no doubt about their social and class origins.

Evidence from another earlier study of twenty-seven large financial institutions, the largest clearing banks, merchant banks, discount houses, insurance companies, and the Bank of England, found that out of a total of 341 directors for whom educational data were available 269 (79 per cent) were educated at public schools and 115 (34 per cent) went to Eton alone. Though much of the detailed work remains to be done, the weight of the evidence is that in 1980 there still was a consolidated, coherent, upper class, enjoying quite disproportionate wealth, power, and life chances, in Britain. The evidence also, though, is of greater mobility than ever previously into this upper class; and of members of this class taking jobs which formerly would not have been regarded as appropriate to their social status.

The upper-class self-image was still very much alive, presented facetiously by Jilly Cooper and by Douglas Sutherland in his works on *The English Gentleman*, less facetiously by Michael Nelson, described by his publishers as 'born in England of a good family ... educated at Bryanston and had a gentlemanly upbringing,' in *Nobs and Snobs*. According to Nelson, 'Britain has continued since the Second World War to be a country made up of many classes, and, though, a gentleman is not class-conscious, he is automatically a member of the upper class of British society.' The upper class, Nelson continues, may be subdivided into three:

First, the recognised aristocracy, accepted as such because of their possession of land, wealth, titles and status; second, the lesser landowners, the 'squires', who sometimes marry into the aristocracy, and, third, the lower-upper class, made up of people who ... have hoisted themselves into the ranks of the upper classes through the right education, service to their country, or marriage.

While the upper-class self-image may be said to have endured, the middle-class self-image had actually become more assertive, as the second quotation from Lynne Reid Banks above might suggest. An even harsher expression of middle-class consciousness emerged from an interview with a woman living in one of London's more expensive suburbs (published by Jane Deverson and Katharine Lindsay in *Voices from the Middle Class*, 1975).

I can't understand people who feel guilty about the working classes. People will always be different, even if everyone has the same houses and the same money. We would always be richer in our minds than the working classes, just by reading books. Labourers can earn a lot of money these days; God, they must have money, the prices they charge! But all they are concerned with is revenge, in the petty ways of their minds. Jealousy and bitching is their main occupation. Look, if everyone had the same amount of money, some people would manage their money better and then things would still be unequal. A person with a different background will live in a different way regardless of money.

Anyway, the Capitalist system helps the poor. If the Stock Market is doing well and the country is richer, that helps the poor. The rich give jobs to the poor. There is always going to be envy, there's always going to be people who are better off than others. It annoys me when people vote Labour out of emotionalism. My best friend voted Labour once, just out of emotion, because she felt it was the right thing to do. Edgar said: 'Are you mad? They are going to nationalise everything and you'll lose all your shares!' She was horrified. 'Oh God, what have I done?' she said. She's mad, completely mad!

There was much talk in the press of the appeal of Thatcherite Conservatism to the middle class. As early as October 1975 David Wood was writing in *The Times* of 'Mrs Thatcher's middle-class uprising'. Subjective comment, as well as the 1979 general election results, suggested that middle-class persons who formerly prided themselves on their progressive sympathies were now swinging away from Labour and back to a more obvious 'class' support of the Conservatives. The best that one middle-class professional who hailed from a working-class background could say was that although he still voted Labour, he no longer cared if the Conservatives won.

The middle class was still the most heterogeneous in educational background. The massive Goldthorpe survey conducted at the beginning of the decade demonstrated that there was indeed mobility out of the working class into the middle class and this trend certainly continued. For those born into the middle class there were opportunities to move up through professional or business success into positions of real influence or power. For the essence of being middle-class in 1980 was that, although life was still easier than it was in the working class, there was no ready access to positions of power; jointly, members of the middle class acting together had influence; singly they had little power. Reports of the Royal Commission on the Distribution of Income and Wealth indicated that it was indeed true, as middle-class people felt in their bones, that differentials between them and members of the working class were steadily being eroded both through taxation, and through the strong bargaining power which certain unions possessed.

As always, clear expressions of working-class self-images are hard to find. However, a survey conducted by Richard Scase in 1972 indicated that 93 per cent of all British manual workers believed that classes still existed in Britain; 29 per cent had an overall image of a two-class society, 60 per cent of a three-class society; 74·8 per cent identified both 'upper, top or higher classes' and the 'working class', and 75·6 per cent identified a 'middle class'; 69·8 per cent allocated themselves to the 'working class', 19·3 per cent to the 'middle class', 5 per cent to the 'lower class', 3·4 per cent to 'the poor', and 1·7 per cent declared themselves 'average people'. If any generalization can be made comparing working-class attitudes in the late forties with those of the seventies, it might be said that a certain optimism and sense of confidence in the former period had now been replaced by a sense of bloody-minded resignation and a feeling of 'once a worker always a worker' and why, anyway, aspire to anything better? Huw Beynon collected some characteristic remarks from Ford workers for his book *Working for Ford* (1973): 'It's the most boring job in the world,' said one:

It's the same thing over and over again. There's no change in it, it wears you out. It makes you awful tired. It slows your thinking right down. There's no need to think. It's just a formality. You just carry on. You just endure it for the money. That's what we're paid for – to endure the boredom of it.

If I had a chance to move I'd leave right away. It's the conditions here. Ford class you more as machines than men.

'It's strange this place,' said another:

It's got no really good points. It's just convenient. It's got no interest. You couldn't take the job home. There's nothing to take. You just forget it. I don't want promotion at all, I've not got that approach to the job. I'm like a lot of people here. They're all working here but they're just really hanging around, waiting for something to turn up . . . It's different for them in the office. They're *part* of Fords. We're not, we're just working here, we're numbers.

As the recession bit more and more deeply, it became as clear as ever it was that the working class is the most vulnerable in modern society. Individuals could escape out of the working class, and had increasingly been doing so over twenty years; but the success of isolated individuals does not affect the status and power of a whole class. However, it would be wrong to deny that the organized working class in Britain had greater power and influence than that in any other country in the world. Governments, whether they liked it or not, had to take into account the views of trade-union leaders. In ordinary industrial disputes, the bargaining power of unions was strong. Very largely, the Edward Heath Conservative ministry at the end of 1973 and the beginning of 1974 was destroyed because he foolishly involved himself in a confrontation with the miners. The Callaghan policies in trying to control inflation were only successful as long as he had the co-operation of the trade unions.

The summing-up, then, must be that class divisions had certainly proved remarkably enduring in Britain but that the lines, both between middle class, upper-middle class, and upper class, and between working class and middle class, were now less firm than ever they had been. Within the working class, the expansion of such occupations as that of lorry driver involved a real physical mobility and freedom uncharacteristic of traditional working-class jobs; the growth of white-coated occupations in the former heavy industries also produced a blurring of the line between working and middle class. In industrial confrontations the self-employed lorry driver, most certainly, allied himself against the organized working class. Yet at the same time unionization was expanding; unions themselves were ceasing to be an exclusive indicator of working-classness.

What, then, is the significance of class in contemporary British society? The study by Butler and Kavanagh of the general election of October 1974 indicated that Labour obtained 49 per cent of the skilled working-class vote, compared with 26 per cent for the Conservatives; and Labour got 57 per cent of the unskilled vote, compared with 22 per cent for the Conservatives. Class, then, remained an important factor in political allegiance.

It was also an important factor in the distribution of political power, as an analysis of the social composition of the first Thatcher Cabinet demonstrates. Margaret Thatcher herself is a symbol of the educational opportunity and upward mobility offered by the British system. From a lower-middle-class background (her father was a shopkeeper in Grantham), she went to a local grammar school and then on to Somerville College, Oxford. It might seem a pleasing portent of the times that hers was a science degree, and that she worked as a research chemist from 1947 to 1951. More significant really was the fact that in 1953 she became a barrister. And one cannot leave utterly out of account the fact that when she married her choice was a very wealthy second-generation businessman (by my definition, a member of the upper class). She herself remained ambivalently both subject to the allure of the upper class, and belligerently a representative of the hard-working middle class.

Nothing ambivalent about the next person in the political hierarchy, however. William Whitelaw (Home Secretary), described in *Who's Who* as a 'farmer and landowner', was educated at Winchester and Trinity College, Cambridge, becoming a regular officer in the Scots Guards; his eldest daughter married the second Earl of Swinton. Nor about the Lord Chancellor. Lord Hailsham had inherited a peerage, disclaimed it, then became a life peer. Educated at Eton, he took a double First (it is an absurd error to think of the upper class as stupid or indolent) at Christ Church, Oxford, and became a Fellow of All Souls, and a barrister. He was MP for Oxford at the age of thirty-one. Most secure of all in his position in the upper class was the Foreign Secretary, Lord Carrington, sixth in succession to a barony created in 1796 (in the Irish peerage) and 1797 (in the British peerage). His mother was the daughter of the second Viscount Colville and he himself married the daughter of Sir Francis McClean. Educated at Eton and Sandhurst, he achieved junior Government office at the age of thirty-two. His many directorships included Barclays, Rio Tinto Zinc, and Cadbury Schweppes. His country house is near Aylesbury, his town house in Chelsea.

The Chancellor of the Exchequer, Sir Geoffrey Howe, embodied the possibility of social mobility over three generations. His grandfather was working-class, a metal worker and union leader in South Wales. His father, a solicitor in Port Talbot, was comfortably middle-class. Howe won scholarships to Winchester and Trinity Hall, Cambridge, where he studied law. He became an extremely prosperous barrister, and received his knighthood in 1970.

Sir Keith Joseph, Secretary of State for Industry, confirmed the position his father, by founding the building firm of Bovis and becoming Lord Mayor of London, and, in 1943, a baronet, had won in the upper class. Joseph was educated at Harrow and Magdalen, Oxford, and, after distinguished war service, was elected a Fellow of All Souls. He became a barrister, and held directorships on Bovis and other companies. Francis Pym, Defence Secretary, is a prize example of the landed gentleman doing rather more than dabble in trade (as a manager with the department-store chain of Lewis's). Pym's father was a Conservative MP; he himself was educated at Eton and Magdalene, Cambridge; his clubs – Buck's, Cavalry, and Guards. The former Sir Christopher Soames (Lord President of the Council), created a life peer in 1978, was educated at Eton and Sandhurst, and married a daughter of Winston Churchill; his main directorships were in finance and banking.

In *Who's Who* James Prior (Employment Secretary) is described as a 'farmer and land agent', though he also held various directorships. After Charterhouse he took a First Class in Estate Management at Pembroke College, Cambridge. Sir Ian Gilmour (Lord Privy Seal) is the third holder of the baronetcy created in 1926. His mother was the daughter of Viscount Chelsea, eldest son of the fifth Earl of Cadogan, and he himself married Lady Caroline Margaret Montagu-Douglas Scott, daughter of the eighth Duke of Buccleuch and Queensberry. It is almost supererogatory to add that Gilmour was educated at Eton and Balliol. The working-class origins of Agriculture Secretary, Peter Walker, have already been mentioned. Walker won his way to a lesser public school, but did not go on to university. Doing well as a successful manager of broker and security companies he set himself up in landed property in Worcester, worth £80,000 in 1970.

Michael Heseltine, Environment Secretary, whose father was a Swansea colonel, was educated at Shrewsbury and Pembroke College, Oxford; his home outside Banbury visibly established him in that upper class whose existence Margaret Stacey had recognized in the first Banbury survey. Educated at Winchester and New College, Oxford, George Younger came from the Scottish brewing family of that name (less well known for its beer than the rival William Younger's, but famous for its close association with the Conservative Party). His father was the third Viscount Younger of Leckie and he himself held directorships in major brewing and whisky concerns. Nicholas Edwards, Secretary for Wales, a merchant banker, was educated at Westminster and Trinity College, Cambridge, and, in 1980, owned three houses, including a town house in Westminster. The Northern Ireland Secretary, Humphrey Atkins, was the son of a captain in 'Kenya Colony' (as *Who's Who* puts it) and was married to the daughter of Sir Robert Spencer-Nairn. Director of a firm of advertising agents, he was educated at Wellington whence he entered the Royal Navy; *Who's Who* lists his club as Brooks's.

Patrick Jenkin, Social Services Secretary, a barrister holding various directorships, was educated at Clifton and Jesus College, Cambridge. Norman St John-Stevas, leader of the House, was a new arrival in the upper class, his father having been a civil engineer and company director by the name of Stevas, who was able to send his son to Ratcliffe, whence he went to Fitzwilliam College, Cambridge, and then, after taking a First in law, to Christ Church, Oxford. St John-Stevas was for a time a university lecturer in law. John Nott, Trade Secretary, after Bradfield and Trinity College, Cambridge, went on to enjoy the gentlemanly occupations of barrister, merchant banker, and director of various manufacturing companies. David Howell (Energy Secretary), son of a colonel, and educated at Eton and King's College, Cambridge (where he took a First), had entered Parliament at the age of thirty; his club was Buck's.

Neither the Secretary for Education and Science (Mark Carlisle) nor the Chief Secretary to the Treasury (John Biffen) quite had the complete upper-class education of all of their other colleagues apart from Walker and the Prime Minister herself. Carlisle went from Radley College to Manchester University; Biffen started from Dr Morgan's Grammar School, Bridgwater, but arrived at Jesus College, Cambridge. However, the overwhelmingly upper-class composition of this cabinet was reasserted by the last figure on the list, Angus Maude (Paymaster General), a gentlemanly journalist, son of a colonel, educated at Rugby and Oriel College, Oxford, and owner of another of those country houses in the vicinity of Banbury.

The purpose of that quick series of potted biographies was not to pillory the Conservative Party but to indicate the continuing hold of the upper class on political power. True, there was considerably less evidence of upper-class political power in the previous Labour Cabinet; yet what is most significant is that in the avowedly *labour* party such upper-class figures as Michael Foot and Anthony Wedgwood Benn continued to be so important. Of the 1977 Cabinet a quarter had been educated at public schools and Oxford (or, in one case, Cambridge). Otherwise Labour at the top proved to be 'meritocratic' (to use the language of Dr Timothy May) middle-class, rather than working-class.

Was Britain approaching a condition of open class conflict? In the seventies the everyday cold war of the work place many times erupted into large-scale strikes. In January 1979 there were more workers out on strike than at any time since the General Strike of 1926. But there *was* no general strike (as, for single days at a time, there was in France). The British working class was, no more than before, committed to the theory of class conflict; but, for practical economic gains, it was, occupational group by occupational group, prepared to demonstrate both its strength and its sense of apartness from employers, Government, and middle-class society generally. (The point was driven home by the relative failure of the 'day of protest' against Thatcherite economic policies in May 1980.)

It has become a commonplace to attribute Britain's poor economic record to its being a 'class-ridden' society. The epithet is an ambiguous one. In France, to take one instance, the social gulf between management and workers is often at least as great as in Britain; there is more formality and more stress on the dignity of titles and status. There is less educational mobility than in Britain – fewer working-class children at university, for instance. Formality, to the extent of pomposity, is also a feature of American society. Yet it is true that the forms of class are, historically, more deeply entrenched in British society; they were not seriously challenged in the forties, when they might have been, and were only slightly modified in the sixties. In the end, formality and authority in other industrial-ized societies are related to function: a boss behaves like a boss because he is a boss. In Britain a boss behaves as he does because he belongs to, or has been socialized into, a particular social background.

In all the recent British industrial confrontations, the accents stick out: when an employer's representative opens his mouth he immediately associates himself, not so much with employers as such, but with the upper class; if he happens to have a working-class, or regional middle-class accent, we register that immediately. The pride, traditions, and class awareness of the British worker have, over a period extending back into the nineteenth century, brought him to a position where he wages a constant, but usually very mild, cold war against his employer on the factory floor itself. He expresses little ideological hos-tility to the employer, and no desire to expropriate him. Feeling no sense of inferiority, his instinct is to stick among his own kind. He feels little involvement in the success of the enterprise in which he works. The French worker is either much more ideologically committed than his British counterpart, or, committed solely to his family and private interests, he goes in for the occasional ritual protest, typically the one-day strike, but otherwise co-operates efficiently with his employer, either because the day of revolution has not yet come, or because he sees it as in his own private interest to do so. The difference here is not between class and absence of class, but between the different ways in which the historical conditioning of the exact nature of class and perceptions of two classes has taken place. In Britain, the persistence of upper-class power, and the advent of organized working-class power, means that there is a constant refrain of hostility towards the middle-class small businessman who only in the 1980 budget at last received the protection of special legislation.

The differences in social habits and culture are greatest in Britain. The British working man eats one kind of rubbish; many middle-class workers eat a similar, more expensively presented, form of rubbish; the upper class does retain some claim to good taste. Managers in Britain are often distinguished most by their clothes, accents, and manners; since these are their main qualifications, they go out of their way to stress them.

Class is a product of history. The particular nature of class relationships in Britain during the Second World War was probably to her advantage; in the 1970s they were very much to her disadvantage. But other factors come in. The British working class has never joined in the 'American' ethos of expansionism, preferring rather to stand on pride in itself and its older traditions. The quirks and trimmings of class are a British preoccupation, and, in the upper reaches, playing the right part has too often been more important than getting things done. The upper class continued to hold too much political power for too long in Britain because there was no effective challenge to it.

The model of class structure presented on contemporary British television is one which recognizes the existence of class differences, but which sees them as largely related to culture rather than power. Most programmes tend to be set within a self-contained cultural milieu, whether upper-class, middle-class, or working-class, with very little direct evidence of friction between different classes. Programmes presenting class conflict tend to be set in an earlier era.

The Butler and Kavanagh study of the October 1974 election brought out the continuing importance of class in voting preferences; but it also brought out that the single most significant factor now was race: 72 per cent of the 'coloured' vote went to Labour, with only 17 per cent going to the Conservatives. Was race now the single most significant divide in British society, eclipsing even the potency of class? One great irony, and perhaps a revealing one about British society, may be that while class was now being openly spoken about when it was no longer the supreme factor in social inequality that it had been in the 1930s, the well-bred reticence that once enveloped discussion of class had now switched itself to discussion of race, just when race was becoming an especially potent cause of inequality. In introducing a series of interviews made in the late seventies with West Indians living in London and published as *Black Testimony* (1978), an American sociologist, Thomas J. Cottle, remarked that:

In Great Britain there is too little discussion of racial matters; too much avoiding the matter in everyday discourse. To listen to some people is to believe there are no racial problems in the United Kingdom. To listen to others, is to hear the problem called minor, easily resolved, barely perplexing, or exaggerated, or subtle. It is none of these. No one who speaks with West Indian, Pakistani, Indian and Mauritian families living in England would call their circumstances minor, exaggerated, or subtle.

About the least combative attitude Cottle found was that of a labourer who admitted that his friends sometimes regarded him as 'being the good Nigger':

You think a white man's going to lose his job before a black one? Not in a life-time. Immigrants come last and go first, man. Everybody knows that. They start their layoffs and I'll be sitting home with my mother all day and talking with all these guys out of work. Then you'll see me talking politics. But what do I do to protect myself? I stay low and work until I drop. I don't let them think they can break me. They got to see how I'm a bull of a worker. And they'll tell you that too. In their minds, see, I'm just the smallest step up from being a slave. But in *my* mind, I know I'm earning what the next guy earns, the white guy, so I am no slave to *nobody*. To nobody, my friend. They can think *their* thoughts, and I'll think mine. I got the laugh so far because I am working, you see what I mean. They want to arrest me for thinking they're all a bunch of racists? hell, they might just as well go arrest every black man and woman in Britain, child too, believe me. These kids know where it's at.

A thirteen-year-old was rather more cynical:

Where's anything going to change for us? Where am I going to get money to help my mother and grandmother? What do you think my brothers can do about anything? Even if they can, it's a lot of years before any of us will be old enough to do anything. We ain't moving at all, man. The country seems to be slowing down too, these days, but families like mine, we haven't moved anywhere for a long, long time already. And see now what happens. My father can't find work over here, work he's fitted for, something he can do well. Are they keeping him from the good jobs because he's black? I'd say yes, sure they are. But how you going to prove it? How can you prove to these boards they have that this person or that person didn't get a job because they were black? Board people are just going to say, look around at all the white men out of work; who didn't give *them* jobs because of the colour of their skin? Or they'll say, look around where you live and you'll find men like your father working. Maybe it's your father. You can't prove these things to anybody. Board people work for the government. They don't make their own rules. The law says everybody has an equal chance, but anybody can see that's a lie.

A school-leaver unable to find employment remonstrated with his father:

If you don't even read the newspapers to find out what kids like me are going through now I pity you. What the hell you think this is all about, man? You think this is a game I am playing, running all over this city begging people to make up work for me to do? Deliver little parcels for them or wipe up floors? You think it's going to get better, that suddenly the government's going to hand down a million new jobs for people? You know what they got planned? They got this thing so worked out it makes me sick. They got a plan that all the little coloured kids, we're told to leave school and think about jobs and making money. Then you know what happens? A few of us get our little rotten work so we're helping them, right? But the most of us, we don't get anything.

Shortly this youth took to organized car stealing and was later sent to borstal.

Many West Indians had a clear picture of how they believed individual whites saw them:

> You are unwanted. You are here because some higher order official let you stay, not because I want you. Yet it is my position and not the official's position that is threatened by your presence, your very being. You should have been stopped before you arrived, you should be sent back even if you have been here for a while. You only create problems. You want my job, you want my food, you want to live in my home, you want to use my school, my hospital, my stores. But don't take it personally; I have no quarrel with you as a person. It's immigration I cannot tolerate.

Cottle also recorded the views of a fifty-year-old white dairy worker from the Midlands:

> It is a crime, all of it. First they come here where they don't belong, and they know it. Then they want their relatives and their relatives' relatives. And would you believe, the government lets them have anything they wish, at any time they wish. But help those of us already here? no, they haven't an ear for that. I suppose the next step will be the government telling us *we* don't belong here anymore because we're sixth generation, or tenth generation. All you have to do is look at a map and you can see how small the country is. There isn't any room for these people. The laws on immigration are so confused the MPs themselves haven't a clue to what they mean. But they turn their back on it. They just turn their back on it. But help the people who've been here these hundreds of years? oh no. We're the new immigrants. I see what happens in countries where all of this has taken place. This isn't new to the world, you know. But can we learn from it, do you suppose? I should have thought so, but I am pessimistic about it now. I don't see but that they've let it go on too long. They should never have let in those people, people who make all these demands, and complain about their circumstances. There are no jobs for them, no money, the schools are crowded where their children go. It's no good at all.

Then, more emphatically, this white testimony continued:

> They're going to bring down this country if they're not careful. They'll topple it. The rich will leave and the rest of us will go it alone with them. It will come down. You remember what I tell you. But

there will be blood before it happens because people here won't take it. We've asked for nothing special, but we'll start asking now. That's the only way to stand up to this. You know, I talk about this and I feel my body reacting to those people. It's not just my mind. It's my whole person. Oh, you'll see changes now. They've already started

West Indians quite clearly felt that racist attitudes in white society spread far beyond the small minority who through the National Front openly advocated violent confrontation with immigrant communities. Much of the National Front support came in decaying urban areas where there were large immigrant populations. Among Jeremy Seabrook's interviewees was one who readily explained why he fought for the National Front:

I don't want parts of my country to become no-go areas, where I feel I can't walk without the risk of being knifed or mugged. I don't want to be with black people, I don't want a multi-racial country. Why should I? I've got nothing in common with them, they don't want to mix with me anymore than I do with them. Why should I be forced to live with them? I want to be able to go into a pub, I want to be able to go to work without seeing a black face. The National Front is saying the sort of things I want to hear. I wouldn't be cruel. If I ran over a black in my car, I wouldn't just leave him lying in the road; I'd kick him into the gutter. I don't want them here. I want them to leave. I understand that this might be a bit disruptive. If the barricades do go up, it won't be the middle class on one side and the working class on the other; it'll be white on one side and black on the other, with just a few race traitors on their side. I want to be just with our own. I don't want to live in a system that falls over itself to favour blacks. If there's anything going in this country, I want it for myself. We've suffered enough in the past, and now it's our turn. We've had one flabby government after another saying, 'We've got to learn to live together.' Well, why? They don't have to live with them, killing goats, wailing at dusk and fasting and being a nuisance.

Predictions about the likelihood of serious racial violence went back some time. The report of the Hunt Committee on Immigrants in the Youth Service back in 1967 had declared that 'If England is not to be the scene of race riots' then 'the time for action is now'. 'Tomorrow', it concluded, would be 'too late'. In 1976, Mark Bonham-Carter, Chairman of the Com-

munity Relations Commission, warned that Britain's black
population, 40 per cent of whom were born in Britain, would
not settle for second-class citizenship 'in exchange for a higher
standard of living and the prospect of some employment. They
are British, and they take the phrase "equality of opportunity"
for what it means. I have no doubt we have not kept pace
with the expectations of British-born blacks.' At this very time,
the Callaghan Labour Government did introduce a new Race
Relations Act which declared all forms of discrimination illegal,
and set up a Commission for Racial Equality with powers of
enforcement. Some commentators took the view that it is not
possible to legislate for people's attitudes. However, legislation
is important for establishing what is held to be the norm of
correct behaviour in any society.

The basic problems were appalling housing, lack of job opportunities, particularly for the young, the mistrust felt between
immigrant communities and the police, and, more simply, the
ineluctable vagaries of human behaviour. On the last point one
can again quote Cottle's 'good Nigger':

There are four pubs around here where some of the men go for
lunch or after work. All I have to do is put my head through
the door of all those places and I know I'm not wanted in there. So
I don't go. You think I don't know I should, that I have to go in
there if I want things to open up in Britain? A good-looking black
girl, she can go in there, they'll be happy to have her maybe. But a
dirty worker, man from the local construction site, black man, they
don't want him, so I am glad to sit in the car and talk, because lunch-
time is when the segregation of staff starts up all over again.

There is abundant evidence on the penultimate, and more
critical, point: almost every black felt himself to be a potential
'sus' (suspect) and to be subject to constant police harassment.
The police, indeed, had problems of their own and the National
Police Federation Conference in 1971, devoted to community
relations, spoke feelingly of the police being placed on top of a
pressure cooker.

The complicated and ambivalent nature of relationships
between the police and immigrant communities was brought
out at successive Bank Holiday West Indian festivals at Notting
Hill. There was evidence there, as elsewhere, of genuine police

attempts at fraternization. But there was also appalling violence, thieving, and destruction of property. Community leaders claimed that by their very presence in force the police provoked violence. The police claimed that their very presence was essential to restrain criminality. On the late afternoon of Wednesday, 2 April 1980, and on into the night, a police raid on a club in the poverty-stricken St Paul's district of Bristol led to rioting in which nineteen policemen and six other people were taken to hospital, and in which a bank, other buildings, and police cars were burnt out, with at the same time much looting and vandalism. At one stage the police had been forced to withdraw totally from the area, before coming back with heavy reinforcements. The riot was said not to be a race riot, but one against the police: many of those arrested were white.

It must always be remembered that the immigrant communities themselves are not homogeneous. Ironically, the most energetic and aggressive group, the West Indians, were probably in many ways the most assimilable; it was the Indians and the Pakistanis, generally industrious, often prosperous, and frequently high achievers at school, who more obviously presented the alien ways which stuck in the craw of xenophobic Britons. On 23 April 1979 the National Front deliberately held a meeting in the Town Hall of Southall, a predominantly Asian community in West London. Four thousand policemen were drafted in to confront 3,000 anti-National Front demonstrators. A large number of these were Asians, but there were also many whites; and it was a white teacher, Blair Peach, who was killed that day, quite possibly at the hands of a member of the Metropolitan Special Patrol Group.

Race might well be seen, then, as a more significant, and certainly more dangerous, divide in British society than class. By contrast, the fury of nationalism was much abated. The Scottish National Party did stunningly well in the October 1974 election: gaining eleven seats, it also put at risk a further thirty-five Labour-held seats and seven Conservative seats. While the issue was far less clear-cut in Wales, it certainly seemed throughout most of the seventies that devolution must be granted to Scotland if total separation was to be avoided. Yet when the referendum came in March 1979, only 32 per cent of the Scots (a clear majority of those voting, though, it should be stressed) and 12 per cent of the Welsh actually voted for devolution. Such issues, it was clear, were still minor compared with older class, newer race, and universal economic questions.

At the end of 1973 and the beginning of 1974 press, television, and political platforms were dominated by the question 'Is Britain ungovernable?'. The year 1974 was indeed unprecedented for violent death on the British mainland; that fact, taken along with the miners' strike of 1973–4, the gathering race problem, and the apparent strength of Scottish and Welsh separatism, did suggest that perhaps traditional British social cohesion was breaking down at last. In July 1974 an IRA bomb attack at the Tower of London killed one woman and badly injured forty-one children. In October and November there were IRA pub bombings near army barracks in Guildford and Woolwich: seven were killed. Then at Birmingham in November, in a horrific pub holocaust, twenty-one were killed and 162 injured. The forty-fifth fatality occurred in June 1974, in Red Lion Square, London, Kevin Gateley being killed when a Trotskyist counter-demonstration met a National Front demonstration. Actually, the worst violence associated with a mining strike had taken place in February 1972 at the Saltley Coke Depot, Birmingham: in 1973–4 the mine workers' leaders deliberately enforced restraint upon their pickets. The other violent industrial event of the early seventies was associated with the building workers' strike in the summer of 1972, and arose out of the primitive sub-contracting conditions in that industry, known as 'the lump': the menacing intimidation carried through by pickets at Shrewsbury resulted in three prison sentences. What really made 1974 such a bloody year was the activity of the IRA; hence the enactment of the 1974 Prevention of Terrorism Act.

British attitudes towards the Irish had always been, to say the least, ambivalent. Throughout the period studied by this book Irish jokes based on the premiss of the utter stupidity of the Irish were rampant (for example, an Irishman is asked to explain why he signs his name with three crosses: the first two are for 'Patrick Murphy'; the third, it transpires, is 'for my degree from University College, Dublin'). Most Britons did not discriminate very closely between citizens of the Irish Republic and citizens of Northern Ireland. As violence escalated, the attitude revealed in public opinion polls was very much that of 'a plague upon both your houses'. A clear majority believed that British troops should be withdrawn from Northern Ireland allowing both factions, increasingly perceived in Britain as illiterate bigots, to fight things out for themselves.

In Britain violence broke out again in June and July of 1977, during a strike at the Grunwick film-processing factory in West London. Grunwick was run by a tough self-made small businessman, himself of Asian origins; his factory largely employed Asian labour. The attempt at Grunwick to secure basic trade-union conditions for the employees became a *cause célèbre* of the left, bringing in not just Trotskyites, but also respectable leaders of the Labour Party. 'This is the Ascot of the left,' one demonstrator declared. 'It is essential to be seen here, best of all to get arrested.' During the most violent phases, ninety-seven policemen were injured, one very seriously by a milk bottle.

The factors, then, which contributed to the 'ungovernability' thesis, or at least to the view that traditional British tolerance and non-violence were breaking down, were: Edward Heath's failed confrontation with the miners in 1973–4; IRA terror attacks (involving in 1977 the death of a distinguished surgeon, and in 1979 of a leading Conservative politician, Airey Neave); the abandonment by public workers of older civic restraints upon their right to strike (putting patients' lives in danger, for instance); the activities of the National Front; the counter-activities, and involvement in strikes, of Trotskyist groups; the development of the tactic of the flying picket; and the increasing use at demonstrations of the Metropolitan Police Special Patrol Group. There were ugly new scars on the face of British society, to be sure. But against these can be placed trade-union restraint and the social contract observed between 1976 and 1978. And even in the gloomy year of 1980, talk of ungovernability and insurrection had rather less plausibility than it had had in 1974.

14. *Living Standards*

Year by year throughout the 1970s the Central Statistical Office publication *Social Trends* contained special articles on aspects of recent social history. In 1975, in keeping with what was said in the previous chapter of the way in which class now dared to speak its name, the article was 'Social Class'. The 1980 edition, the tenth issue, featured an article, 'Changes in Living Standards Since the 1950s', which covered both 'material living standards' and 'the rôle of publicly provided services'; in, therefore, borrowing for the title of this chapter the rather colourless phrase 'living standards' I shall be putting together topics 5 and 6 of my original list of major areas of social change: social welfare and material conditions. The article itself is very far from gloomy, the tone being set by a cover drawing in which a family of six, perched on a ration book dated 1951, give place to a family of four wheeling a supermarket trolley full of provisions. 'Consumerism' – the growth of supermarkets, the availability of credit for the purchase of durable consumer goods, and, latterly, the use of credit cards for the whole gamut of purchases from alcohol to dining-room suites – was indeed a central phenomenon of the age.

Tory radicals in the 1960s had argued that as society became more affluent the need for the Welfare State would wither away. In actual fact, as the majority grew more affluent the needs of the individuals and groups left behind were more sharply revealed. Conservative and Labour spokesmen voiced differences over the respective weighting to be given to collectivist initiatives or market forces in the provision of welfare facilities; but as far as welfare policies affected individual members of society there was striking continuity between the policies of the Labour Government which fell in 1970, the Heath Conservative Government which fell in 1974, and the Wilson and Callaghan Labour administrations which lasted till

1979. Just how far the Thatcher Conservative administration after 1979 is bringing about fundamental policy changes (as distinct from changes imposed by financial stringency) it is as yet too early to say. Over the major part of the decade (and on into the 1980s, I personally would hazard) social policy was determined by six main factors. First, there was the developing awareness of the new types of personal deprivation constantly being revealed in a high-spending consumer society. Secondly, there was a new and far more sophisticated approach to the problem of job protection, deriving partly from a recognition that too often in the recent past working-class jobs had remained rather less secure than any others. Thirdly, in a time of mounting inflation, more elaborate attention was given to the question of income protection. Fourthly, basically on grounds of administrative and financial efficiency, there were alterations in administrative structures (in part related to local government reform) and attempts to avoid making superfluous benefit payments. Fifthly, a factor running against the first three, and in some respects the fourth as well, a worsening economic situation enforced greater attention to questions of economy. Sixthly, demographic changes, and above all the slowing-down in population growth in the middle of the decade, forced changes in broad planning targets and priorities.

Within the realm of income maintenance and social security, the major piece of legislation, the Social Security Act passed by the Heath Conservative Government in 1973, was essentially a consolidating Act. As far as recipients were concerned, not a great deal changed when the provisions of the new Act came into force in January 1976. Income loss due to unemployment continued to be covered through Unemployment Benefit, dependent upon the payment of National Insurance contributions, and Supplementary Benefits. To qualify for Unemployment Benefit the unemployed person must have paid, or been credited with, fifty weekly contributions in the previous calendar year. Payment does not begin till after three days of unemployment and ceases after one year, though eligibility for benefit can be reviewed after the payment of thirteen contributions. The Earnings Related Supplement does not become payable till after two weeks of unemployment and ends after twenty-six weeks. Where there is no entitlement to Unemployment Benefit, or where such entitlement has become exhausted, Supplementary Benefits come into play, as they do also if a man's National Insurance benefit is below the Supplementary Benefit scale, though, where relevant, the wage stop is applied. Penalties apply where unemployment is voluntary or due to misconduct or where, in the case of a single man, other employment in the area is available. In the former two cases a disqualification for six weeks can apply; in the latter the single man can be refused benefit after four weeks. Though persons on strike could not themselves receive Unemployment Benefit or Supplementary Benefit they could, and this was a matter on which some Conservatives became increasingly outspoken, receive such benefits on behalf of their dependants.

The rather unsatisfactory Redundancy Payment Scheme of 1965 remained in force; but with, after 1974, a new range of devices designed to protect employment, or at least income. The major innovation was the Employment Protection Act of 1975 whose provisions covered the right not to be unfairly dismissed, entitlements to a written statement of terms and conditions of employment, guaranteed pay, time off work for trade-union duties, and also redundancy pay, minimum periods of notice, and maternity rights. It also covered suspension from work on medical grounds and an employee's rights when the employer becomes insolvent. The Act, as we have seen from Chapter 12, could not act as a bulwark against industrial recession. Nor could various job creation schemes, including the Employment Subsidies Act of 1978, whereby payments were made to employers to enable them to retain or recruit employees, reverse the tide. The Labour Government sought to achieve the aim of income maintenance in old age through linking social security pensions to the cost of living index, and through pressing for the adoption of private schemes whose basic feature was the provision of a pension related to the level of earnings on retirement (such as, for instance, the Universities Superannuation Scheme – USS – in replacement of the older FSSU scheme).

Sickness benefits, for which the self-employed as well as the employed make contributions and therefore are covered, are paid on a rate related to earnings for twenty-six weeks, after which there is an inexhaustible invalidity benefit paid at the basic sickness benefit rate. In practice there are considerable inequalities in the way different social classes are treated, it being quite customary in professional middle-class employments for sick employees to go on being paid their salary, whereas manual workers become immediately dependent upon social security benefits. Employed women who pay the full rate of National Insurance contributions are entitled to maternity benefit enabling them to stay off work for some time before and after confinement. On the birth of a child a maternity grant can be paid provided either the father or the mother has an adequate record of National Insurance payments.

Those disabled at work receive Industrial Injuries Benefits. Otherwise, the disabled have to depend upon Supplementary Benefits subject to a needs test. From October 1972 Attendance Allowances have been payable to those forced to give special attention to the disabled. A unique product of the Heath Conservative Government's desire to bring back some voluntary element into the Welfare State was the provision in 1973 of £3 million to set up the Family Fund, administered by the Joseph Rowntree Memorial Trust on behalf of the Government, to provide grants to the parents of children under sixteen suffering from severe congenital handicaps. For the first six months after widowhood the Earnings Related Widows Allowance is paid at a rate higher than the basic Unemployment and Sickness benefits. What happens after six months depends on the age and responsibilities of the widow. The needs of widows and orphans may also be covered by occupational pension schemes. As a general rule these various benefits come to an end if the widow re-marries, or, more unsatisfactorily, if she is deemed to be cohabiting with a man. Though stuffiness, and even harshness, continued in regard to the vexed question of cohabitation, there was a general humanizing of attitude towards single-parent families. Where a woman was entitled to maintenance, but was finding difficulty in actually getting it, the Department of Health and Social Security would pay Supplementary Benefits at the full rate and then endeavour to recover the maintenance payments itself. In the administration of Family Income Supplement, a non-contributory

scheme introduced by the Heath administration to provide benefits for low-income families with dependent children, single-
parent families were treated on a level with two-parent ones.

Though social security was undoubtedly patchy and inadequate in certain areas, Government commitment in this area
did not in any way contract in the 1970s. Even making allowances for inflation, the actual increase in Government expenditure is made very clear from Table 4.

Changes in the National Health Service very much follow
the same pattern. The major Act, again passed by the Heath
Conservative Government, was the National Service Reorganization Act of 1973: however, services for the consumer, as
a leading authority has put it, 'have not changed. Patients see
the same family doctors and attend the same hospitals to see
the same specialists.' The essence of the re-organization was the
replacement of the much criticized tripartite structure set up by
the Act of 1946 by what was intended to be a more unified
system, but which, in the upshot, proved more complex and
bureaucratic than the old structure. At the top, there was still
the Secretary of State, advised by the Central Health Services
Council and served by the officers of the Department of Health
and Social Security. At the next level all services were integrated within the fourteen Regional Health Authorities. As part
of an intended move towards efficiency and greater professionalization, the chairmen of these Authorities are paid; and
advice is provided by the Regional Advisory Committees,
representing the Health Services' staff, and given statutory
recognition. Thirdly come the ninety Area Health Authorities,
which took over all the functions of the old Hospital Management Committees and Local Executive Councils, as well as
most of those of the local authorities. Chairmen are appointed
by the Secretary of State, the rest of the members being
appointed by local authorities, universities, and the regional
health authorities, and have to include at least one doctor and
one nurse. Unfortunately there was a serious and disruptive
mis-match between these Area Health Authorities and the new
local government units.

The miracle of the National Health Service, if newspapers
and television were anything to go by, was not that it did so

Table 4: Government expenditure on social security benefits

Central government current expenditure	Year ended 31 March										£ million
	1968/9	1969/70	1970/71	1971/2	1972/3	1973/4	1974/5	1975/6	1976/7	1977/8	1978/9
National insurance:											
Retirement pensions*	1,578	1,663	1,818	2,092	2,422	2,894	3,751	4,898	5,777	6,739	7,719
Widows' benefits and guardians' allowances	159	168	174	203	228	254	323	409	451	485	525
Unemployment benefit	132	135	158	250	219	182	227	473	582	655	660
Sickness benefit	362	401	394	338	306	325	372	460	538	636	688
Invalidity benefit	—	—	—	96	208	255	339	475	596	740	887
Maternity benefit	39	39	42	44	44	44	48	57	84	96	126
Death grant	11	12	11	13	13	14	14	15	15	16	16
Injury benefit	35	34	33	32	33	35	36	40	47	51	52
Disablement benefit	63	64	69	75	83	92	116	152	175	200	226
Industrial death benefit	8	9	9	10	12	14	18	23	26	30	31
War pensions	124	124	127	136	150	164	204	258	283	310	340
Family allowances	310	354	354	359	354	359	359	554	567	906	1,858
Supplementary benefits:											
Old persons	215	233	253	286	285	284	318	419	491	644	757
Unemployed persons	79	80	95	155	191	150	200	381	575	579	706
Sick persons	72	76	81	84	85	96	118	129	134	152	159
Other persons in need	80	100	115	140	154	185	237	306	387	452	484
Other non-contributory benefits:											
Old persons' pensions	—	—	8	24	28	29	32	36	38	38	37
Family income supplement	—	—	—	5	11	14	14	14	20	28	30
Attendance allowance	—	—	—	6	25	38	66	102	136	175	193
Mobility allowance	—	—	—	—	—	—	—	—	8	21	72
Invalidity pension	—	—	—	—	—	—	—	12	37	48	126
Lump sums to pensioners	—	—	—	—	81	3	3	—	—	98	—
Administration	143	167	186	230	246	292	376	538	608	675	747
Total government expenditure	3,410	3,659	3,927	4,578	5,178	5,723	7,171	9,751	11,575	13,874	16,490

*Including lump sum payments to pensioners amounting to £79 million in 1973/4 and £90 million in 1974/5

Source: Central Statistical Office

much but that it managed to survive at all: the rumbling malaise of the sixties, apparently, had become feverish crisis. The facts and figures are less conclusive. All had never been completely well with the National Health Service – has it ever been with health provision anywhere in the world? The tale of the seventies is a mixed one: advances in some areas, retreats in others, but certainly not one of unrelieved gloom. Crude international comparisons show Britain spending a lower proportion of the National Income on health than other industrialized countries. Yet anyone who has encountered the sheer terror with which the prospect of hospitalization is faced in many walks of life in North America, or anyone, even, who has encountered the system of retrospective reimbursement of medical expenses to be found on the European Continent, will be hard put to it to maintain that Britain has inferior services. It is true that qualified medical staff are poorly paid in Britain compared with their counterparts overseas; it is also true that the British service is rather heavily dependent at various levels upon immigrant personnel: the passing of the Medical Act 1978 implicitly recognized that some Asian doctors were not as well qualified in all aspects as they ought to have been.

In general, the National Health Service in the later seventies was distinguished by greater participation at local level than ever before, though most informed commentators doubted whether more efficient management had been achieved. The general practitioner service improved throughout the decade: in 1973 there were 2,386 patients per doctor; in 1978 2,312 (2,148 in Wales and 1,875 in Scotland). On the other hand, the number of fully staffed hospital beds was in decline: 437,000 in 1973 to 395,000 in England and Wales in 1978. The average length of time that people spent in hospital fell, and the average number of patients in hospital each day fell from 436,000 in 1971 to 380,000 in 1978. Taking a longer time-span the number of people treated as in-patients rose from about 5 million in 1961 to over 6·6 million in 1977. In general, waiting-lists steadily lengthened, though there were fluctuations: the total queue in 1976 was 722,000, which actually fell to 715,000 in 1977, before rising to 801,000 in 1978. Total public expenditure on the Health Services rose by 10 per cent at constant prices between

1973–4 and 1978–9, but an alarming and accelerating proportion of expenditure was going on drugs and other medicines. The share of the pharmaceutical services rose by 17·4 per cent between 1951 and 1978. In the same period the shares taken by the general medical, the dental, and the ophthalmic services fell by 5·8, 7·3, and 4·3 per cent respectively. From the middle seventies contraceptives became free through the National Health Service, though the problem remained that too few people availed themselves of this facility. In the opinion of most experts the reformed abortion law of the sixties was now working humanely and under effective supervision, and was much in the interests of the health and well-being of women in general. Equally, a major aim of the National Health Service was that all women having their first babies should have them in hospital. In 1960, 66 per cent of all births had been in hospital; by 1977, 98 per cent of all births were in hospital, and practically all women having their first babies had the confinement there.

Attempts at developing private medical services had not been strikingly successful in the 1960s. Now, in a time of constant rumours of crisis, long waiting-lists, official encouragement to employers to provide welfare schemes, and the new conception of unions, particularly among professional workers, as corporations representing all the interests of their members, there was up to 1975, and again after 1977, a great increase in private medical care through group schemes (though, at the same time, there was actually a slight decline in the number of individual subscribers). Group health schemes contained about 672,000 subscribers in 1978, with most or all of the contributions being paid by employers. Many of these schemes covered dependants, so that, in all, company health insurance schemes were covering about 2·4 million people. Private hospitals and nursing homes contained about 34,500 beds (many of these for the use of wealthy overseas, rather than British, patients).

In 1945 the fundamental housing problem had been that too many people did not have a home of their own, that too many people were crammed into decaying, inadequate properties: in short, that there were too few houses and too many of these were below the standard proper to a civilized community. By

1980 there were, in global terms, more dwellings than there were households and the vast majority of the population did have the basic facilities of inside toilet, bathroom, and so on. The characteristic slums of this era were the heartless public housing estates built in the fifties and sixties and now stuck on a descending spiral into Hades as, a natural target for frustration and vandalism, they increasingly became dumping grounds for problem families. Authority recognized the problem, as authority for a hundred years had recognized the problem of the traditional slums. On paper, new policies of conservation and renovation, and, indeed, of evacuation and even destruction of housing stock less than a quarter of a century old, were now in force, but, alas, the massive sums necessary to remedy the sins of yesterday were not available. The main concern in the post-war years had been with providing housing for the working class as a class: by the late seventies, as was the case in so many other aspects of welfare policy, the problem was no longer seen as a class one, but as one relating to distinctive deprived groups, in this case, black and Asian immigrants, the homeless, and gypsies.

Throughout the United Kingdom in 1978 there were about 19,901,000 households while at the same time the actual number of separate dwellings totalled 21,101,000. In every region there existed more dwellings than families to fill them, though in London the margin was very narrow indeed. Yet many people seeking homes were unable to find them. The trouble was that, as a survey carried out in 1977 indicated, there were about 729,000 dwellings standing empty for various reasons: around 127,000 were being converted or modernized and were therefore uninhabitable; a sizable number of the remainder belonged to those prosperous enough to own second homes.

House building danced in erratic time with the economy. In 1968 413,700 houses had been built. In 1971 the figure was 350,600, in 1972 319,300, in 1973 294,100, in 1974 269,500, in 1975 313,000, in 1976 315,200, in 1977 302,700, and in 1978 279,200. Within these figures there was a significant shift away from public construction to private construction. In 1978 152,000 houses were built within the private sector and only 136,000 in the public sector. Owner-occupation was on the advance, as the figures for the different types of tenure in Table 5 show.

Table 5: Stock of dwellings: change and tenure

| Stock of dwellings – at end of period (millions): | 1951–60 | 1961–70 | 1971–4 | 1975 | Thousands and millions | | |
					1976	1977	1978
Owner-occupied	6·97	9·57	10·57	10·76	10·96	11·16	11·39
Rented from local authorities or new town corporations	4·40	5·85	6·09	6·40	6·56	6·70	6·79
Rented from private owners	4·31 }	3·77	3·42	3·19	3·09	3·01	2·93
Tied accommodation	0·93 }						
Total	16·60	19·18	20·10	20·35	20·61	20·86	21·11

Source: *Social Trends* (1980)

Again we must remember the variousness of British social geography. Whereas in the country as a whole 54 per cent of dwellings were owner-occupied, with 32 per cent rented from local authorities, and 14 per cent from private owners, the figure for owner-occupation was as high as 62 per cent in south-eastern areas outside of Greater London (where it was only 48 per cent) and 63 per cent in the South-West; in Scotland, the only part of the United Kingdom where local authority housing at 54 per cent accounted for more than half of all dwellings, it was only 35 per cent. There was, of course, a correlation between housing type and social class. But more and more the line of demarcation was occurring within the working class itself. Skilled workers were joining with the professionals in buying houses; more and more it was unskilled workers who formed council tenants.

There are simple measurements of housing standards. A dwelling is judged to be overcrowded if it falls below the 'bedroom standard'. This standard allows one bedroom for each married couple, one each for other men and women aged twenty-one or over, one each for two people of the same sex aged ten–twenty, one for any person aged ten–twenty together with a child under ten of the same sex, and one for any person aged ten–twenty not covered by the above, with one for each two of any remaining children and one for any child remaining. Other major indicators of below-standard housing are the lack of the sole use of a bath or shower and the lack of the sole use of a W C inside the building. A new indicator, and very much a sign of the times, was that of whether or not the house had central heating. As Table 6 shows, there has been considerable all-round improvement since 1971.

Overcrowding and lack of amenities were most heavily concentrated in immigrant households. Overcrowding was more prevalent in Scotland than elsewhere in Britain; but on the whole, largely because of the high proportion of recent public authority housing, Scotland was well off for basic amenities.

A number of pressures combined to push immigrants into the worst decaying areas, often ones scheduled for eventual demolition. Public concern over the special problem of the homeless, officially defined as those housed in local authority temporary accommodation, came to a head in 1974. A number of voluntary organizations, such as Shelter, had already come into being in the 1960s. In 1974, following a recommendation made in the Seebohm Report on the homeless, practical responsibility for providing accommodation for the homeless was vested in the housing authorities rather than the Social Services. The 1974 Government circular 'Homelessness' urged local authorities to work closely with the voluntary housing movement and be ready to make loans or grants to help them. Finally, increasing attention was given in the seventies to the plight of gypsies. Although the Caravan Sites Act of 1968 appeared to require local authorities to provide sites for gypsies, in fact most local authorities took advantage of the exemptions in the Act. All indications suggested that the number of travellers and gypsies was on the increase.

For much of the population, however, the crucial problem was the gigantic inflation in house prices through the 1970s. Although modest Government and local authority support was given to some first-time house-buyers, at no time did the number of mortgages available match the demand. If all forms of public expenditure on housing, including loans and grants in the private sector as well as subsidies to public-sector housing, are

Table 6: Housing standards: by tenure, 1971 and 1978

Percentages

	Percentage of households								Total sample size (= 100%)	
	below bedroom standard		lacking sole use of				with central heating			
			bath/shower		wc inside building					
	1971	1978	1971	1978	1971	1978	1971	1978	1971	1978
Owned outright	3	2	12	5	13	6	39	52	2,654	2,634
Owned with mortgage or loan	4	3	4	2	5	2	57	73	3,206	3,478
All owner-occupiers	4	3	7	3	9	3	49	64	5,860	6,109
Rented from local authority/New Town	10	6	3	2	5	2	24	43	3,691	3,999
Rented privately unfurnished	8	4	33	19	37	18	15	28	2,043	1,309
Rented privately furnished	19	14	58	52	57	51	17	27	320	283
All tenures	7	4	12	6	13	6	34	52	11,914	11,700

Source: *Social Trends* (1980)

taken together, such expenditure was in 1978–9 15 per cent up on 1973–4, 8 per cent down on 1976–7, and 3 per cent up on 1977–8.

Of all the major issues of social policy in the seventies, education engendered most controversy. The Labour Government after 1974 pushed forward vigorously with its policy of directly absorbing public-sector grammar schools into comprehensive schools and indirectly pressuring 'independent' schools to do the same by withdrawing their 'direct grants'. With various degrees of intensity Conservatives opposed this universalist policy, as indeed did some Labour supporters when faced, as parents, with the problem that overall social good might conflict with the educational prospects of their child. In fact, the debate over whether or not the absorption of grammar schools into comprehensive schools meant a lowering of standards or not was a confused one. Alas, both sides seemed more concerned to make a case than to get at objective facts. But whether well-founded or not, fears were spreading among parents and educationists alike that standards in British schools were not as high as they might be. Independent schools now had to charge far higher fees but, along with the public schools, they tended to prosper as it became clear that many parents would prefer to buy their way out of a state system which they increasingly distrusted. The Labour Party at last brought positive proposals for ending the privileged position of the public schools into its programme; though once more, between 1974 and 1979, nothing was actually done. Labour, at the very least, could be accused of inconsistency, and indeed of a hostility towards the middle class, thrown into relief by its tenderness towards the upper class, when in pushing through its policies of making the entire state secondary system comprehensive, it left open increasingly expensive independent and public schools for the privileged to escape to.

The arguments for a universal comprehensive system, as with the arguments for a universalist national health service, are very strong indeed. But they become seriously weakened when loopholes are left. Beyond that, it became apparent that, as in the United States, comprehensive schools in certain better-off areas had higher standards than comprehensive schools in impoverished areas. Thus, the comprehensive principle in itself was very far from abolishing inequalities. Altogether the total number of school pupils declined slightly after 1977, which would probably stand out as the peak year of the century, to 11,221,000. Of these 614,000 were in assisted or independent schools.

At another level, probably the most serious educational problem towards the end of the decade was the high level of teacher unemployment and of unemployment among the academically qualified in general. Even before the return of the Thatcher Government in 1979 public-spending cuts were affecting all aspects of higher and further education, as well as schooling in general. If public expenditure at constant prices on education is taken as 100 for 1977–8, it had stood at 102 in 1973–4, 104 in 1976–7, and was slightly up again to 102 in 1978–9, before the more drastic cuts struck.

In introducing the concept of the Welfare State as it emerged in the post-war years, I suggested that apart from the four major areas of social concern, a welfare state could also be taken to embrace a miscellaneous range of other pieces of social legislation. Such other legislation, indeed, indicates changes in the areas of social concern. In the 1970s, apart from questions of race and sex discrimination which I deal with elsewhere, the major special concerns were with the environment and consumer protection. Under the latter head, one might note the Control of Pollution Act 1974, the Community Land Act 1975, and the Inner Urban Areas Act 1978, designed to assist the regeneration of inner-city areas; and under the second head, such legislation as the Consumer Safety Act of 1978.

If we take together the economic and geographical aspects discussed in Chapter 12 together with the social policy issues just discussed, we arrive at the actual living conditions of British people in this period. Broadly, British people in the late seventies were healthier and had higher life expectancy than ever before, but one or two killers of the contemporary age were strengthening their grip, particularly cancer and heart disease.

On the vexed matter of real income the long-term perspective is well worth bearing in mind. Using 1975 prices, average earnings for a man in manual work rose from the equivalent of £31 a week to £54 a week between 1951 and 1975. The proportionate increase for women was rather greater. Put another way, a manual worker with average earnings would have had to work thirty-four minutes to buy a pint of beer in 1950, but only eighteen minutes in 1977.

For all of their intrusive quality, and the agony they caused, high-rise flats housed only a minority of British people. In fact four out of five households were accommodated in houses not flats. The traditional terraced housing of the early part of the twentieth century still provided dwellings for one quarter of all households. Families or individuals with private households of their own totalled 97 per cent. The official handbook, *Britain 1979*, expressed the essence of British aspiration, even if a slightly embellished view of reality: 'Many British families now live in houses grouped in small terraces, or semi-detached or detached, usually of two storeys with gardens, and providing two main ground-floor living rooms, a kitchen, from two to four bedrooms, a bathroom, and one or two lavatories.' Over one half of all families owned their own homes, though half of these were still paying off mortgages. One third of all families moved house every five years.

Spending patterns did not alter drastically in the seventies from those established in the first era of affluence. In many respects it was more of the same: in the late seventies about 50 per cent of households had a telephone, about 52 per cent use of at least one car, and 11 per cent use of at least two cars, 88 per cent a fridge, 71 per cent a washing machine, but only 3 per cent a dishwasher. The big development in central heating has already been noted; by 1978 natural gas was being piped to fourteen million homes, and nearly six million used it for central heating. The most significant new modern convenience was the deep-freezer. In 1970 only about 4 per cent of households owned one, by 1972 this had risen to about 8 per cent, and by 1978 to 41 per cent. Correspondingly there was a sharp rise in the 1970s in the purchase of frozen foods. Five other areas, which tell us something about the fashions and fads of the time, are also of significance. Traditionally the British had been addicted to unhealthy white bread, tasting of tissue paper. Yet 12 per cent of all bread eaten in 1977 was of the wholemeal type and there was a general increase in the consumption of 'health' foods. Secondly, an enormous boom was apparent in do-it-yourself. In 1978 over one billion pounds was spent on do-it-yourself products: house-holders (often women) pasted nearly one million kilometres of wallpaper and used about one hundred million litres of paint. Over roughly the same period, to move to another significant area, it was reckoned that forty-four million pairs of jeans were bought, and that about four in every ten people bought at least one pair of jeans over a twelve-month period. Fourthly, in 1974 a small, but steady, expansion in the use of pedal bicycles began. Finally, while tobacco sales declined, sales of alcohol, and most particularly sales of wine, increased.

This chapter began with a reference to the essay 'Changes in Living Standards Since the 1950s' published in *Social Trends* No. 10, the 1980 edition. There a summary was attempted:

Perhaps there are three changes which stand out amongst the others. Firstly, the range of opportunities open to young people widened enor-mously. For example, as the three decades moved on, increasing pro-portions of young people made use of the opportunity to continue education after the statutory minimum school-leaving age. The same group of people could afford to buy their own radios, hi-fis, and cars; and, later on, they could afford to move into homes of their own at increasingly earlier ages.

Secondly, women – particularly mothers – were more likely to have some sort of paid job in the 1970s than in earlier years. This meant that the proportion of families with more than one earner increased.

Thirdly, people at work were entitled to longer holidays as the years went on, and enjoyed a small decrease in the number of hours that they worked each week. Thus working people had more time for other pursuits such as DIY and leisure activities.

The first of these points brings out a difficult issue in regard to the pace of social change. Over three decades no doubt what is said about young people was true; yet, in 1980, what struck observers most was the bleak outlook which faced young school-leavers and, indeed, at a more prosperous level, the prob-lems now facing first-time home-buyers.

It would be absurd to deny that, whatever the deeper economic realities, the British were still enjoying unprecedented levels of material prosperity at the end of the 1970s. But this was to make the problem of being a have-not in a have society particularly serious; and it meant too that unemployment was a drastic threat to those with heavy hire-purchase commitments on the appliances of affluence.

However, the final words of the essay in *Social Trends* read as follows:

It is not possible to produce a figure, or set of figures, which shows that we are x per cent better off than we were in 1951. It is clear that there was a substantial improvement in real disposable incomes and in material conditions between the 1950s and the 1970s, but many of the changes described in this Commentary are simply *differences* in the ways people live – whether they are for the better or worse is left for the reader to judge.

It is in the next chapter, in considering questions of customs and behaviour, the family, and social deviance and law and order, that I move towards the difficult area of the quality of life.

15. 'Gimme a Man After Midnight'

The title is that of a hit song of 1979 by the pop group Abba. Many were the signs of a world turned upside down as far as relations between the sexes were concerned. Earlier in the decade a woman agony columnist in a London evening newspaper, replying to a nervous young man who said that when entertaining young women in his bedsitter he was embarrassed by the prominent position of his bed, advised that since the bed was the most important item of furniture on such occasions he should use every device to make it the focal point of the room. Another woman journalist, speculating on the possibility of a male contraceptive pill, pointed out that the important thing about the old-fashioned male sheath was that at least one could see that it was on. A standard truism to Malcolm Muggeridge and other pundits of his generation had been that women are incapable of being humorous about sex. In fact, the most hilariously bawdy novel of the time was Molly Parkin's *Switchback* (1978). Less than a generation before, women were not supposed to think the thoughts expressed in this and many other books, let alone set them down in print. The opening lines of *Switchback* could have been designed to bring apoplexy to the traditionalists:

Blossom Tree opened her eyes. It wasn't light yet, but she had been rudely awakened (an apt description, she thought) by her husband's heavy erection twitching between her warm buttocks. Nosing its way in like a determined torpedo.

'Bugger me!' she exclaimed crossly. 'I don't know about that!' and sliding over to face him she took his tool in her hand. The firm touch seemed to satisfy the taut, questing flesh; by the time Blossom had drifted to sleep once again, her handful had subsided to nothing.

Meanwhile, some 290 miles away in London, Blossom s twin, June Day, was awakening too. But in quite different circumstances. The man sleeping beside her was a stranger as far as she could tell. She felt cautiously. Circumcised. Nothing much to write home about, neither dressing to left nor to right, but centrally and in the perpendicular – Christ – suddenly there was *heaps* to write home about!

For a time, the woman's magazine *Cosmopolitan* (founded in 1972) had published pin-up pictures of nude males, but these soon disappeared; apparently women actually preferred looking at pictures of nude females, so that those now regularly appearing in the *Sun* and other popular newspapers could scarcely be represented as the exclusive products of male chauvinism. However, male strippers were increasingly in demand at women's clubs and women's outings. 'Role reversal' was a modish, though probably not very exact phrase (rendered for commercial purposes as 'unisex'). Catherine Storr published a very funny novel, *Unnatural Fathers* (1976), which postulated the idea of males actually giving birth. More relevant, perhaps, to the reality of changing social attitudes in this sphere was an advertisement for a convenience food broadcast on commercial radio: after repeated complaints from her ill-mannered husband, the housewife discovers the magic of this particular convenience food; but the punch-line is that she then divorces her husband 'and marries a much nicer man'.

The key feminist tract of the 1970s, as already mentioned, was Germaine Greer's *The Female Eunuch*, reissued as a paperback in 1971. Referring to the suffragette era as 'the first feminist wave', Dr Greer declared her book to be 'part of the second feminist wave': 'The new emphasis is different. Then genteel middle-class ladies clamoured for reform, now ungenteel middle-class women are calling for revolution.' In a work of high literary quality and deep scholarship, she made some disturbing points:

Women have very little idea of how much men hate them . . . The universal sway of the feminine stereotype is the single most important factor in male and female woman-hatred. Until woman as she is can drive this plastic sphere out of her own and her man's imagination she will continue to apologize and disguise herself, while accepting her male's pot-belly, wattles, bad breath, farting, stubble, baldness and other ugliness without complaint   Is it too much to ask that women be spared the daily struggle for superhuman beauty in order to offer it to the caresses of a subhumanly ugly mate?

But let us leave questions of the relationships between the sexes (to which I return in discussing the family) and turn to other aspects of customs and behaviour. Commercial radio makes a good starting point. Commercial broadcasting of more or less continuous pop music from 'pirate' ships had begun in 1964, but had been squeezed out by effective Government counter-action. Under the Heath Conservative Government licensed local radio stations were set up. They clearly met a felt need, and the advertisements, broadcast as separate inserts, not, as in America, by the disc jockey himself, were not noticeably more irritating than the kind of condescending self-indulgent chat which still too often formed the official notion of informality as presented on BBC local radio. Local radio, of both kinds, at any rate, did represent and enhance a spirit of local participation and involvement, a mode of the sixties which developed impressively in the seventies.

Participation, involvement, consumer protest and action, these were all present in the sixties, but they were dominant motifs in the seventies. The Campaign for Real Ale was founded in 1971, and really burst into significant effectiveness around the middle of the decade. In the 1960s the 'big six' brewery combines had gone hell for leather in fulfilment of the theory that what the nation wanted was a handful of bland beers each supported by a brand name, heavily advertised. Small breweries were bought up and either converted into making big-name beer or, more often, closed down; as the motorway boom reached its peak it was believed that a few massive breweries producing pasteurized beer could deliver it to every corner of the kingdom. That cost accountants make lousy beer is to be expected; with a major petrol crisis on the way, even their economic forecasts were shaky.

Real beer is not pasteurized, and should not be served under carbon dioxide pressure. Unlike continental and North American lager-style beers, it is intended to continue 'conditioning' in the barrel. It therefore has a relatively short life, and needs to be handled and served with skill and care. By the late seventies the big breweries were in retreat. Watney's, who had been the leaders in the movement towards massification and gasification, employing the idiot television slogan 'Watney's Red Revolution' and painting all of their pubs red, now brought back two traditional bitters, and began to scrape off some of the red paint. Even more of a classic case is that of Whitbread's. This historic family firm had been taken over, its beautiful old brewery in Chiswell Street on the borders of the City of London closed down, and a modern beer factory built at Luton beside the M1 motorway thirty miles north of London. Whitbread's then bought up many local breweries and, final mad tribute to the idea of the brand name, marketed a whole range of different-tasting beers as 'Whitbread Trophy'. By the late seventies the Trophy labels were being ripped off and good local beers were being given their proper names back and also being served properly, without benefit of carbon dioxide.

However, repentant sinners should not gain their rewards too easily. A nice parable of the new balance between the local brewer of traditional ales and the conglomerate-owned national brewer could be seen in the relationship between the two breweries Shepherd Neame and Whitbread Fremlins which stand opposite each other in the small Kent town of Faversham. In April 1980, the Chairman of the former, Robert Neame, also Chairman of the Kent County Council Finance Committee and of the South-East England Tourist Board, was able to declare: 'It has really paid off remaining independent. Fremlins previously had the reputation of being Kent's premier brewers. That accolade has now passed to us.' Although Whitbread Trophy was now once again being called Fremlins Bitter, 'It's difficult,' Mr Neame commented, 'for them to regain their reputation. Even if they restore the old name, people realize who controls them.' None the less, the revival of real ale remained a relatively minor phenomenon compared with the expansion of the market for lager – most of it brewed in Britain (despite foreign names) and of poor quality.

In the gloom of the seventies, not all of the battles went to the big battalions, nor were the righteous always vanquished. It is sometimes said that social behaviour and fashion go in cycles, or that innovation is inevitably followed by reaction. Thus the sixties, a time of radical change (which it certainly was), is said to have been followed by the conservative seventies. In fact, in much of what is most important in manners and life-styles, change is cumulative. Perhaps violence, race tension, and terror-ism are the most important social phenomena of the seventies; yet the decade was also increasingly characterized by a greater tolerance, by a progressive breaking-down of rigid stereotypes in social relationships. No doubt when old rules and old customs lose their force there is uneasiness and even aggression. Yet most often the confrontation and challenge had taken place in the sixties; in the seventies there was much more genuine acceptance for, in the cliché, 'doing your own thing'. If stereotypes were collapsing as to the respective rôles of 'them' and 'us', governors and governed, media magnates and viewers, producers and con-sumers, men and women, so too were they collapsing with re-gard to the respective rôles of age and youth. Still in the sixties, style in appearance and dress was very much a function of age. For generations, nay centuries, it was accepted that as a person moved through the progression so decisively defined in Shakes-peare's 'All the world's a stage' so the appropriate style and the appropriate manner must be adopted. Lines, as far as fashion was concerned, were perhaps more vertical than horizontal in the later seventies: many different styles co-existed in the same age group, and the same styles could be observed over different age groups. Here, in itself, was another aspect of the loosening-up of society. Fashion – that is to say something determined by 'them' on behalf of 'us' – no longer asserted its old tyranny: more and more (within, of course, the limits always imposed by the human desire to conform with one's peer group, however that is defined) individuals chose to dress and present themselves as in-dividuals.

Among the young, certainly, there were exaggerated fashions pertaining to different cliques and sects. The new stylized groupings of the seventies had been the Skinheads, who ex-pressed an exaggerated reaction to the long hairstyles of the sixties, and the Punks, who, with dyed hair and clownish make-up (for both sexes), brought a genuine verve and colour to teenage style. In the later seventies there were revivals from earlier decades: Teds (who, without sideburns, emerged as Rockabilly Rebels), Mods (sometimes smartened-up Punks). and Rockers. 'Skins' took to pork-pie hats and thereby became Rudies. But these are all segmentations within one basic age group: they did not represent one consolidated youth style ranged against the whole of the rest of society.

The single biggest leisure activity of the majority of all British people was watching television. The number of viewing-hours had risen fairly sharply at the end of the sixties, but held steady, with perhaps a very slight increase, in the seventies. In the 1977–9 period, average hours viewed per week were sixteen in the summer and twenty in the winter. Children and the elderly tended to watch the most television, while women watched more than men; but the differences between the different categories were not very marked. The largest audiences would be recorded for royal occasions, major sporting events, light entertainment, and certain specially popular films, and varied from twenty million for light entertainment and fifteen–twenty million for sporting events or films to seven–eight million for documentaries and five–six million for current affairs. The average number of hours of radio listened to per week in 1978–9 was about nine hours, of which about seven and a half hours was provided by BBC radio, with the remainder provided by commercial and independent local radio.

An official Household Survey carried out in 1977 attempted, by asking questions about activities participated in over a four-week period, to identify and quantify major leisure activities apart from watching television. Top of this list came 'going out for a meal or a drink': 71 per cent of men had done so in the four-week period, 57 per cent of women (but what a daft bureaucratic category: what almost all of the men and most of the women had actually done was visit the pub). Next came listening to records or tapes: 64 per cent of men and 60 per cent of women. Then came reading books (57 per cent of women and 52 per cent of men – figures almost certainly about as high as would have been found in any other country in the world). After that, for men, came house repairs and do-it-yourself (51 per cent, 22 per cent of women) and gardening (49 per cent, 35 per cent of women) and for women needlework and knitting (51 per cent, as against a not altogether surprising 2 per cent for men). Other activities in which women appear to participate more than men were attending leisure classes (3 per cent women to 1 per cent men), dancing (16 per cent women against 14 per cent men), social and voluntary work (9 per cent women as against 8 per cent men), and going on outings to the seaside, the country and parks (7 per cent, 5 per cent, and 4 per cent as against 6 per cent, 5 per cent, and 3 per cent respectively) and on visits to historic buildings, and theatre, opera, and ballet (9 per cent and 6 per cent, as against 8 per cent and 4 per cent respectively). The last two groups of figures may have represented women's continuing responsibility in regard to entertaining children. However, when it came to visiting museums and art galleries the men had it by 4 per cent to 3 per cent.

Other important activities included walks, climbing, etc. (lumped together as 'countryside activities'), involving 31 per cent of men and 27 per cent of women; going to the cinema, involving 11 per cent of men and 10 per cent of women; amateur music and drama, involving 4 per cent of men and 3 per cent of women; home-based games of skill, 21 per cent of men and 16 per cent of women; and hobbies, 12 per cent of men and 3 per cent of women. After a steady decline since the fifties, cinema attendances actually staged a rally in 1978: the characteristic new phenomenon, which enjoyed an enormous expansion in the middle 1970s, was the multi-screen complex, in which three small cinemas performing simultaneously were housed in the gigantic antediluvian shell of a 1930s cinema. Watching football was still a major pastime, though it no longer held the modish appeal it had attained in the 1960s. In face of the counter-attraction of colour television and the deterrent of football hooliganism attendances were holding up reasonably well. Of outdoor sports in which people actually participated, football was also the most popular. The 1977 Household Survey showed 6 per cent of men interviewed as having played football within the last four weeks. The most popular sport of all was darts, involving 15 per cent of the men and 4 per cent of the women interviewed. Betting on horses, dogs, or through football pools was a fairly consistent activity among men in different social groups: it was an activity of 29 per cent in the Household Survey, and, also consistently across social classes, of 11 per cent of women. Bingo, however, was very much an activity of women in the semi-skilled and unskilled groups: 17 per cent of women in this group as against only 6 per cent in the professional and managerial group. On average, 5 per cent of men indulged in bingo.

Throughout the sixties an English historian, a long-time exile in the University of Glasgow, had been wont to speak of 'the Misery (Scotland) Act', his all-embracing explanation of the killjoy tedium of Scottish social life. Suddenly, in the late seventies, Scotland shot ahead of her southern neighbour in one traditionally fraught area. As a result of Section 64, Subsection 3, of the Licensing (Scotland) Act of 1976 (there was no English counterpart) certain pubs were enabled to stay open all day, from eleven in the morning till eleven at night. The crucial clause read:

> After considering the application and any objections made thereto, a licensing board may grant an application for the regular extension of permitted hours if, having regard to the social circumstances of the locality in which the premises in respect of which the application is made are situated or to activities taking place in that locality, the board considers it is desirable to do so ...

Officially, a holiday is a period of four or more nights away from home considered by the respondent to be a holiday. On this basis, the total number of holidays taken by British people rose from twenty-seven million in 1951 to thirty-four million in 1961, to forty-one million in 1971, and up to a peak of forty-nine million in 1973: the figures in 1976 and 1977 were forty-five million and forty-four million respectively, then there was a revival in 1978 with the figure going up to forty-eight million. In 1978, also, the figure for holidays abroad was at its highest yet: nine million, as against eight million in 1977 and 1973, seven million in 1971, four million in 1961, and two million in 1951. By far the most popular foreign destination was Spain, taking a good thirty per cent of all foreign holidays.

New overseas influences on British customs and leisure activities were strongly marked by the middle seventies. British society was showing the effects of continental travel, of closer commercial links with Europe brought about by membership of the EEC, and of having growing Asian and West Indian communities located within its midst. Often now the traditional fish-and-chip shop might be run by Indians, Pakistanis, or Greeks, offering curry or kebabs in addition to the old standard fare. For almost every sector of the market there were Italian restaurants, Chinese restaurants, of varying levels of sophistication. Shops and markets offered avocados, mangoes, peppers, artichokes, and aubergines. When consideration is given to the racial views described in Chapter 13, and to the growing evidence from opinion polls of hostility to the Common Market, it has to be said that Britain in the later seventies had acquired a new cosmopolitanism without shedding its old xenophobia.

For the country as a whole there was no change in the secular decline in religious observance, though there was in the seventies a definite growth in fringe religion – Moonies, gurus, and so on – and also a quite striking expansion of interest in astrology. Openness to outside influences, both American and oriental, was one factor here; as to the other bases of religious or quasi-religious need at a time of decline in institutional religion, it is only possible to speculate.

My opening remarks were concerned with sexual attitudes; on sexual behaviour, none of the evidence suggests that there was anything in the way of a puritan reaction in the seventies. The most thorough and up-to-date survey of sexual behaviour among teenagers and women in their early twenties was that published in April 1980 in *19* magazine, based on questionnaires filled in by 10,000 readers. The majority (77 per cent) of those responding fell within the age range sixteen–twenty-four, though there were also younger girls and older women. Some of the results, therefore, were manifestly less representative than others. Of the relatively small number of those aged sixteen or less, fully 46 per cent said that they were not virgins. In each cohort the number claiming virginity declined: at seventeen, 43 per cent; at eighteen, 22 per cent; at nineteen, 17 per cent; at twenty–twenty-one, 12 per cent; at twenty-two and over, 8 per cent. Taking all girls under twenty-one, and this is probably the most reliable and representative statistic, 26 per cent claimed to have had their first sexual experience before the age of sixteen. Of all sexually experienced girls (again a slightly less representative statistic) 39 per cent claimed to have had sexual experience at under sixteen years of age. Of sexually experienced single girls 72 per cent had had two or more partners. Over one half of those who started sex early had had four or more partners, and a quarter claimed to have had ten partners or more.

What, then, were the implications for that enduring institution, marriage? Evidently, as the organizers of the survey commented, 'the virgin bride has become a rarity in our society'. However, 77 per cent of all those participating in the survey disagreed that marriage was becoming old-fashioned and obsolete. Only one in ten said that they would prefer unmarried living together to marriage; but eight out of ten said they would be willing to live with their man with or without reservations or marriage prospects. From subjective evidence it is clear that the condition whereby couples live together in a relatively stable relationship without actually being married had become an accepted social institution, though the incidence was not in fact widespread enough to show up significantly in official statistics. The number of first marriages was certainly in steady decline in the 1970s: first marriages for both parties numbered 377,000 in 1971, 273,000 in 1976, and 266, 000 in 1977. Here, certainly, was a reflection of the change in attitudes of younger people towards marriage. But the overall popularity of marriage as an institution was sustained by the increasing number of second marriages. The divorce rate rose slowly, and stood at 10·4 per thousand of the married population in 1977; on the other hand, the average age of the re-marriage of divorced people was falling. The figures, then, suggest, not a destruction of marriage, but a greater and more flexible range of options: stable unmarried relationships, later marriages, more frequent divorce, more frequent re-marriage. The convenience food commercial was not so wide of the mark.

Some traditional customs, still detectable in the early fifties, such as 'churching', appeared to have died out altogether. Attitudes towards children had continued to soften, yet Britain in many respects remained one of the most backward countries in the world in this area. While corporal punishment of children was against the law in Saudi Arabia (much featured in the press as a brutal, atavistic Muslim state) it remained in existence in many British, and, above all, in Scottish schools. Unlike Scandinavian countries, Britain had no special legislation protecting children's rights against, for instance, their parents.

From within families, the problem given most attention was

that of how to handle teenage children. Self-evidently, the statistics of teenage sexual behaviour cited above contained within them their own problems for parents. Then there was violence, drink, drugs, and even just sheer waywardness. The drug scene of the late seventies was rather smudgier than that of the sixties: facts were even less certain; voices of both takers and opponents were, in keeping with the more tolerant pluralistic trends already mentioned, much less strident; there was even a strong do-it-yourself element. If there was any general problem of addiction and abuse among children and young people it was rather in relation to alcohol; and here their elders scarcely set a good example. The major new development of the mid-seventies was that of sniffing glue, and this became quite a widespread open-air habit among young males, particularly on housing estates. Surveys, however, suggested that glue was simply a cheap alternative to alcohol which would be resorted to as soon as the funds were available.

The avowed use of cannabis may have reached a peak early in the seventies, when perhaps about a third of all students in higher education were indulging, with about half that figure among young people of the same age group outside higher education, and perhaps 10 per cent of school pupils. But it may well be that the total number of cannabis users remained at least the same throughout the seventies. Some authorities believed the habit was spreading among working-class youth, including skinheads. What was certain was that use of cannabis was becoming much more private. Whereas it was difficult at the beginning of the seventies to be in a university and not be aware, at least, of its use; in the later seventies those who were not involved tended to have no contact with those who were. At the same time, the attitudes of the law became rather more sensible and humane: first-time offenders caught in possession of cannabis had risked a prison sentence in the early seventies; thereafter, at most, they risked a fine.

Far other was the case with the hard drug heroin. By 1980 there was far more heroin around in the country than there had ever been before, and an organized black market on a scale unknown in 1970. Even the official seizure figures give some indication: in 1973 a little over 3 kg were seized; by 1978 the

figure had risen to 60 kg. The situation had not yet reached
the seriousness of, for instance, New York, where much crime
was directly related to drug addiction, but some experts predicted that, while abuse of cannabis was scarcely a problem, the
growth of heroin addiction, apart from the personal damage
done to addicts, could become a further cause of violent crime
in Britain.

Overall there was actually a decline in the number of serious
criminal offences recorded by the police in 1978 and 1979, and
a decline in the number of persons prosecuted. However, crimes
of violence against the person, and crimes by young people,
particularly personal violence and vandalism, increased. Although rape had, very properly, become a matter for serious
concern and protest among feminist groups, the number of such
offences actually slightly declined also.

What perhaps helped most of all to colour attitudes about
the direction British society was taking and to spread dis-
enchantment among the articulate was the number of cases
involving corruption and conspiracy. It is hard to be sure
whether those in authority, in the civil service, in local government, in the police, in financial institutions, were really becoming more corrupt, or whether the police were becoming more
zealous and public morality, if one can use such a phrase,
becoming less tolerant of high jinks on the part of those who
in a former era might well have contrived concealment behind
the majesty of office.

To cope with a great diversity of problems there were the
police forces (still under the control of local authorities, not
of the central Government) totalling 120,000, including 8,890
policewomen: one policeman to every 450 members of the
population, in fact. As noted in Part Two, increasing the
numbers might not necessarily affect the detection, or even the
prevention, of crime. But, without doubt, when it came to riot
and civil disturbance, the forces were often dangerously
stretched. They were now, however, grouped together more
rationally than had been the case in the forties and fifties. For
the whole of Great Britain there were now just sixty-seven
regular police forces, ranging in size from about 130 in the
remoter parts of Scotland, to about 21,200 in the Metropolitan

Police. The particular problem within the realm of law and order which gained most publicity at the end of the decade was that of gross overcrowding in Britain's prisons: prison strikes and demonstrations, of which there were many, would, experts predicted, soon culminate in some great explosion.

In general, as indicated in Part Two, the police tended to have the respect and support of the British people. How far they had had the support of submerged minorities in the past is dubious. But the clear message of the seventies was that they were very definitely faced with the active hostility of disinherited youth, white as well as black. In witness to this the 1980s began with the quite spectacular violence in St Paul's, Bristol, at Brighton and Scarborough a few days later on the Easter Bank Holiday of 1980, and then on the evening of the Easter Monday at Finsbury Park in North London. The omens were not good; but taken all in all it would be absurd to say that they were all bad. The two contrary elements suggesting hope on the one hand, and despair on the other, form the title of my next chapter.

16. Tolerance and Confrontation

Previous chapters in Part Three have indicated why, as mentioned in the Introduction, by the end of the 1970s books and articles were being published on different variations of the 'Is Britain Dying?' theme. Apart from the problems of the economy, race, and civil violence, some writers also pointed to Britain's poor performance, after the excitements of the sixties, in the realms of intellect, arts, and entertainment.

It certainly appeared that while such painters as Elizabeth Frink, David Hockney, and Bridget Riley continued to produce excellent work, they had no true successors. London theatre was probably still the best in the world, but economies were showing, and again there seemed nothing quite to match the innovations of the sixties. British art merged anonymously into the major international trends; and these trends, blurring the distinctions between 'high art' and popular art, stressing literalness and 'super realism', pushing political messages, and emphasizing feminism and homosexuality, were not themselves of a sort to assist the revelation of distinctively national or personal genius.

The best dramatists, Pinter, or Tom Stoppard (*Rosencrantz and Guildenstern are Dead*, 1967; *Jumpers*, 1972), say, had made their names long since. This would hold true too for poets and for musicians. Innovation tended to be at the unspectacular, and perhaps necessarily transient level, taking the form of multimedia events and of happenings involving audience participation. However, it was in the mid-1970s that the National Theatre at last entered into its magnificent new architectural complex and thereafter continued to present a range of plays which could by no stretch of the words be deemed conservative or unimaginative.

The most significant development in the indigenous novel

was, as hinted at at the beginning of the previous chapter, the emergence of the liberated woman novelist. However, such writers as Angela Carter and Fay Weldon seemed, in their very different ways, to run against the problem that in the real contemporary world there was no prospect of full women's liberation as feminists envisaged it; woman's own nature seemed to be against it. Thus some feminist writers took off into various forms of fantasy, surreal or futuristic worlds where alone, they seemed to be suggesting, women could be completely free. Angela Carter's *The Passion of New Eve* (1977), set in a horrifically violent America of the near future, has a handsome predatory man captured by a women's group and subjected to an operation which turns him into a highly desirable, and vulnerable, young woman. The vulnerability, as much as the unconquerability, of women appeared to be major themes in *Sweet William* (1975) by Beryl Bainbridge, and *Praxis* (1978) by Fay Weldon. If, where it is possible to identify social and political trends in creative writing, one such trend stressed the woman's viewpoint, another tended to take a rather right-wing view of society. The tone of Tory sourness had been well struck in Kingsley Amis's poem of the sixties 'A Tribute to the Founder', republished in the *Collected Poems* of 1979.

> By bluster, graft, and doing people down,
> Sam Baines got rich, but, mellowing at last,
> Felt that by giving something to the town
> He might repair the evils of his past.
>
> His hope was to prevent the local youth
> From making the mistakes that he had made:
> Choosing expediency instead of truth,
> And quitting what was honest for what was paid.
>
> A university seemed just the thing,
> And that old stately home the very place.
> Sam wept with pleasure at its opening.
> He died too soon to weep at its disgrace.
>
> Graft is refined among the tea and scones,
> Bluster (new style) invokes the public good,
> And doing-down gets done in pious tones
> Sam often tried to learn, but never could.

That tone had become a dominant key by the mid-seventies, giving a special power to Amis's own masterpiece, *The Alteration* (1976), in which he created a Britain as it might well be had the Reformation never taken place. While back in the fifties the 'popular' espionage-and-thuggery novels of Ian Fleming eventually abandoned their cold war complexion, the 'quality' spy novels of John Le Carré were increasingly informed by a sense of the barbaric obscurantism of the Soviet régime. Malcolm Bradbury's *The History Man* (1975) was portrayed as a nasty, lefty, trendy, university sociologist. However, the *Daniel Martin* of John Fowles's big novel of 1977, a highly successful British Hollywood screen writer, managed to preserve liberal and even social-democratic attitudes in musing on the structural weaknesses which had made Britain a feeble, sluggish country compared with the USA. A conversation between Piers Paul Read's *A Married Man* (1979) and his sister and brother-in-law

made him most pessimistic about his ideals; for his sister and her husband seemed to exemplify a new bourgeoisie which had expropriated and exploited the Welfare State. Instead of scrambling to save money to send their children to private schools they schemed to get them into some chosen comprehensive which, because word had gone around among like-minded members of the state-employed élite, was then packed with the progeny of up-and-coming couples while the children of the working classes were relegated as before to the second-class schools.

All the paradoxes of Britain's record in science and technology sharpened in the seventies. Much had been done in the sixties to develop science teaching in all types of secondary schools, yet in the seventies there was a swing back in student choices from science to arts subjects. There was still a strong élitist atmosphere about university science, yet, despite economic stringency, British scientists retained their enviable eminence in the international community. Developments were particularly arresting in 'the life sciences', in microbiology, molecular biology, and immunology: the 'physicists' war' had become the 'biologists' peace'. Basically it was the achievements in immunology which made possible the transplant surgery which attracted so much attention in the press. Most attention of all was focused on the arrival, early in 1979, of the world's first 'test-tube' baby, resulting from the partnership of Robert Edwards, physiologist at Cambridge University, and Patrick Steptoe, gynaecologist at the distinctly unfashionable Oldham General Hospital. Peter Medawar, himself one of the most illustrious figures in the realm of immunology, emerged (in partnership with his wife) as *the* science philosopher to rival Sir James Jeans of an earlier age: the elegant and profound *The Life Science*, by P. B. and J. S. Medawar was published in 1977. In the world of technology much attention was focused on the silicon chip developed in the United States which made possible very complex computerization within a small space. In the 1960s, research into robot technology at Hawker-Siddeley and Guest Keen and Nettlefold was as far ahead as any in the world, and significant advances were achieved at the University of Nottingham in the early 1970s. Yet there was remarkably little practical sign of the micro-electronic revolution in the Britain of the seventies. Its most obvious manifestations appeared to be in pocket calculators, new cash registers in shops, and sophisticated children's toys. While from the very beginning of the seventies the Japanese, and in lesser degree other West European countries, exploited the possibilities of automated 'robot' factories, in Britain really significant developments only came at the very end of the decade. The automated Mini Metro factory at Longbridge, Birmingham, was shown off to the press in September 1980. None of the robots were of British manufacture. It was right at the time when unemployment was soaring alarmingly that a number of other firms announced lay-offs due to automation based on micro-electronic robot technology. Never was the failure to integrate technological and social planning shown up more sharply

However little understanding there was of the relationship between science and technology and society and government, there was probably till the early seventies general acceptance of the view that science and technology offered great boons to society. Only in the seventies, with the development of the environmental movement, the growth of fears about the uses to which 'data banks' might be put, and the questioning of the effect on the human mind of constant exposure to television, did this fundamental liberal–optimist assumption begin to be questioned. Again, as with so many of the issues raised by science and technology, this was a worldwide, not a purely British matter. In fact – to extend further the whole paradoxical nature of the matter – Britain could be singled out as making particularly effective use of the potential of television: many drama series, both contemporary and classical, and such general service programmes as *The World at War* (on ITV) or *The Voyages of Charles Darwin* (on BBC) were the admiration of the world. As the Medawars rightly said, 'Most of the problems that beset mankind call for political, moral and administrative rather than scientific solutions.'

There were serious problems at humbler levels. Some of the less healthy features of the book industry have already been noted. But only in the middle seventies did the proud position still held by British publishing in face of all rivals begin to disintegrate. Book prices shot up; hitherto impregnable firms turned in large trading losses; retrenchment and redundancy struck suddenly and often arbitrarily; North Americans found it no longer sensible to order British books, nor indeed to seek to have their own works published by British publishers. Among popular bestsellers, the rage was for works of terror, and, above all, occultism and exorcism: almost all the market leaders were American–originated.

The story of the press is not much happier. Thus a further Royal Commission on the Press (the second since the war) was set up in May 1974. In its *Final Report* (July 1977) the Commission noted that sales of national dailies had fallen from 15·8 million per day in 1961 to 14·0 million in 1976; while the provincial press generally prospered the national press was in a condition of recurrent financial crisis. The Commission divided the press into a number of categories: first the 'qualities' – *Daily Telegraph, Sunday Telegraph, Financial Times, Guardian, The Times, Sunday Times,* and *Observer* – and the 'populars' – *Daily Mirror, Sunday Mirror, Daily Express, Sunday Express, Sunday People, Daily Mail, Sun,* and *News of the World* (later there arrived the appalling *Daily Star*); 'the *Morning Star*' (the Communist Party newspaper), said the Commission, 'does not fit easily into either classification'. Next came the weekly 'Journals of Opinion': *Economist, Spectator, New Statesman, Tribune,* and *New Society.* Then the 'Alternative Press', creation of the sixties, well nourished in the seventies: *Gay News* (which, launched in 1962, had a bigger circulation than the *Spectator* or *Tribune*), *Private Eye* (which had at one time achieved a circulation of 100,000), and *Time Out* (steady sale of about 48,000). The Commission's next groupings were the 'Provincial Mornings', of which there were now only twelve in England and Wales, compared with eighteen in 1948 (Scotland still had four), and the 'Evenings', of which nine had closed since 1961, leaving no single provincial city with more than one evening paper (London had two, though they were to be amalgamated in November 1980). Finally the Commission came to a series of categories, either launched, or greatly expanded, in the seventies: 'freesheets', product of participation and consumerism, providing information on entertainments and tourist attractions, financed by advertisements; immigrant newspapers; 'general periodicals', including the old war-horses like *Reveille* and *Titbits,* the newer specialist magazines orientated towards pop music, say, or Do-It-Yourself, and the increasingly explicit sex magazines; and the 'women's press' made up of the more traditional weeklies and monthlies such as *Woman* and *Good Housekeeping,* the newer 'emancipated' monthlies such as *Cosmopolitan* (founded in 1972), the firmly feminist organs such as *Spare Rib* (also founded in 1972), and the mass of girls' magazines which form such an important source for the student of changing moral attitudes.

This varied progeny of Gutenberg's epochal invention was in fact (with minor exceptions) owned by ten large companies, four of which were, in the last analysis, controlled from outside Britain: the Thomson Organization, Atlantic Richfield, News International (the Australian owners of the *Sun*) and Beaverbrook Newspapers (ultimately owned by the French finance company, Générale Occidentale). The six others were: Reed International (formed by a merger with IPC in 1970), S. Pearson and Son, Associated Newspaper Group, Guardian and Manchester Evening News Ltd, Daily Telegraph Ltd, and Morning Star Co-operative Society.

In addition to the menace of mergers, the Commission also identified four other major problems: the invasion of privacy by 'investigative' reporters; the weakness of the Press Council in maintaining the highest journalistic standards; the growing control of the major alternative source of information, television, by the newspaper companies; and poor industrial relations:

One debilitating legacy to national newspapers from the post-war days of easy profits and weak management has been the exceptionally high earnings of print workers and a disposition among publishers to yield easily to threats of unofficial action. Industrial relations in Fleet Street have been notoriously bad for a generation and their improvement has been the regularly falsified hope of everyone who has attempted to set the industry on the path of modernisation.

Throughout 1979, indeed, Times Newspapers were paralysed as managers and men failed to agree over the introduction of computerized techniques. When their representatives appeared on television to express their differences and, ultimately, to explain their agreement, their accents, naturally, were those of, on the one hand, the public-school-educated upper class (represented in this case by Marmaduke Hussey) and, on the other, the intrepid London artisanry.

How far, then, were social and political values changing? What of that secular Anglicanism of which I have spoken once or twice? In the previous chapter one of my main arguments was that, contrary to what was being said about the disintegration of traditional values, it was the continuing vigour of the Anglican tradition which permitted a peaceful accommodation to consumerism, participation, youth culture, and feminism. Tolerance had not fled the country. But there could be no gainsaying the facts of violence simmering on the surface, and, as a new decade opened, more frequently bursting devastatingly into the open.

It is particularly difficult when dealing with a past so immediate that it merges into the present, to distinguish between what actually was happening and what political and social commentators hotly in pursuit of fundamental causes and universal remedies declared was happening. Here, I choose four major areas of the political and industrial history of the seventies, none of which clearly demonstrates a disintegration of values, a continuation of values, or a replacement of one set of values by another. As always, the areas overlap and inter-relate. They are: first, trade unions, industrial relations and strikes; second, developments (a better word, here, than changes) in the way in which national economic and social decisions were arrived at, sometimes described, though in my view quite inadequately, as representing a move towards 'corporatism'; third, the position of the Labour Party, appearing at one moment as the country's national governing party, at another as a body ready at any moment to splinter between right, centre, and left elements, while at the same time apparently choking in apathy and lack of funds; and, fourthly, the radical Conservative attitudes of Thatcherite conservatism which, it can be argued, helped to hold Labour, the trade unions, and the left together in the middle years of the decade, and then, after 1979, began to effect a reorientation of political and social values.

As noted in Part Two there was a great and rising upsurge of strike activity between 1968 and 1972. As we also saw, there are different ways of measuring the intensity of strike activity. Taking the number of days lost, these reached their peak figure of 23,909,000 in 1972. There was then a sharp reduction to a figure little above that for 1969, 7,197,000. As the Heath confrontation intensified and Labour Governments took over in confused circumstances, the figure more than doubled again in 1974 to 14,750,000. The prime years of the social contract, 1975 and 1976, had figures back around late sixties' levels of, respectively, 6,012,000 and 3,284,000. There was a slight up in 1977, and then a slight down again in 1978, the figures, respectively, being 10,142,000 and 9,405,000. In 1979, as the social contract collapsed, the figures rose up beyond the proportions of the 1926 General Strike. Within these figures the central phenomenon was that, in keeping with the trend beginning at the end of the sixties, strikes were now not so often small-scale, unofficial efforts, but frequently involved large unions and many workers, and had official backing. It appeared as though strikes were becoming more 'political' than 'industrial' in purpose (though, as I have already suggested, there is some unreality about this distinction). The weight of trade-union leadership was thrown against the Heath Government's Industrial Relations Act and in favour, till the very end at least, of Labour's social contract and policy of wage limitation. In formulating the stages of the wage policy and the concomitant bargains struck in the social contract, the Labour Government was operating in close co-operation with the trade-union leadership; and there may well be truth, too, in the story that Heath had hoped to work in much closer collaboration with the trade-union leadership than his policies of confrontation would suggest. Certainly, in July 1976, he gave his support in this respect to the Labour Government: 'The agreement between the Government and trade unions' was in the national interest especially since 'those countries which had had greater success in dealing with the industrial situation were those which had the closest form of consultation with both sides of industry'.

The phenomena of flying pickets and 'secondary picketing' had been introduced in the early seventies. Then in 1974 the miners' leaders deliberately acted to restrain violence. But the issues remained live ones even during the period of relative quietude in industrial relations in the middle seventies, coming to the fore again in the Grunwick strike, and then much more forcefully, in the steel strike of 1980. Truly the energies of activists in earlier generations of the trade-union and Labour movement had been directed much more towards the traditional activities of propaganda and organization than towards picketing and intimidation. Yet the new type of picketing was little more than an up-dating and intensification of the activism of the hunger marchers in the thirties. Certainly it could be held to be undesirable in that it became a focal point for militants on both left and right who had little to do with the trade-union movement, that it was liable to create violence, and that it interfered with the livelihood of employers and employees not in any way directly involved with the particular strike in question. To that extent there was a case both for legislation and for a return to the kind of self-discipline which the British trade-union movement had so long exercised.

Despite the revived interest in workers' control and industrial democracy in the 1960s little had been done. The whole saga of industrial democracy in the later seventies tells us much about the contemporary trade-union movement and its attitudes, and very much suggests, not that radical, disruptive, ideas were taking over, but that the traditional stance had shifted little. However, with a Labour Government back in office after 1974, and a General Council of the TUC, together with the most influential trade-union leader of the time, Jack Jones of the Transport and General Workers', strongly committed to their own version of industrial democracy, the matter was very much back on the agenda. Furthermore, the Government began to surmise that the extent of worker participation in management in European countries, particularly West Germany, might have something to do with their greater economic success. In his first address as Prime Minister to the Labour Party Conference in 1976, James Callaghan spoke of successive Governments having 'failed to ignite the fires of industrial growth in the ways that Germany, France, and Japan, with their different political and economic philosophies, have done'. Worker participation schemes, on Government directions, were introduced into the British Steel Corporation, British Leyland, and Chrysler.

Yet there was still great resistance to the whole concept from within the trade-union movement itself: opposition was particularly strong from the Electricians, the Engineers, and the General and Municipal workers. Among the public at large, it appeared that something over half of all adult employees did favour worker participation in management, but that most people were against industrial democracy being imposed by law. There was public opposition, too, among trade-unionists as well as non-trade-unionists, to the TUC scheme, whereby worker directors would be nominated through trade unions; there was also opposition to any idea of worker directors being in a majority on boards. As governments so often did in such circumstances, the Callaghan Government in December 1975 appointed a Committee of Inquiry under the Chairmanship of Lord Bullock. The Bullock Committee had an enormously difficult task in front of it and in the end produced a majority report, a minority report, and a note of dissent. Basically the Bullock Report proposed that its scheme for industrial democracy would only come into practice in a company where at least one third of the employees expressed a wish for such an arrangement. But where the scheme did come into effect workers' representation on the board would be controlled entirely by the trade unions. It was on this point that the minority – desiring that representation should be directly from the workforce as a whole, not through the unions – split from the majority. An elaborate scheme for the composition of boards would ensure that though in appearance there would be 'parity' between employers and employees, the addition of a co-opted 'third group' meant that workers' (or, in effect, union) representatives could never be in a majority, and thus could always escape responsibility for serious, or unpopular decisions. At the same time the Report went out of its way to stress that unions would still retain their traditional independence.

As was to be expected, the proposals were not well received. Employers drew back now from the prospect that industrial democracy might become a reality; liberals (in all parties) joined with the minority in opposing the vesting of control of workers' representation exclusively in the hands of the unions; and such union leaders as John Lyons, General Secretary of the Electrical Power Engineers' Association, expressed the old reservations: 'Employee representatives on boards à la Bullock will tie the unions into the management process.' Thus when the Labour Government came to frame its own proposals on the subject they departed quite far from Bullock. The Government proposed a two-tier scheme, with worker representation only on a 'Policy Board', not involved in the day-to-day running of the company, which would be reserved to a more traditional 'Management Board' exclusively composed of the usual 'professional' managers; even on the Policy Board, workers' representatives would have no more than one third of the seats. Elections for these seats would be carried out by the workforce as a whole, not through trade unions. Once more, little had been done to implement the proposals by the time the Labour Government fell from office.

Several of these issues bring us towards the heart of the discussion as to whether Britain was or was not becoming a corporatist society. One of the few political leaders who boasted of running a corporatist state was Mussolini, the Italian dictator, so the term has a pejorative quality to it. It implies that instead of the country being ruled by a democratically elected parliament, major decisions are made through bodies representative of various vested interests (in particular trade unions and employers' associations) interacting directly with the government. That ordinary Members of Parliament have been losing influence since the late nineteenth century is a historical truism. That MPs carry less respect than they once did among their peer groups in the upper and middle classes is also true; how much they actually meant to the masses in the nineteenth century is a moot question. But direct influence upon Parliament and government by vested interests and pressure groups is nothing new whatsoever. As modern society has become more complex, so the balance of forces behind political decision-making must become more complex. Political commentators have focused attention on such pressure groups as: the Child Poverty Action Group whose campaigning and lobbying did much to bring about the introduction of Child Benefits; the Abortion Law Reform Association and the Society for the Protection of the Unborn Child which between them provided much of the ammunition for the parliamentary debates on abortion; and the National Association for Mental Health which did much to reorientate the National Health Service towards this traditionally neglected and suspect area. In an ideal world it would be better if MPs themselves had control of the research facilities offered by such organizations; but on the whole these pressure groups cannot unreasonably be seen as representing that element of participation and commitment which was one of the more encouraging legacies of the sixties, husbanded and developed in the seventies.

In the general election of February 1974, 78·8 per cent of the electorate voted, a figure which, marking a reversal of the trend of declining electoral participation since the fifties, suggested that political apathy was not going to be a cardinal sin of the seventies. Labour polled half a million less votes than they had in the election they lost in 1970, but the Conservatives lost still more seriously at the hands of Nationalists and Liberals. With 37·9 per cent of votes cast the Conservatives returned

297 MPs; Labour with 37·1 per cent of votes cast actually returned 301 MPs; the Liberals with 19·3 per cent had 14 MPs, the Scottish Nationalists with 2 per cent and the Welsh Nationalists with 0·6 per cent had 7 MPs and 2 MPs respectively. Nevertheless, events which followed suggested that Labour really was establishing itself as the natural governing party. With the old flair and skill Wilson ran a minority Government till October when he chose his moment for a further general election. This time Labour polled 39·2 per cent of all votes cast to 35·9 per cent for the Conservatives. By traditional standards Labour's majority was still tiny, yet Wilson, and then Callaghan, seemed to govern with confidence. There was a desperate sterling crisis in the late summer of 1976, but thereafter, despite continuing recession and very high unemployment, there was something of a recovery, and it appeared that inflation was being brought under control. Fear of what an alternative Conservative Government under Mrs Thatcher might do helped to keep the unions and the left in line.

However, for a younger generation of militants there was no joy at all in seeing a Labour Government presiding over wage controls, high unemployment, and spending cuts. Within many sections of the party the grouping known as the Militant Tendency gained in strength. Outside of the party much unfavourable comment was evoked by the behaviour of leftist students in generally making it impossible for right-wing opinions to be heard in student unions or at student meetings. This sort of totalitarian intolerance did suggest that serious flaws were developing in the Anglican tradition of fair play and free speech. As the Labour Government went into the dismal winter of 1979 and on to electoral defeat, the problems within the party came out into the open. Was the survival of Labour as a broad-based, non-ideological, institution, designed primarily for the purpose of getting workers' representatives into Parliament, now menaced? Many of the objectives on which Labour had set its sights in the thirties and forties had indeed been accomplished. The social contract had committed the Labour Government to bringing 'about a fundamental and irreversible shift in the balance of power and wealth in favour

of working people and their families'. But how high a priority
was to be given to that aim, compared with just somehow
trying to keep the economy afloat? Traditionally the broad-
based non-ideological Labour Party had been a factor for
stability in British society; in 1980 it was still too early to say
that it was now ceasing to be so.

It would be a mistake to see the Conservative election victory
of 1979 as marking anything like a revolution in British social
and political values. Self-evidently, most of those who believed
in consensus politics or some form of collectivist socialism continued to do so. On the other hand, already in the seventies
politicians in the Labour Party as well as in the Conservative
Party were claiming that trade-union powers must be curbed
and that encouragement must be given to thrift and enterprise.
As long as inflation was running at a few per cent per year
it was generally taken by politicians, privately if not publicly,
as being no bad thing; but as inflation rose sharply in the
seventies greater credence was given to arguments that above
all it was the duty of governments to provide for a stable
economic environment in which each individual could plan his
future on a rational basis.

However, whatever a few self-conscious political theorists
might think, whatever the developments in the Labour Party,
whatever the truth or falsity of the fears that Britain was becoming a corporatist society, and whatever the activities of the
trade unions, great interest still attaches to the fundamental
views, or lack of them, of the ordinary mass of the British
people. A much cited worldwide Gallup opinion survey conducted in 1977 suggested that, on their own valuation, the
British people were among the happiest in the world. Of course,
this evidence could be interpreted in two opposite ways. Some
commentators, such as the American author of *Britain: The
Future That Works*, argued that it was better to be happy and
relatively poor, than relatively prosperous and subject to stress
and unhappiness. Other commentators, particularly those of a
Thatcherite cast, saw the poll as indicating the very thing that
was wrong with Britain, a determination to put personal tran-
quillity and happiness far ahead of hard work and serious endeavour. That this – whether one saw it as a good thing or

a bad thing – was true of a large section of the British people seemed to be confirmed by a *New Society* survey carried out on 28 April 1977. In a sample of 1,081 adults nearly twice as many considered it better to work only for as long as was necessary to live a pleasant life than considered it more important to work as hard as they could for as much money as they could get. Most of those interviewed appeared to be fairly content with their incomes and over half considered that a rise of £10 a week or less was all that they needed to live without financial worries. These results were consistent across all social classes.

Had the British always had such attitudes? If not, how far back did they go? The nation, or at least certain members of it, had surely shown great energy and initiative in the period of the building-up of the British overseas Empire from Elizabethan times onwards, and still more so during the period in which Britain became 'the workshop of the world'. It was in the inter-war years, J. M. Keynes thought, that the British upper class, many of whose fathers had built up industrial empires in the nineteenth century, began to become complacent and unadventurous. Perhaps, with the diffusion of affluence throughout society after the Second World War, this complacency percolated down through all classes of society.

Most commentators writing at the end of the decade were concerned with 'crisis': crisis in the economy, crisis in law and order, crisis in racial and industrial relations. From the point of view of the survival of the nation as a whole as a stable and relatively prosperous (as, of course, in comparison with the rest of the world Britain undoubtedly was) society these commentators may very well have been right. But from the point of view of the vast majority of the British people, as little interested as ever in major national concerns, the most significant changes in values were probably those related to sexual mores and social relationships: the tight little society of the late forties had expanded much, and the movement begun in the sixties, towards more humane, more civilized, and more libertarian attitudes and towards a more comprehensive notion of what should be included in the term social welfare, continued on its upward trajectory right to the end of the 1970s.

Then again, perhaps these changes loomed so large only because of the essential conservatism and insularity of the British people. The ultimate irony of 1980 was that the task of blasting the British out of their conservative ways was in the hands of a government labelled 'Conservative'.

Conclusion
The Confusions of History

A good deal of the debate over 'What Went Wrong?' was in the end concerned with economic, rather than social history. Economic performance, of course, is related to social conventions and social attitudes. But, since economists are scarcely agreed among themselves, it is not for a social historian to pronounce on the rightness or wrongness of the economic policies of successive governments. What can perhaps be said is that if Britain has indeed, since 1945, had a 'mixed economy', in many ways the mix was not exactly the right one: too much emphasis on large units, whether public or private, too little on small business enterprises.

As Isaac Kramnick points out in *Is Britain Dying?*, recent critiques take three forms, depending upon the politics of the critic:

> The conventional left in Britain and elsewhere sees a crisis and assigns the blame to bankers, managers, and the class system. The right in Britain and elsewhere, especially in America, sees a crisis and indicts unions, socialism, and intellectuals. The radical left also sees a crisis, but one that undermines the entire social order of capitalist Britain. While still pointing to the conventional villains – profits, exploitation, and international bankers – it has more stridently added another in recent years: the Labour Party serves in its view as a 'guarantor of the post-war capitalist order', diffusing pressures from below which threaten the system.

It is not true that Britain has a class system and other countries do not. But it does seem that the particular forms of class in Britain, valuable in assisting social unity during the trials of the Second World War, have increasingly become a liability in the post-war world. Managerial attitudes have been too much related to maintaining the outward symbols of an upper-class status and too little towards managing efficiently. Unions in

Britain have, in fact, practised 'secular Anglicanism' far more than they have practised militancy or pursued grossly disruptive goals; but, having deeper roots than any other working class in the world, the British working class has more and more concerned itself with maintaining the *status quo* than with the higher productivity through which alone higher living standards could be attained. Standards of public service, as seen for example among bus drivers, ticket collectors, and delivery men, are notoriously and self-evidently low. The service is to the group, and the rules of the job; not to the community.

To call oneself socialist has, indeed, often meant the repetition of antiquated shibboleths bearing little relationship to the changing nature of British society. Nationalization of steel could not hold back the unfavourable tides of the world market; nationalization of British Leyland did little to improve appalling management–union relations. Within their own spheres British intellectuals have produced work of great interest, if not of world-shattering import. No doubt it is in keeping with the long tradition of Anglicanism and pragmatism that no politician, nor any group of politicians, has ever presented a thorough-going intellectual critique of Britain's problems. The shibboleths of the left have simply been met by refurbished shibboleths from the right. Between them, Labour and Conservative Governments both did in fact implement many of the reforms which the critics were advocating from the later fifties onwards. The Labour Governments of the sixties carried out considerable reorganization in central Government; the Conservatives in the early seventies launched major local government reform. Ironically, neither reform quite produced the results expected. Certainly, the Labour Party continues to be a force for stability rather than for radical change in British society. But it is hard to believe that the remedies of the radical left would do more than take from the British that contentment which, according to the opinion polls, they were still evincing in the late seventies.

If we turn to purely social problems those attracting most attention, particularly from foreign commentators, include race relations, the decline of the inner city, and the abysmal deterioration of many public services. On the first point, xenophobia and prejudice remain well-marked facets of the British character while upper-class politicians have simply shown a lamentable complacency in believing that a verbal reiteration of a lack of prejudice was a substitute for positive policies directed at genuine integration. On the latter two points, one important key, quite certainly, was that explained by Anthony Sampson, the author of two perceptive studies, *Anatomy of Britain* and *Anatomy of Britain Today*. The inadequate and grossly expensive underground and bus services provided in London, he pointed out, resulted from the fact that those upper-class and upper-middle-class people who actually make the major decisions never themselves have to travel by London's public transport. They do travel by rail and air, and thus Inter-city rail services in particular, and air services to some extent, are of a rather high quality. This point, related to the nature of class in Britain and the lack of a participatory political culture, despite all the developments of the late sixties and seventies, must be a central one in any assessment of 'What Went Wrong?'.

Some foreign commentators have been kind, though from the middle seventies onwards never as optimistic about British prospects as they had been a decade earlier. François Bédarida, writing in 1977, concluded his book *Contemporary British Society* with these remarks:

> The British are now reduced to the common lot, to the level of a decent European average. We must agree, however, that the islanders do hold some important cards in their hand. The asset of a civilization going back many centuries is unlikely to fade away in quite such a fleeting manner. The creativity of the last twenty years in the sphere of culture and the art of living are a sign of various untapped resources. In the world of today England has definitely ceased to be a great power strutting proudly in the first rank of nations, but it is up to the English to continue to be a great people.

If we turn back to the simple 'How It Was' theme then what has to be stressed, as all Government surveys at the end of the seventies were doing, is that real living standards for almost everyone had risen greatly since the post-war years. There were new sources of conflict and tension, but for the great majority horizons were wider, aspirations higher, and opportunities for their fulfilment larger. The most desperate problem was that economic set-backs and technological change meant intolerably high levels of unemployment and, above all, dismal prospects for many of the country's school leavers.

Essentially what we are faced with is a complicated historical legacy in which former strengths seem to become weaknesses and remedies emerge as worse than the evils they were intended to cure. How far back in history do we have to go to find the roots of current ills? The thirties was a pretty dismal decade in Britain, yet then it was France which seemed the more obviously conservative, stagnant, and socially divided nation; and would anyone really prefer the Germany of Adolf Hitler? So we do have to focus attention again on the war. It did bring change, but also complacency and a reinforcement of older structures (while other countries were forced to build anew). Too much of the reconstruction of the Era of Consensus was in rhetoric rather than reality. The tradition of secular Anglicanism helped society to adjust to the changes of the sixties, but more and more it assumed the form of a self-congratulatory conservatism.

If it is true that the faith in consensus and civic solidarity of the British have helped to bring the nation to a point where even 'the level of a decent European average' begins to seem beyond its grasp, it is also clear that the simple nostrums of the radical right will no more work wonders than did the simple nostrums of social democracy. Neither thirty-five years of social development, nor the confusing bequest of the war which preceded it, can be wished away. But an understanding of these thirty-five years is a first step towards the preparation of sane, considered remedies which will cash in on that humane spirit which, despite everything, has been a characteristic of British society since 1945.

Note on Sources and Guide to Further Reading

All serious historical work must be based on primary source material, that is material originated, within the period studied, by individuals and groups pursuing their own particular purpose, rather than consciously striving to provide comprehensive accounts for posterity. The writing of such accounts is the task of historians, and their accounts form 'secondary sources'. The line is blurred when one is dealing with contemporary history: none the less it is still, even in the period since 1945, not really very difficult to distinguish between 'raw' primary material and the more consciously composed secondary accounts.

At the time this book was finished the unpublished archive materials in the Public Record Office were not available beyond 1950. However, from my point of view, this was no great loss: it is easy to get hold of masses of other primary material central to the study of social history. Basic to this study have been: (a) STATISTICS, most conveniently supplied in the HMSO *Annual Abstracts of Statistics* and also, since 1970, in *Social Trends* published annually by the Central Office of Information; (b) ACTS OF PARLIAMENT (always worth checking, since statutes frequently get curiously misquoted) and OFFICIAL REPORTS, i.e. reports of Government departments, committees and Royal Commissions (useful examples for students are *The Report of the Ministry of National Insurance for the Period 17 November 1944 to 4 July 1949* (1950), *The Report of the Committee on Broadcasting (Pilkington Report)* (1961), and *The Report of the Royal Commission on Standards of Conduct in Public Life 1974–1976* (1976)); (c) SOCIAL SURVEYS, including those carried out in the early years by the Central Office of Information, those carried out at the same time by the private research organization Mass Observation, and those increasingly carried out since by academic sociologists, for example, the two studies by Margaret Stacey and her associates, *Tradition and Change: A Study of Banbury* (1960) and *Power, Persistence and Change: A Second Study of Banbury* (1975).

All of which, to give the zest of personal experience, must be blended with (d) the fascinating range of PERSONAL RECORDS running from the private diaries of Hugh Dalton at the British Library of Political and Economic Science, private letters relating to the first year of peace housed at the Imperial War Museum, and the many invaluable un-published collections in the Modern Records Centre of the University of Warwick to such published diaries as J. L. Hodson's *The Way Things Are* (1947) and autobiographies as *The Greasy Pole* (1965) by Reginald Bevins or *The Double Helix* (1968) by J. D. Watson. NEWSPAPERS (e), while often suspect when used as evidence for that vague entity 'public opinion', are invaluable for social reportage; under the general heading of 'the press' are, apart from the major national and local papers, the vast range of publications which give deep insights into the concerns of special interest groups, the women's magazines, the pop music publications, and, say, the newspaper of the Campaign for Real Ale (since 1971). I should add that the files of *New Society* (since 1963) offer a unique and invaluable resource for survey material and social commentary. Finally (f) FILMS, NOVELS, TELEVISION PRO-GRAMMES, PAINTINGS, BUILDINGS, of which I have given specific though, I would admit, arbitrary instances in the course of my text, and (g) the plethora of MISCELLANEOUS PRINTED SOURCES, running from party Conference Reports and policy statements, such as the Conservative Party's *The Industrial Charter* (1948), through volumes of polemics, such as Hugh Thomas (ed.), *The Establishment* (1959) or Isaac Kramnick's *Is Britain Dying?: Perspectives on the Current Crisis* (1979), to major seminal works such as Peter Winch's *Idea of a Social Science* (1958) or P. B. and J. S. Medawar, *The Life Science* (1978), are all invaluable sources.

As yet there are few secondary accounts of British social history since 1945, the main serious contender being Pauline Gregg's sound and comprehensive *The Welfare State* (1967); almost all of the more recent books published so far have concentrated on political history. Most rounded is C. J. Bartlett, *A History of Post-War Britain 1945-1974* (1977). The clearest guide is Alan Sked and Chris Cook, *Post-War Britain: A Political History* (1979). There are good points in David Childs, *Britain Since 1945: A Political History* (1979), though it becomes rather rushed towards the end. R. Eatwell, *The 1945-1951 Labour Government* (1979) is a serious, but highly condensed, political history. Another serious, if rather basic, study is *British Politics and Government 1951-1970: A Study of an Affluent Society* (1974) by Mary Proudfoot. Peter Calvocoressi, *The British Experience 1945-75* (1978) is a stimulating personal account, and V. Bogdanor and R. Skidelsky (eds.), *The Age of Affluence 1951-1964* (1970) contains useful, if rather traditional, essays on one part of the period.

In the realm of sociology, Trevor Noble, *Modern Britain: Structure and Change* (1975) is a deeply thoughtful work; Eric Butterworth and David Weir (eds.), *The Sociology of Modern Britain* (revised edition

1977) brings together a series of useful essays. Judith Ryder and Harold Silver, *Modern English Society* (revised edition 1977) is a brave attempt to bring sociology and history together which does not always quite come off. *Change in British Society* (1978) by A. H. Halsey provides a stimulating overview.

Both François Bédarida in *A Social History of England 1851–1975* (1979) and Alfred Havighurst, *Britain in Transition: The Twentieth Century* (revised edition 1979) contain only very short final chapters on the period since 1945, but are important as giving the considered judgements of a distinguished French and a distinguished American historian respectively.

The standard of pop history has gone up immensely in recent years and there are a number of stimulating volumes covering parts of the period under review. Michael Sissons and Philip French (eds.), *The Age of Austerity 1945–1951* (1963) contains a series of illuminating essays. *The New Look: A Social History of the Forties and Fifties in Britain* (1963) by Harry Hopkins is still well worth consulting. Christopher Booker and Bernard Levin both wrote brilliant individual accounts of the 1960s, *The Neophiliacs* (1969) and *Pendulum Years* (1970), respectively, but the former's *The Seventies* (1979) proved to be a disappointing collection of previously published journalistic pieces. More rewarding here is Norman Shrapnel's *The Seventies: Britain's Inward March* (1980).

Now let me take the eleven major topics of social change which I identified in the Introduction, indicating the main secondary, and a few primary, sources.

1. Social Geography

Jean Mitchell (ed.), *Great Britain: Geographical Essays* (1962) provides a good basic tour round the country and also offers some insights into liberal intellectual attitudes at the beginning of the sixties. The series on Industrial Britain published by David and Charles and edited by David M. Smith is excellent, and contains such titles as *The North-West* (1969) by the general editor, *The North-East* (1969) by John House, *The Humberside Region* (1970) by Peter Lewis and Philip Jones, *South Wales* (1972) by Graham Humphrys, and *The Steel Industry in Post-War Britain* (1974) by David Heal. Other useful books for the Celtic fringes are *A Geography of Scotland* (1977) by K. J. Lea and *Wales: A New Study* (1977) edited by David Thomas. There are points about both geography and education to be gleaned from a much-reprinted textbook, *Geography of the British Isles* (latest edition, 1978) by N. J. Graves and J. T. White and, at the other extreme, there is fascinating contemporary detail to be found in West Midlands Group,

Conurbation: A Survey of Birmingham and the Black Country (1948). An interesting survey of one single town (Swindon) is *An Awkward Size for a Town* (1967) by Kenneth Hudson. R. K. Kelsall, *Social Structure of Britain: Population* (fourth edition 1979) and R. M. Williams, *British Population* (second edition 1978) are useful brief guides.

2. Economic and Technological Change

K. Warren's *Geography of British Heavy Industry Since 1800* (1976) moves us towards the second of my topics. Here essential information is furnished by the two volumes of *The Structure of British Industry* (1958) edited by D. L. Burn and by the same author's *The Steel Industry 1939–1959* (1961). Derek H. Aldcroft, *British Transport Since 1914* (1975) is a standard work. On a vital subsection of this topic direct primary evidence is to be found in R. Fraser (ed.), *Work: Twenty Personal Accounts* (1968) and *Work II: Twenty Personal Accounts* (1969), while useful essays are included in *Men and Work in Modern Britain* (1973) edited by David Weir; *Work and Well-being* (1975) by Peter Warr and Toby Wall is an excellent general survey. Kevin Hawkins gives a doleful subject a brilliantly stimulating discussion in his *Unemployment* (1979). A particular economic phenomenon of considerable social significance is studied in Oliver Marriott, *The Property Boom* (1967). *British Nationalisation 1945–1973* (1973) by R. Kelf-Cohen is the most authoritative recent work on its subject, and an interesting Tory critique is John Burton, *The Job Support Machine* (1979), while the model study of private industry in the post-war years is *Unilever 1945–1965: Challenge and Response in the Post-War Industrial Revolution* (1968) by Charles Wilson. There is, revealingly, no adequate account of technological developments within the purely British context, but an international perspective is provided by such works as Eli Ginzberg (ed.), *Technology and Social Change* (1964). The most recent book on one of the most critical technological developments is Carl Djerassi, *The Politics of Contraception* (1980).

3. Social Class and Social Structure

The literature on social class is enormous. My own approach is explained in my *Class: Image and Reality in Britain, France, and the USA Since 1930* (1980), which contains an extensive, though by no means exhaustive, bibliography. Useful recent books include: John Westergaard and Henrietta Resler, *Class in a Capitalist Society: A Study of Contemporary Britain* (1975), a Marxist analysis; John H. Goldthorpe, *Social Mobility and Class Structure in Modern Britain* (1980) and A. H. Halsey, A. F. Heath, and J. M. Ridge, *Origins and Destinations: Family,*

Class, and Education in Modern Britain (1980), both based on detailed empirical sociological research; and Ivan Reid, *Social Class Differences in Britain: A Sourcebook* (1977). Jilly Cooper, *Class: A View from Middle England* (1979) is entertaining and often very near the mark. For direct insight into the upper-class ambience see Harold Nicolson, *Diaries and Letters 1945–62* (1968) edited by Nigel Nicolson and *Chips: The Diaries of Sir Henry Channon* (1967) edited by Robert Rhodes-James. The education of the upper class can be studied in Jonathan Gathorne-Hardy, *The Public School Phenomenon* (1977). Vital works, containing important primary material, are Colin Bell, *Middle Class Families: Social and Geographical Mobility* (1968) and the three volumes by J. H. Goldthorpe and his associates, *The Affluent Worker* (1968–9). Basic, though still incomplete, factual information can be found in the *Reports of the Royal Commission on the Distribution of Income and Wealth* (1975 onwards). Brian Jackson, *Working Class Community* (1968) is indispensable. Superb on the unions is R. Taylor, *Fifth Estate: Britain's Unions in the Modern World* (1982).

4. Social Cohesion

For the various elements involved in the question of social cohesion there are: Nicolas Deakin, *Colour, Citizenship and British Society* (1970), Sheila Patterson, *Immigration and Race Relations 1960–67* (1969), and Thomas J. Cottle, *Black Testimony: The Voices of Britain's West Indians* (1978); Christopher Harvie, *Scotland and Nationalism* (1977), Karl Miller (ed.), *Memoirs of a Modern Scotland* (1970), and Alan Philip, *The Welsh Question: Nationalism in Welsh Politics 1945–1970* (1975); R. Clutterbuck, *Britain in Agony* (1978), Kevin Hawkins, *Management of Industrial Relations* (1978), and Colin Crouch, *Class Conflict and Industrial Relations Crisis* (1977); Germaine Greer, *The Female Eunuch* (1970) and Anna Coote and Tess Gill, *Women's Rights* (1974); and Tessa Blackstone, Kathleen Gales, Roger Hadley, and Win Lewis, *Students in Conflict: L.S.E. in 1967* (1970).

5. Social Welfare and Social Policy

In the later post-war years the distinguished academic M. Penelope Hall established herself as the unchallengeable authority on the evolution of social welfare. This eminence was charmingly recognized in the collection of essays edited by John Mays, Antony Forder, and Olive Keidan entitled *Penelope Hall's Social Services of England and Wales* (ninth edition 1975), a work as indispensable now as Penelope Hall's original study was in its day. Another useful collection of essays is *Social Welfare in Modern Britain* (1975), edited by Eric Butterworth and Robert Holman. J. B. Cullingworth has two standard works,

Housing Needs and Planning Policy (1960) and *Housing and Local Government* (1966). A longer perspective is provided by John Burnett, *A Social History of Housing 1815–1970* (1978).

6. Material Conditions

For material conditions it is best to go back to primary statistical and survey material. For the early part of the period there is, for example, *Poverty and the Welfare State* (1951) by B. S. Rowntree and G. R. Lavers. For the later part there is an important essay in *Social Trends 10* (1980). The annual Government publication, *Britain: An Official Handbook*, though it inevitably puts a pleasant gloss on everything, is a good guide to all aspects of life in Britain. John Burnett has a pioneering work, *Plenty and Want: A Social History of Diet in England from 1815 to the Present Day* (revised edition 1979).

7. Customs and Behaviour

Another part of the social survey of York carried out by Rowntree and Lavers, *English Life and Leisure: A Social Study* (1951), takes us into the realm of customs and behaviour. Two classics here are Geoffrey Gorer's *Exploring English Character* (1960) and Tom Harrisson's *Britain Revisited* (1962); otherwise much can be learned from official surveys. James Walvin has written some useful brief guides: *Leisure and Society 1830–1950* (1978), *Beside the Seaside* (1978), and *The People's Game: A Social History of British Football* (1975). Christie Davies, *Permissive Britain: Social Change in the Sixties and Seventies* (1975) is a collection of excellent essays rather than a comprehensive history. The question of drug-taking is thoroughly, and sensitively, discussed in Kenneth Leech, *A Practical Guide to the Drug Scene* (revised edition 1974); also helpful is N. Imlah, *Drugs in Modern Society* (1970). Sexual behaviour among young people was analysed by M. Schofield, *Sexual Behaviour of Young People* (1965). Another useful book by Kenneth Leech is *Youthquake: The Growth of a Counter-Culture through Two Decades* (1973).

8. The Family

For the family, indispensable surveys are Peter Wilmott and Michael Young, *Family and Kinship in East London* (1957) and *Family and Class in a London Suburb* (1960), and Colin Rosser and Christopher Harris, *The Family and Social Change* (1965). Geoffrey Gorer provides fascinating detail on moral attitudes and much else in *Sex and Marriage in England Today* (1971).

9. Social Deviance and Questions of Law and Order

Law and order, and all that, are dealt with by Brian Abel-Smith and

R. Stevens, *Lawyers and the Courts* (1966), Don Campbell, *Police, the Exercise of Power* (1978), and Ben Whittaker, *The Police in Society* (1979). A brilliant study, written from the rather distinctive Marxist viewpoint of the 'Birmingham school', is Stuart Hall, Chas Critcher, Tony Jefferson, John Clarke, and Brian Roberts, *Policing the Crisis: Mugging, the State, and Law and Order* (1978).

10. Intellectual, Scientific and Artistic Development

For developments in what I loosely termed 'culture' there is first of all John Sutherland's *Fiction and the Fiction Industry* (1978). More traditional is Volume 7 of the *Pelican Guide to English Literature: The Modern Age* (revised edition 1973) edited by Boris Ford. Drama is well catered for in John Elsom, *Post-War British Theatre* (second edition 1979). Two original critical studies are Rubin Rabinovitz, *The Reaction Against Experiment in the English Novel 1950–1960* (1967) and Blake Morrison, *The Movement: English Fiction and Poetry of the 1950s* (1980). For 'high music' the best introduction is the final chapter of Percy M. Young, *A History of British Music* (1967). Richard Middleton, *Pop Music and the Blues: A Study of the Relationship and Its Significance* (1972) is a book of stunning verve and originality. The pop music scene can be further explored through such publications as Gavin Petrie (ed.), *Rock Life* (1974) and David Downing, *Future Rock* (1976). For art one goes to exhibitions and studies catalogues. However, if the exhibitions are over one can consult such books as John Rothenstein, *Modern English Painters: Wood to Hockney* (1974), John Russell's *Henry Moore* (1968), and Edward Lucie-Smith's *Art in the Seventies* (1980). For architecture Paul Thompson's section in *A History of English Architecture* (1979) by Peter Kidson, Peter Murray, and Paul Thompson is reliable; Charles Jencks, *Modern Movements in Architecture* (1973) is idiosyncratic. The perfect guide to the world of design is Fiona MacCarthy in her *A History of British Design 1830–1970* (1979).

For science there is J. G. Crowther, *Science in Modern Society* (1967) and Hilary and Steven Rose, *Science and Society* (1969); I have already mentioned J. D. Watson's first-hand, fascinating, though no doubt fallible, record, *The Double Helix: A Personal Account of the Discovery of the Structure of D.N.A.* (1970). For intellectual developments generally, the final chapter of Michael Biddiss, *The Age of the Masses* (1977) manages, in short and breathless space, to be incredibly stimulating. *The Twentieth-Century Mind: History, Ideas, and Literature in Britain*, vol. III, 1945–1965, edited by C. B. Cox and A. E. Dyson contains in its separate essays the facts and names I have not been able to cram into my own book. Religion figures with appropriate faintness in some of the social surveys already cited: to find out why, try the primary survey, *Puzzled People: A Study of Popular Attitudes to Religion* (1948) by Mass Observation and the brief history, *Religion in Britain since 1900* (1962) by G. S. Spinks. Best of all are the three *Sociological Yearbooks of Religion in Britain* (1968–70), edited by David Martin.

Three Royal Commissions on the Press (chaired by Sir William Ross 1947–9, Lord Shawcross 1961–2, and Professor O. R. McGregor 1975–7, respectively) provide solid, magisterial reading on this ever-important topic (1949, 1962, and 1977), which can be amplified in one direction by A. C. H. Smith, *Paper Voices: The Popular Press and Social Change 1935–1965* (1975) and in another by *The Cecil King Diaries* (1972 and 1975). Raymond Durgnat, *The Mirror for England: British Movies from Austerity to Affluence* (1970) is fascinating though often far-fetched; Roy Armes, *A Critical History of British Cinema* (1978) is more reliable. The authoritative work on radio and television is Volume 4 of Asa Briggs's *History of Broadcasting in the United Kingdom*, entitled *Sound and Vision* (1979).

11. Social and Political Values, Institutions, and Ideas

Within the realm of social and political values and institutions, works which now have the status of powerful primary sources are: Richard Hoggart, *The Uses of Literacy* (1957), Tom Maschler (ed.), *Declaration* (1957), Michael Shanks, *The Stagnant Society: A Warning* (1961), and Anthony Sampson, *Anatomy of Britain* (1962) and *Anatomy of Britain Today* (1965). There is much valuable survey material, spiced with apt comment, in Philip Ziegler, *Crown and People* (1978). For industrial relations there are the *Report of the Committee of Enquiry on Industrial Democracy (Bullock Committee)* (1977), the original, though, I think, in the end misguided, *Industrial Politics* (1979) by Robert Currie, and *Strikes* (revised edition 1977) by Richard Hyman, which is a fine example of Marxist analysis shaped by the facts of the real world. The fullest development of the notion of the growth of corporatism in British society is Keith Middlemas's *Politics in Industrial Society* (1979), where, however, the main emphasis is on the period before 1945; the recent period is studied more intensively in Michael Moran, *The Politics of Industrial Relations* (1977). The *Report of the Royal Commission on the Civil Service (Fulton Report)* (1968) was largely written by Lord Crowther-Hunt (as he became); interest, if not total objectivity, therefore, attaches to *The Civil Servants: An Enquiry into Britain's Ruling Class* (1980) by Peter Kellner and Lord Crowther-Hunt.

Finally, on the theme of 'What Went Wrong?' there is the book of that title *What Went Wrong?. Working People and the Ideas of the*

Labour Movement (1978) by Jeremy Seabrook, the American-originated *The Future That Doesn't Work* (1977) edited by R. Emmett-Tyrrall, Jr, and the all-American reply *Britain: A Future That Works* by Bernard D. Nossiter (1978). A further American contribution, apart from Kramnick, is *The United Kingdom in 1980: The Hudson Report* (1974); note also Michael Stewart, *The Jekyll and Hyde Years* (1977), revised edition, *Politics and Economic Policy in the United Kingdom Since 1964: The Jekyll and Hyde Years* (1982).

The gaps in this fragmentary survey are fully covered in John Westergaard's standard bibliography, *Modern British Society* (latest edition, 1979), which, however, somehow contrives to avoid mentioning any of my own works on twentieth-century social history. All too soon, no doubt, this slight book of mine, *British Society Since 1945*, will be taken by the next generation of historians as but one poor primary source amid the torrents with which *they* have to contend.

Index